## About this book

These essays on postcolonial subje̶⎯⎯⎯⎯⎯⎯⎯̶⎯⎯⎯ntiers of critical theory by illuminating the contradictory p̶⎯⎯⎯⎯⎯⎯aments Africans confront in strikingly different parts of the continent at the start of the twenty-first century. The focus is on the making of subjectivities as a process which is political, a matter of subjugation to state authority; moral, reflected in the conscience and agency of subjects who bear rights, duties and obligations; and realised existentially, in the subjects' consciousness of their personal or intimate relations.

The notion of agency is interrogated, without lapsing into the new Afropessimism. The essays recognise postcolonies troubled by state decline and increasing exploitation, dispossession and marginalisation, but avoid Afropessimism's reduction of subjects to mere victims. Even more against the grain of conventional postcolonial studies is the radical questioning of the force of 'modern subjectivism' in struggles for control of identity, autonomy and explicit consciousness, and through artistic self-fashioning in globally driven consumption.

With substantial cases based on autobiography, personal experience and long- term scholarly fieldwork in countries as diverse as Madagascar, Kenya, Uganda, Sudan, Botswana and Cameroon, the book opens out a fresh field for comparative research and theory on postcolonial transformations in intersubjectivity. This is to take seriously the people's perception, so widespread in postcolonial Africa, that to live life to the full is to live it in interdependence, in conviviality, if possible; that care and respect for others – indeed, civility – is a precious, and indeed, precarious condition of survival and as such is the object of recognised strategies for its conscious defence; and that because significant others are opaque – never being totally knowable – uncertainty, ambivalence and contingency are inescapable conditions of human existence.

# Postcolonial Encounters

A Zed Books series in association with the International Centre for Contemporary Cultural Research (ICCCR), Universities of Manchester and Keele.

*Series editors*: Richard Werbner and Pnina Werbner

This series debates the making of contemporary culture and politics in a postcolonial world. Volumes explore the impact of colonial legacies, precolonial traditions and current global and imperial forces on the everyday lives of citizens. Reaching beyond postcolonial countries to the formation of external ethnic and migrant diasporas, the series critically theorises:

- The active engagement of people themselves in the creation of their own political and cultural agendas;
- the emerging predicaments of local, national and transnational identities and subjectivities;
- the indigenous roots of nationalism, communalism, state violence and political terror;
- the cultural and religious counter-movements for or against emancipation and modernity;
- the social struggles over the imperative of human and citizenship rights within the moral and political economy.

Arising from the analysis of decolonization and recolonization, the series opens out a significant space in a growing interdisciplinary literature. The convergence of interest is very broad, from anthropology, cultural studies, social history, comparative literature, development, sociology, law and political theory. No single theoretical orientation provides the dominant thrust. Instead the series responds to the challenge of a commitment to empirical, in-depth research as the motivation for critical theory.

For full details of this list and Zed's other subject and general catalogues, please write to:
The Marketing Department, Zed Books, 7 Cynthia Street, London N1 9JF, UK
or email Sales@zedbooks.demon.co.uk • Visit our website at: http://www.zedbooks.demon.co.uk

# Postcolonial Subjectivities in Africa

EDITED BY

## Richard Werbner

Zed Books

LONDON & NEW YORK

*Postcolonial Subjectivities in Africa* was first published in 2002 by
Zed Books Ltd, 7 Cynthia Street, London N1 9JF, UK and
Room 400, 175 Fifth Avenue, New York, NY 10010, USA

Distributed in the USA exclusively by Palgrave, a division of
St Martin's Press, LLC,175 Fifth Avenue, New York, NY 10010, USA.

Cover design by Andrew Corbett
Designed and set in 10/12 pt Bembo
by Long House, Cumbria, UK
Printed and bound in the United Kingdom
by Biddles Ltd, Guildford and King's Lynn

All photographs in Chapter 2 are from the personal collection of Heike Behrend

A catalogue record for this book
is available from the British Library

ISBN    Hb 1 85649 954 5
        Pb  1 85649 955 3

Library of Congress Cataloging-in-Publication Data
has been applied for

# ◎ Contents

## Afterword – The Personal, the Political and the Moral
Provoking Postcolonial Subjectivities in Africa

# ◎ Notes on Contributors

**Heike Behrend** is Professor of Anthropology at the Institute of African Studies, University of Cologne, Germany. She has conducted extensive field research in Uganda and Kenya on war, religion and media, and is currently studying discourses and practices of photography in Eastern Africa. She has written numerous articles and co-edited *Snap Me One. Studiofotografen in Afrika* (1998); her latest book is *Alice Lukwena and the Holy Spirits War in Uganda* (1999).

**Deborah Durham** is Associate Professor of Anthropology at Sweet Briar College. She has been conducting research in Botswana over the past twelve years, focusing primarily on members of the Herero community from Mahalapye, and on how people realise cultural and ethnic identities in the context of liberalist democracy. More recently, she has been studying 'youth' as a social concept in Botswana, and in anthropology more broadly. She has published articles and contributions to collections on Herero life, political culture in democratic Botswana, and youth.

**Sharon Elaine Hutchinson** is Associate Professor of Anthropology at the University of Wisconsin-Madison. She has been carrying out periodic field research in South Sudan since 1980. Her 1996 book, *Nuer Dilemmas: Coping with Money, War and the State*, was co-winner of the 1997 Amaury Talbot Prize. She is currently developing a second historical monograph that concentrates on war-provoked social and religious transformations among the Sudanese Nuer.

**Jok Madut Jok** is Assistant Professor of History at Loyola Marymount University in Los Angeles. After education in Sudan, Egypt and the United

States, he received his doctorate in anthropology from the University of California, Los Angeles. His book, *Militarization, Gender and Reproductive Health in South Sudan*, was published in 1998.

**Michael Lambek** is Professor of Anthropology at the University of Toronto. He is the author of two books and numerous articles on the Malagasy speakers of Mayotte and has recently begun publishing his research on the royal ancestral cult and historical consciousness among Sakalava in Mahajanga, Madagascar. His work in press includes *A Reader in the Anthropology of Religion* (Blackwell) and (edited with Ellen Messer) *Ecology and the Sacred: Engaging the Anthropology of Roy A. Rappaport* (University of Michigan Press).

**Karen Middleton** holds a Nuffield Foundation Fellowship at Oxford University and is currently writing an environmental history of southern Madagascar. She has conducted extensive anthropological field research among the peoples of the Karembola region, and is author of a number of articles on gender, kinship and ritual. She is Deputy Editor of the *Journal of Religion in Africa* and editor of *Ancestors, Power and History in Madagascar* (Brill, 1999).

**Francis B. Nyamnjoh** is Associate Professor in the Department of Sociology at the University of Botswana. He has researched and written extensively on Cameroon, where he was until October 1999 Head of the Department of Sociology and Anthropology at the University of Buea. He is currently completing a study on media and democratisation in Africa in the 1990s, and has published widely on media and communication in Cameroon and Africa. He is also a writer of fiction, and his novels include: *Mind Searching* (1991), *The Disillusioned African* (1995) and *A Nose for Money* (forthcoming). He is an editorial board member of *Critical Arts*, *Ecquid Novi*, *Pula* and *International Journal of Comic Art*.

**Akira Okazaki** teaches intercultural communication and anthropology at Kanagawa University, Japan. He studied at the School of Oriental and African Studies, University of London, where he wrote his PhD thesis after conducting fieldwork among the Maasai and the Gamk. He has travelled extensively in Africa and written widely on world music, on a conflict between men and women among the Maasai, and on the sociality of dreams among the Gamk. He was elected to the first Evans-Pritchard Lecturership, All Souls College, University of Oxford.

**Paul Stoller** teaches anthropology at West Chester University of Pennsylvania. The author of numerous publications, his most recent books include *Sensuous Scholarship* (1997), a collection of essays, and *Jaguar: A Story of Africans in America* (1999), a novel. He is currently conducting field research among West African immigrants in New York City.

**Richard Werbner** is Professor of African Anthropology and Director of the International Centre for Contemporary Cultural Research at the University of Manchester, and currently Professorial Fellow in the Department of Sociology at the University of Botswana. Among his books are *Ritual Passage, Sacred Journey (1989), Postcolonial Identities in Africa (1996), Memory and the Postcolony (1998)* and *Tears of the Dead: The Social Biography of an African Family* (1991), for which he received the Amaury Talbot Prize of the Royal Anthropological Institute. He has carried out long-term research in Zimbabwe and Botswana, on which his current book in preparation is *Renegotiating Postcolonial Citizenship*. He is co-editor-in-chief of *Social Analysis*, and a member of the editorial board of *Journal of Southern African Studies, Cultural Dynamics,* and *Journal of Religion in Africa*.

**Susan Reynolds Whyte** is Professor of Anthropology at the Institute of Anthropology, University of Copenhagen. She has carried out ethnographic fieldwork over many years in Uganda. Her monograph, *Questioning Misfortune: the Pragmatics of Uncertainty in Eastern Uganda*, was published by Cambridge University Press in 1997.

To our postcolonial creditors in Africa

# ◎ Introduction

## Postcolonial Subjectivities:
## The Personal, the Political and the Moral

Richard Werbner

## Changing Subjectivities and the *Longue Durée*

These essays on postcolonial subjectivities cross the frontiers of critical theory by engaging in analysis of the contradictory predicaments Africans confront in very different parts of the continent at the turn of the twenty-first century. In the first half of the book, we give most attention to problems of consciousness, conscience and the Other. In the second, the issues we foreground are more centred on uncertainties, subjection and the subjunctive. But our major interest throughout is in the ways that subjectivities are currently changing in African postcolonies, often in very ephemeral ways, and yet are constrained by intractable conditions, some of very long duration.

We reject views that start from the generalities of globalisation the world over and thus subvert understanding of the subjective ambiguities and ambivalences in Africa's distinctively postcolonial predicaments. Our approach challenges the tendency to argue as if one familiar mode of subjectivity, modern subjectivism, is irresistibly on the march, everywhere becoming the dominant mode. At the heart of our arguments is an intertwined pair. 'the subjective' and 'the intersubjective'. We are well aware that phenomenologists from Husserl to Merleau Ponty have laboured long and hard to convince us that one without the other is a nonsense. Their point is that only when we lapse into individualist delusions, or perhaps schizophrenia, can we forget that the intersubjective is ever and always the ground of the subjective; that there is no subjectivity prior to intersubjectivity. Following the phenomenologists, it is difficult to define a certain line dividing the subjective from the intersubjective. But it is doubtful that we need to do so, to make a timeless definition outside history.

Instead, our interest is twofold, in historicising intersubjectivity and in the actual intertwining of subjectivity and intersubjectivity. First, we seek to problematise a current postcolonial phenomenon, according to which subjects are compelled to be aware and concerned about their interdependence, even their mutual entanglement – they come to perceive that being implicated with significant others has a special importance for their own consciousness; that such implication is vulnerable or even uncertain, under current postcolonial conditions; and that they must act strategically to realise and defend it. This interest in historicising intersubjectivity has largely been neglected in postcolonial studies, and our volume opens out a fresh field for research and theory on the postcolonial transformations of the intersubjective. Our second and related interest – in the actual intertwining of subjectivity and intersubjectivity – is in the ways that people actively negotiate or play off one against the other, from one postcolonial moment to another.

We start from people's own perceptions of how the subjective is implicated in the intersubjective – it is an empirical matter, for discovery and not *a priori* assertion. We criticise the unreflexive projection of subjectivities as universals. At the same time, we take care to disclose postcolonial efforts to reach beyond past limits of subjection, in some cases even to receive from outsiders new ways of turning oneself into the Other, intimately, publicly, or perhaps for a passing moment in play or ritual.

In analytical terms, subjectivities may be defined as *political*, a matter of subjugation to state authority; *moral*, reflected in the conscience and agency of subjects who bear rights, duties and obligations; and *realised existentially*, in the subjects' consciousness of their personal or intimate relations. These terms are not exhaustive, of course. There may be consumer subjectivity, arising in subjection to a global market, and that may conflict with subjugation to state authority. There may be playful or aestheticised self-fashioning, and this may reflect an adoption of the latest, most fashionable ways of being wholly Other and the actual appropriation of modern subjectivism, all of which may proceed through new, virtually global struggles to control identity and command highly explicit consciousness.

## The Ambiguities of Subjection and Subjugation

An obvious difficulty in all this is the slipperiness of the terms in common use for subjective processes. Important examples are subjugation, which is not always used in a sense restricted to the power of the state to dominate and make the subject, and subjection, which is often associated with disciplinary processes but is used even more broadly as virtually an umbrella term for the making of the subject, in almost any sense, usually several at once. We cannot claim to have resolved the ambiguities by imposing a standard vocabulary – the literature is already too richly engaged for that, and the ambiguities brought together by the multiple senses of our basic terms are too much the very stuff of actual discourses.

Instead, by recognising that subjectivity is an ambiguous concept, including intersubjectivity (or at least not easily defined apart from it), and by calling on its various senses, our approach problematises the relations between the personal, the political and the moral during remarkably unlike postcolonial transformations. None of these relations can be grasped by using a simplistic dichotomy, such as Mahmood Mamdani's influential distinction between citizen and subject (1996; see also Comaroff and Comaroff 1999:23), between the right-bearing person entitled to justice and living under the rule of law as a citizen of the state, on the one hand, and on the other, the subject under so-called customary authorities, such as the kings, chiefs and their staff deployed by the colonial state under indirect rule.

Basic in our approach is the recognition, as Francis Nyamnjoh puts it, that Africans 'are both citizens and subjects ... sometimes they are more citizen than subject and sometimes more subject than citizen' (Nyamnjoh 2001). Our arguments consider how far subjectivities are determined by discourses, political economy, state structures, and personal dispositions. We open out the notion of agency in order to bring it beyond the analytic limits of individualism and the lone heroic actor. The relative autonomy of social actors, like the very category of the subject, is taken to be problematic under changing postcolonial conditions. We debate where and how marginalisation, dispossession and exploitation form the grounds of subjectivities in very different postcolonies. We also find the 'fun spaces' (P. Werbner 1996, 2001) where, as in rap music and smartly dressed up portrait photography, people indulge in the pleasures of playful self-fashioning.

## Beyond the Heroic Individual

Arguing in our first chapter that the current theory of the subject needs to give as much attention to morality as it does to power and desire, Michael Lambek illuminates the self-fashioning of Nuriaty, a woman living in Mayotte – a place he calls a postmodern colony (a would-be postcolony, only for a minority of its people in an earlier, passing moment), because of its seemingly anomalous refusal to sever ties with France. Nuriaty surprises Lambek himself. When Lambek first knew her in 1975, Nuriaty was a local or domestic medium; she was tied to the spirits of her family, speaking their language in possession, and serving as a curer for a narrow set of clients within her own community. By 1995, on Lambek's more recent return, Nuriaty has taken on an unexpected capacity, and at some risk to herself. She has become the medium of the Sultan, an ancient authority figure of national importance, and speaking an archaic dialect not her own, Nuriaty has not merely reinvented herself, in the way that mediums usually do, she has achieved the ability to reach beyond her past limits in culture, identity and marginalised experience by creatively intertwining the personal and the public, the moral and the political. Even more striking is her newly achieved capacity to project, for a greater audience in a wider public arena, a consciousness – and conscience, Lambek stresses – of history. With visions from her dreams of past heroes weeping, she cries for respect and dignity at a time of felt rupture in the face of rapid change which threatens to marginalise her and people like her.

There is an obvious difficulty in this analysis which Lambek addresses forcefully. Is agency more a question than an answer here, as Richard Fardon insightfully remarked in a conference discussion of this chapter? For the subject herself, none of this remarkable capacity – the cultural inventiveness, the moral judgment or the appeal to the wider good, during spirit possession – is her own. She is not a heroine of self-fashioning or a morally judicious virtuoso in her own eyes. Instead, she is the subject of the ancestor; the agency, as it is perceived, is the spirit's. In brief, the moral practice starts from a denial of agency. The paradox is that it is the very undergoing of subjection which constitutes her as a persuasively influential and dignified subject in intersubjective relations.

Following Roy Rappaport, Lambek resolves the paradox by subsuming it in a more general predicament of moral practice. His theoretical statement of the predicament is this:

In assuming responsibility and rendering themselves subject to specific liturgical, political and discursive regimes and orders, people simultaneously lay claim to and accept the terms through which their subsequent acts will be judged. People are agents insofar as they choose to subject themselves, to perform and conform accordingly, to accept responsibility, and to acknowledge their commitments. Agency here transcends the idea of a lone, heroic individual independent of her acts and conscious of them as objects.

In these terms, for a more rounded picture of historical consciousness, Lambek himself invokes Aristotle and his notion of situated judgment, an interest which Susan Reynolds Whyte pursues in her concept of 'situated concern' but following the pragmatist philosophers, especially John Dewey. Even more broadly, Lambek points to the importance of an Aristotelian approach for a postcolonial anthropology that addresses the practical wisdom of everyday life (see Whyte, below, on pragmatism and practical wisdom).

It might be thought that Heike Behrend's chapter on popular photography and postcolonial subjectivities in Kenya takes us back to desire and the heroic individualist subject, now become a global player. All too familiar, at first impression of her Kenyan subjects, is the obsessive consumer in the world market for new things American, for freshly hegemonic youth fashions, body poses, slang, popular styles and cultural experiences, no less than for the latest magazines and consumer goods, above all 'the real thing' in new clothes. For Kenyan urban youth, there is a radically 'desired other', the African American from the ghetto, and it is as if the global success of the African-American culture industry (see Basu and P. Werbner 2001), marketing the bits and pieces of urban rap and hip hop, has come home to urban Kenya and given youth as avid consumers the means for heroic self-fashioning, for individual assertion, for autonomy, and even for resistance.

All of that, with its echoes of the late Foucault on aestheticised self-fashioning, is merely part of the story, however. Behrend moves us beyond that first impression through a very subtle unpacking of the playful ways that, in particular, one Kenyan youth, Peter, and his friends enter into social exchange around images of themselves as 'the desired other'. Stylised after the African-American, their images obliterate the friends' own ethnic differences and thus represent them renewed as autonomous individuals.

What seems to fascinate Peter and his friends is not the inner being, the individual's soul so to speak, or its revelation. Instead, they look to the very surface of the body, posed and clothed as a work of art. Photographed, it must become beautiful enough to be not Kenyan but of the radically 'desired other', poor like themselves yet able to resist and express protest against oppression, violence and marginalisation. Then it becomes possible for the poor urban youth to give of their enriched selves to each other by mutually exchanging their portrait photographs, by competitive display of their constantly traded, ever changing collections in albums, and, every few days, by sharing their gendered fantasies in admiring if sometimes critical comments on their images (always of peers, never of family or parents). Hence they do much more than merely buy, sell and consume, competitively and ostentatiously, 'the real things' from America – they are not mere pawns of the global market. They put their imagined selves at the disposal, even the mercy, of each other. Their aestheticised social exchange of peer self-images constitutes, around an imagined world, an actual intensity of shared intersubjective reality for their own generation, to the exclusion of their elders. Momentarily and in a theatre of their own imagination, as it were, these urban Kenyan youths realise the subjective emancipation of peers.

Behrend quotes a song of Peter's, yearning for travel to get beyond 'the sack full of lice' God has given the youth at home in the city. Home in the city is where they feel harried by the police, uncared for, and branded, because they are out of work and have no decent clothes. Seen in this light, their social exchange around African-Americanised portrait photography provides, as a postcolonial counter-reality, something of an escape to a distant undomesticated place or, perhaps, an exotic space of imaginary refuge from confinement at home in the city, in miserable poverty under one of the most repressive postcolonial regimes in Africa (on Tanzanian barbershops as sites of powerful transcendence, see also Weiss 1999, 2000).

Behrend finds that, inspired by the African-American example, Kenyan rapping with lyrics of conscious protest against the police and the ruling regime is expressive of resistance to subjugation by the state. But Behrend also makes us understand how ephemeral the moments of playful resistance are. If each photo reflects back a 'frozen gaze', subjectifying and at the same time objectifying the photographed person, few photos, if any, last long in a single collection, being passed readily in trade from one collector to another. The lyrics themselves are haunting in their expression of unease and loss, and for the subjects as well as for us the photos, like the freeze pose in breakdancing, catch a glimpse of the beautified autonomous self that is fleeting, an instant of real pleasure, but a mere instant nonetheless. An ironic twist is that Peter himself gets lost from sight, leaving his imaginary traces behind. Behrend returns to search for him and his current collection in vain – even for his best friends, Peter disappears, becoming in Behrend's representation virtually an icon for the momentary, passing subjectivity in the postcolony. Yet if Peter is untraceable in person, in his and his friends' images from his driving obsession with the appearance of the radically 'desired Other', his pleasing traces endure. His images await you.

## Subjection in Endemic Civil War

Seen against our second chapter and Behrend's illumination of a postcolonial appropriation of modern subjectivism – a subjectivity constituted by artistic self-fashioning, globally driven consumption and the struggle for control of identity, autonomy and explicit consciousness – the third chapter by Akira Okazaki is deliberately subversive and polemical. From the very start of his chapter about subjectivities among Nuba and Gamk in a war-torn borderland of the Sudan, Okazaki demands that we suspend our own subjective biases. Okazaki removes us from the ease of a familiar, even too familiar subjectivity in order to open out a different perspective on postcolonial subjectivities among marginalised, dispossessed and exploited peoples. Importantly, they are also peoples confronting endemic civil war exacerbated by the disabling legacy from a colonial policy of 'divide and rule'. Wider debates about resistance as a postcolonial strategy are central to Okazaki's analysis.

Okazaki's method is not only critical but also regionally comparative in a way that is a rare accomplishment in postcolonial studies. Okazaki uses one of his cases – that of Nuba – for deconstruction. The first step in his argument is to break down certain current theoretical assumptions. These are Eurocentric assumptions, he argues, which give a higher value to the achievement of autonomy, self-determination, and explicit consciousness in resistance. Pursuing such achievement along with the objectification of their own culture makes Nuba all the more vulnerable to subjugation – they offer armed resistance but their very survival is left in grave danger. Against that comes Okazaki's other case – that of Gamk – and his original deconstruction of the valorised subjectivity serves as the basis for a recovery of the significance that a non-violent alternative, realised through dreaming consciousness, has for survival.

The term 'dream consciousness' is problematic, Okazaki recognises. On the surface, it would appear to stand for an individualist illusion. It conveys, to the unwary, misleading ideas of the individual subject, the lone dreamer, and private experience, as it were prior to the social. Using 'dream consciousness' for Gamk dreaming as a non-violent strategy in the face of war, oppression and exploitation, Okazaki is himself much aware that he might be taken to be exaggerating the force of the subjective in resistance. But Gamk dreaming forms a dream consciousness that is social, not individual consciousness, and it also forms the conscience as a capacity of moral judgement not by the individual alone but together with the significant others who participate in giving a dream its meaning. Indeed, for Gamk, there is no dream at all until people, often many people, make it exist in the public domain as a shared meaningful reality. Gamk dreaming is a profoundly intersubjective activity. The constant public preoccupation with dreams in formation, with their uncertainties – and they are frequently re-imagined in meaning over time – is a hallmark of Gamk cultural and social life under the pressure of dislocating change.

The consequences are far-reaching. Latent social problems are dealt with by Gamk through dreaming by bringing them out for public interpretation and counteraction, often in ritual. In their dreaming, Gamk rework the moral ambiguities and ambivalences of their lives. Even further, Okazaki argues, their dreaming makes Gamk reflexive; they reach a heightened awareness, one might say a meta-consciousness, that moral ambiguities, ambivalences and uncertainties are an inescapable condition of their present existence. In accord with that, rather than taking up arms against power that subordinates them, Gamk demonise power and resort to ritual to ease its force over them. Here the conclusion that Okazaki draws from his comparison of Gamk with Nuba is that it is the Gamk strategy for survival, not the Nuba one for resistance, that renders them less vulnerable in the face of the unwelcome outside intervention in their lives. Even beyond that, his argument as a whole raises a broad challenge for postcolonial studies of estrangement, of the defence by people of a sub-jectivity of their own under the aggressive threat from overpowering strangers (on such estrangement see Werbner 1989, Chapter 4). Okazaki wants us to become far more reflexive so that we call into question much that is often taken for granted about autonomy in personal self-formation, political self-determination, and the importance of different forms of consciousness in postcolonial resistance to subjugation.

But what happens to the definition of identity, self and other in processes of postcolonial subjection when civility ends, when subjects of mutual respect become mere objects of violation in inter-ethnic conflict? How are we to understand the remaking of subjectivities in the post-colonial encounter with escalating violence and aggression directed by the people against themselves, albeit political violence driven mostly from beyond their region, both by pressure from a consortium of international petroleum companies and by the ruling regime of the postcolonial state itself? Addressing these questions in our fourth chapter, Sharon Hutchinson and Jok Madut Jok extend the regional comparison within war-torn Sudan to rural communities of Nuer and Dinka in the south. Like the Nuba and the Gamk of the nearby borderland, Nuer and Dinka have also had to endure the efforts of the postcolonial state to divide and rule, imposing another version of the old colonial policy, by funding rival military elites for the sake of control over an oil zone.

Under conditions of rapid polarisation and militarisation, during the 1991–9 period, the ethnic other ceased to be the subject of ethical restraints on inter-ethnic conflict among these neighbouring, culturally related and intermarried peoples, who share a recognised common ancestry. Before then, the lives of women, children and the elderly were sacrosanct; they were never intentionally killed in battle. Slaying them was a direct affront against God as the ultimate guardian of human morality, and it was felt to visit the slayer or some member of his family with divine anger in the form of terrible illness, sudden death and other afflictions.

What Hutchinson and Jok show is that the devaluing of the ethnic other from ethical subject to brutalised object – the end of inter-ethnic civility – has devastating consequences for the postcolonial subjectivities of Nuer and Dinka. It leads to a vicious increase in aggression which is gendered and inwardly directed; it magnifies the powers of men over women. The vulnerability of women to violence and rape becomes much greater, even at the hands of their male 'protectors' from their own ethnic group, and not merely from enemy troops. In brief, the ending of inter-ethnic civility brings with it a profound shift in people's moral reasoning and personal consciousness which is most grievous for unarmed women and children. It is, Hutchinson and Jok suggest, 'a distinctive turn in their postcolonial subjectivities' which extends to their very concepts of what ethnicity is.

In the past, Nuer and Dinka differed significantly in their concepts of ethnicity, a difference which Hutchinson and Jok relate to their colonial and precolonial history, starting from the famous nineteenth-century expansion of Nuer eastwards across the White Nile into Dinka- and Anyuak-occupied lands. In this long era of predatory expansion, the ethnic divide from the Other, like the social distance between insider and outsider, meant one thing for encroaching immigrant communities, the Nuer, and another for Dinka, the encroached. It was an ethnic divide that was not equally permeable from both sides.

Assimilation of strangers suited the Nuer, who did their best to make ethnic outsiders feel like insiders. Nuer competed for leadership among themselves by gathering in and winning the loyalty of as many co-resident Dinka and Anyuak clients as possible. In accord with that, Nuer conceived of someone as being one of themselves (Naath) and 'a real person' or 'a true human being' (*raam mi raan*) primarily by how he or she behaved; biological parentage mattered less. Hence Hutchinson and Jok call this era's Nuer concept of ethnicity 'performative'.

Virtually the mirror opposite was true among Dinka and in relation to their own identity, Jieng. The Dinka concept of ethnicity was 'primordialist', in Hutchinson and Jok's terms. Dinka made the most of blood-rich metaphors of procreative descent among themselves; for them, Jieng was a hereditary identity as was the ethnicity of the Other, Naath. Their primordialist ethnicity, obviating assimilation, suited Dinka in their efforts to resist being swallowed up by their Nuer neighbours.

In recent years, with the escalating militarisation and political violence against unarmed non-combatants, the ethnic divide has become less permeable and more sealed on both sides. With that, also, has come a change in the Nuer concept of ethnicity, moving closer to that of the Dinka, the shift being part of what Hutchinson and Jok call 'a more "primordialist", if not "racialist" way of thinking about their ethnic "essence"'. Nevertheless, Hutchinson and Jok find the signs of a possible reversal of this adverse trend, and 'hope that the atmosphere of inter-ethnic peace created by the 1999 Wunlit Peace Conference will continue to reawaken Nuer and Dinka men and women to the historical fluidity and permeability of their ethnic identities for the greater good of the South'.

## Vulnerability, Conviviality and the Domestication of the Subject

Underlying the approach in Hutchinson and Jok's chapter and, indeed, in much of the first half of this book, is a concern with the force and consequences for human vulnerability of the changes in postcolonial subjectivities. There is of course, a global context for our shared human vulnerability; it is 'a world of hegemonies of all kinds', to use Francis Nyamnjoh's phrase, in which we are all more or less vulnerable, when it comes to being able to be who we are as agents in relationships with others, and when it comes to articulating and defending our collective interests.

Given that global context, and building on public debate in Cameroon about the notion of *convivialité culturelle*, in the fifth chapter Nyamnjoh introduces his own concept of 'conviviality' (see also Nkwi and Nyamnjoh 1997; Nyamnjoh 1999). 'Conviviality' is a matter of interdependence and intersubjectivity; it is the congenial fellowship, often lighthearted, merry, and even hilarious, created between active agents otherwise perhaps in competition or even conflict with each other but determined to empower and not marginalise each other.

Nyamnjoh's aim in writing of conviviality is to understand better how postcolonial subjects can transcend their vulnerability while they negotiate their subjection through relationships with others. Conviviality is the light side of subjectivity in the postcolony, the darker side being the one Nyamnjoh foregrounds in much of his other writing, including his remarkable first novel, *Mind Searching* (1991) (on connivance and the *commandement* in Cameroon and other postcolonies, see also Mbembe 1992a, 1992b, and R. Werbner 1996). 'Cameroon constantly needs', Nyamnjoh observes, 'to balance the tensions of a triple colonial heritage and other multiple identities that have made it "Africa in miniature" (cf. Mbock 1996) and, also, a paradise of paradoxes.' The question is, Cameroonian academics, journalists, writers, politicians and clergy themselves now ask: how can Cameroon survive in 'harmonious coexistence', when it is 'threatened by political, religious, ethnic and economic differences and inequalities'? What can keep such a postcolony united 'despite its internal contradictions and differences'? How can its people realise their agency and subjectivity effectively while drawing upon multiple and disparate cultural repertoires?

No one believes in the existence of simple answers, or that the hard lessons of disenchantment with the state will easily vanish in a new wave of optimism. But the point is a matter of consciousness: that the questions are being publicly raised and the answers openly debated in a conscious quest for a survival strategy in the postcolony as an "Africa in miniature". Nyamnjoh carries the debate forward by exploring 'the imperatives of conviviality' in the light of his own and others' subjective experience in the *fondoms* or kingdoms of the Cameroon grassfields. There, he suggests,

> Agency and subjectivity have meaning only as domesticated agency and subjectivity: the freedom to pursue individual or group goals exists within a socially predetermined frame that emphasises conviviality with collective interests at the same time that it allows for individual creativity and self-fulfilment.

Nyamnjoh reflects on the changing social significance of individual success, his own along with others', in the grassfields. His own biography as 'a prince in every sense but blood', and having different fathers and several mothers, is a revealing case. He recalls his early identity crises, his most elaborate, highly prestigious wedding – 'the wedding of the year' – his marriage, and his academic accomplishments. He shows that, at present, significant others make concessions to each other, mutually negotiating fresh options which 'would certainly have sent shock waves through the *fondom* some ten years back'. While regional ideas of domesticated agency and subjectivity have been remarkably resilient, many people, including *fons* or kings and their queens, also share the sense that one must move with the times, be open to a wider world and to new ways of doing and being, including trendy imports from the USA. They try to merge the indigenous and the exogenous 'to create modernities that are not reducible to either but superior to both'. Rather than retreating from the uncertainties involved, they seem confident in their capacity to adapt and be adaptable. It all runs radically counter, Nyamnjoh concludes, to what modernisation theorists and their critiques widely predicted. Nyamnjoh's recognition of the importance of the fostering of intersubjective creativity and interdependence in the course of domesticating the subject has broad implications for postcolonial theories of agency and subjectivity in Africa.

## Moral Uncertainty, Civility and the Contradictions of Interdependence

But how do Cameroon's postcolonial subjectivities appear, if seen in the light of others at another extreme of the continent? Or rather, what does a further comparison illuminate, if we consider postcolonial subjection not, as in Cameroon, where the predatory state has made citizens connive in the certainties of the gross abuse of power, but instead where the sense of uncertainty arises all the more because of great expectations, still vibrant, for democracy, civic virtue and, in a locally much loved phrase, 'empowered' citizenship? In the sixth chapter, building on Achille Mbembe's representation of the grotesque banality of power in the postcolony (Mbembe *ibid*.) and pursuing the contrast in an extreme alternative at the other end of the continent, in Botswana, Deborah Durham discloses a paradox of optimism. With the very opening out of faith in a better future, of great expectations and opportunities for personal success, community development and ambitious advancement on merit comes not assured certainty but perplexing uncertainty about subjection to power (for her complementary analysis of the ironies in postcolonial indeterminacy, see Durham 1999). 'For many in Africa', Durham argues, 'are less zombified by the certainties of the abuse of power on the grand scale, than puzzled by the moral grounds on which they themselves can take effective action.'

Durham redirects postcolonial studies of subjection to the problems of effective pragmatics in the face of moral puzzlement. She makes her case through a richly nuanced analysis of the moral and political discourses around the failure of a Herero candidate to be appointed to chiefly office despite winning an election in one of Botswana's biggest railway towns, currently its railway headquarters, the ethnically diverse 'urban village' of Mahalapye. Some of this postcolonial story might seem familiar to Africanists brought up on Max Gluckman's famous notion of 'intercalary roles' (Gluckman 1949) and the colonial classics of the Manchester School about hereditary village headmen. But against the grain of that, the postcolonial version on elected office is surprising, and the intercalary notion itself needs revision to apply to the postcolony, Durham shows. She finds that it is based on the assumption of distinct spheres, such as the domestic and the political, which the role articulates or intercalates. Hence it obscures what postcolonial analysis needs to reveal – and, indeed, Durham herself does reveal: the subtle ways that multiple models of civic participation and political subjectivity are simultaneously present in overlapping, closely interrelated contexts. Even further, moving beyond that notion frees Durham's approach to examine the local predicaments of urban villagers who encounter the actual contradictions of a liberal democracy. On the one hand, it is a democracy that has the rhetoric of ethnically undifferentiated citizenship with ideals of liberalism, of free and fair elections and of individual accomplishment through self-improvement; that has a civil bureaucracy promising advancement on merit; that has uniform civic buildings spread across the country. On the other hand, it also swings between using a technocratic or centralised bureaucratic logic and an electoral or populist one; it fosters a tension between the *ad hominem*, divisive rhetoric of party politics and the consensual language of shared values in the village forum or *kgotla*; it has a government and public sphere which provide 'few models for discourse about communities as means to success, or more particularly as moral means to success – either as "tribal" groups, or more recently as villages'.

For me there is a great temptation, reflecting on the minefield of perplexing uncertainties in Durham's case, because I am writing this Introduction in Botswana during a time of national soul-searching about the rights and privileges of minorities, including the Herero. I am tempted to follow the leads in Durham's analysis of the Mahalapye case as they extend into ongoing debates about urban elites and minorities elsewhere in the country, but I must reserve that for another discussion, given our present limits (Werbner 2001). Here the point worth stressing is that through the Mahalapye case Durham gives us fine access to the actual realities of postcolonial subjection in the ambiguous interplay between the national and the local state. On that basis, she makes us understand how, and at what cost, postcolonial agency is a hybrid, 'hybridized between a strongly asseverated liberalism and the renewed relevance of group experiences' (see also R. Werbner 2000). Even beyond that and *contra* the early Foucault, Durham's argument extends to broad conclusions about the more general importance of uncertainty in political and other social action.

This theoretical interest in contingency, indeterminacy and ambiguity in subjectivity is at the heart of our seventh chapter by Susan Reynolds Whyte. Whyte is concerned to understand, and make us understand also, how people in eastern Uganda are surviving the ravages of the AIDS epidemic. Her argument builds on her prize-winning book, *Questioning Misfortune* (1997) and its demonstration of how John Dewey's philosophy of pragmatism illuminates African pragmatics and the practical wisdom of everyday life. Like Durham, Whyte is careful to make it plain that in no way does her view of postcolonial uncertainties imply that life was more certain in colonial or precolonial times. What has changed in postcolonial transformations is the nature of the uncertainties, not the existence of uncertainty itself (see also R. Werbner 1996). Here Whyte wants to distinguish her approach from that of Achille Mbembe and Janet Roitman in 'Figures of the Subject in Times of Crisis', where they write of a characteristic of the times, the 'profoundly provisional and revisable character of things' (1995:342; see also R. Werbner, *ibid*.). In Whyte's view that leads Mbembe and Roitman into describing a generic subjectivity and a shared cultural pattern abstracted from action. Instead, in line with pragmatism, what concerns Whyte is a matter of doing, of intentional action and especially interaction.

Whyte's approach turns on a concept of the subjunctive; that is, the tentative and the conditional mood – the mood which is responsive to the if and maybe of experience and looks to an uncertain future with both hope and doubt. In eastern Uganda, in the people's own terms, it is a matter of *ohugeraga*, of trying out alternatives, such as one plan of action, then another. It is this subjunctive mood that prevails in subjection to the insufficiencies of health care systems in postcolonial African states, Whyte suggests. Related to the subjunctive, in Whyte's view, is another concept, civility, by which, following Richard Rorty, she means a virtue of practical wisdom recognised by the people themselves, the virtue of attending to others, showing them respect, and recognising 'their moral privilege to an account of how things are'. In everyday life, the exercise of civility which, in turn, relates to a sense of being mutually implicated or interdependent, qualifies how the subjunctive mood is realised, as people cope with the chanciness of postcolonial health care.

The postcolonial quest for a state of bodily and material well-being is also foregrounded by Karen Middleton in our last chapter. Middleton's interest is in moral relatedness, inward-looking subjectivities and the significance of incest for postcolonial subjection among the Karembola of southern Madagascar. Like Whyte, too, Middleton gives prominence to the people's own understanding of the subjunctive – that which, in their phrase, 'makes the self live', and which, she interprets, 'places indeterminacy and precariousness at the very heart of social reproductive processes'. Here, as in Whyte's chapter, among others, the self is, of course, the relational self, implicated in interdependence with significant others, both living and dead. But for Karembola the implication is extreme, very highly elaborated culturally and so intricate that everyone is 'enmeshed in commitments, constraints and influences that extend far beyond known relatives'. Following Whyte's situated understanding even further, Middleton unpacks the significance of people's own perception of embodied subjectivity – their sense that it is 'by eating one another' in sexual intercourse and by 'sharing water and food' that they create the subjectivity which is the most intensely emotional and which they value the highest.

Karembola live in a rural, culturally insular periphery. There are local inequalities of wealth and power among them but these are not based on new advantages in education, political office or entrepreneurship but on the age-old manipulation of networks of gift exchanges, linked to the reproductive powers of people and cattle. Although the rate of outward labour migration by whole Karembola families, moving to settle permanently in cities and their own communities in the distant north, has become high, in their original southern home Karembola remain relatively cut off from such settlers. Moreover, while Karembola speak as if, in the past, foreigners completely colonised their bodies and minds, postcolonial state intervention has been largely ineffective and political autonomy remains considerable.

Because of this peripherality, Middleton has to write against the grain of recent trends in postcolonial studies. These are trends which, to the uncritical, might make her account seem naïve, ahistorical or lost in what Peter Geschiere ironically calls 'Anthropology-land' (1999). Well aware of that, Middleton is careful to position her analysis against the background of a considered review of much recent debate on postcoloniality, expanding world systems, modernity, and historical transformation.

'On standard measures', Middleton observes, 'the Karembola is probably the most "deprived" and marginalised region of one of the poorest countries in the world.' But this observation, inviting outsiders to imagine a hinterland 'peripheral to progress, development and modernity', has to be qualified in subjective terms. It has to be read, Middleton insists, according to the way Karembola themselves imagine their centrality: the way, from the outsiders' viewpoint, they subjectively reverse peripherality.

At the centre, for the blessing of power, purity, fertility and wealth, Karembola place closure, realised above all in marriages in one house, commonly between brothers' children. What appears paradoxical, however, is that 'closure may just as easily end in moral blame and pollution, and become yet another factor Karembola invoke to explain their poverty and their impotency', Middleton reports. She resolves the paradox by revealing more of the dialectics of subjectivity among Karembola, how Karembola seesaw between alternatives, never being quite sure how best they can secure life and having to try, pragmatically, first one option then another, each being open to provisional and contestable interpretations.

'Perhaps. Who's to know?' is a common response among Karembola on hearing of a misfortune or a death and, recognising their human vulnerability, feeling unable to know its cause with any certainty. The Karembola discourse for such uncertainties is about 'a massive skein of intimacies' which the people know they can never disentangle and which they feel has made Karembola-ness and Karembola personhood, even in precolonial times, 'long before the French arrived'. This inescapable heritage from the past is the discourse of intimate entanglement, obsessive for Karembola, which Middleton sums up in the word 'incest'.

'The possibility of incest of one kind or another permeates relations between just about everyone,' Middleton observes, including even strangers in a single moral community. The potential is felt to be greatest between people classed as belonging to different generations, say 'parent' and 'child', but attracted to be sexual partners, as if they were of same generation: their incest conflates the order of generations upon which reproduction is felt to depend. The turning of such potential into actual blame for witting or unwitting transgression of the incest taboos is highly politicised, involving guileful competition for control of divinatory and other discovery techniques to expose incest. Virtually all sexual intimacy, outside the preferred form of marriage, is beyond personal control, at least by the intimates themselves, for they are at risk of being subjected to scandalmongers in the manipulation of public opinion. For Karembola, subjection disciplining intimacy is not by the state but by the pressure from their own entanglement with each other. And the irresistible desire is not for intimacy with the overwhelming Other but with the self, wrestling in the contradictions of the narcissistic self-embrace.

Here the micropolitics of locally situated subjection leads Middleton to pursue her analysis again deliberately against the grain of a fashionable trend in postcolonial studies, particularly of witchcraft. It is the trend redirecting witchcraft discourse, in my view, 'from ahistorical questions of social control, responsibility or micropolitics in interpersonal relations to historical questions of moral and political economy within the state under changing conditions of capitalism' (R. Werbner 1996:1, for a further re-thinking of the limits of this trend, see also Werbner, in press). Middleton's conclusions at once recover the challenging interest in the earlier questions and also go well beyond the much rehearsed answers in order to make better sense of the complex ambiguities in that mode of postcolonial subjection where the people's favourite strategy is to 'lie possum', as self-absorbed as possible. It would be all too easy to simplify these complex ambiguities by appealing to the notion of 'relocalising', as if Karembola were merely recovering the local in the face of global forces or defending a world of their own against postcolonial encroachment from outside. Against that, it is a hallmark of Middleton's approach that it reaches to the *longue durée*, compelling us to reflect, in an open-ended way, upon the continuities from the precolonial to the colonial to the postcolonial in the making of Karembola subjectivities.

## Postcolonial Encounters and Our Continuing Dialogue

Which leads me to the continuities in our own long-term project – the engagement with postcolonial encounters in a series of volumes, each of which has come mainly from meetings I convened on behalf of the International Centre for Contemporary Cultural Research, the Standing Committee on University Studies of Africa, and the Association for Africanist Anthropology. In our Afterword, Paul Stoller reviews more of the debate in papers presented to the most recent of these meetings but not included in this volume.

The first volume, *Postcolonial Identities in Africa* (R. Werbner 1996), arising from the Inter-University Colloquium held at the University of Manchester in May 1994, problematised the multiple identities and plural arenas in African postcolonies. The aim was not to efface ethnicity, the looming obsession in so much of the literature on the politics of identity in Africa, but to cut it down to size by foregrounding the improvisation of many other contested identities. From the very start, the notion of the postcolonial itself had to be taken as problematic: we knew that it resounds with a wealth of meanings beyond the mere 'after' or 'against' the colonial. Hence we began with a review of its currency in mainstream postcolonial studies under the influence of diasporic intellectuals, primarily literary critics and some political scientists (for more recent reviews see Afzal-Khan and Seshadri-Crooks 2000 and Ahluwalia, in press), and we tried to show how the mainstream makes its object of study in order to highlight the contrast with our own departure, which foregrounds the state and state-created domains in the postcolonies themselves. Coming to terms with the very 'post' in postcolonial called for an engagement with the past, both as presence and as absence. We recognised a very broad challenge:

In the postcolonial struggles for authority in public life arises a daunting challenge for analysis, which we take up to show how and why the present reconstructions of personal and collective *identity*, of *social subjectivity* and for *moral agency* draw on the culturally nuanced resources of *social memory* for negation, for affirmation and for playful fun (R. Werbner 1996:4, italics added).

This is the challenge we pursued further both in the next volume, *Memory and the Postcolony* (R. Werbner 1998), with contributions mainly from our panel at the November 1996 Meetings of the American Anthropological Association, and in the present volume, based mainly on contributions to our panels at *Manchester '99': Visions and Voices,* the fiftieth anniversary celebration of the Department of Social Anthropology at the University of Manchester.

It is worth saying that we found that no part of this challenge, no key concept or substantive interest, could be addressed in depth without examining the others also, at least tentatively and perhaps at the edges of our analysis. Each of the volumes has thus had a distinct focus and an overlapping background, in turn bringing into perspective identity, social memory and subjectivity.

The shift in the second volume was to identify the memory crisis in Africa and then clarify its postcolonial significance for the critique of power. We rejected the presentist line which reduces memory to an artefact of the immediate moment, the distorted mirror of current interests, as if memory were merely a backwards construction after the fact. Instead, our historical approach to memory took this as problematic:

intractable traces of the past are felt on people's bodies, known in their landscapes, landmarks and souvenirs, and perceived in the tough moral fabric of their social relations – sometimes the stifling, utterly unwelcome fabric. The very passion in, for and against memory, keeping it alive, burying or killing it, disclosing, registering, textualising and re-creating it [was] also problematic in our analysis (Werbner 1998:3).

The embodied subjectivity upon which our discussions of memory was predicated comes to the fore in our current arguments. Pursuing that throughout much of the book and, as Michael Lambek suggests, also going beyond it, we return repeatedly to the 'domestication of the subject', in Nyamnjoh's phrase, to the implication of the subject in intersubjectivity, to the people's perception, so widespread in postcolonial Africa, that to live life to the fullest is to live it in interdependence, in conviviality, if possible; that care and respect for others – indeed, civility – is a precious and precarious condition of survival and as such is the object of recognised strategies for its conscious defence; that, because significant others are opaque, never being totally knowable, uncertainty, ambivalence and contingency are inescapable conditions of human existence. We return repeatedly, also, to the problematics of postcolonial morality in tension with power, including state power and more diffuse social power, and the consequences of this for the autonomy of postcolonial agency. And recognising that subjection is a playful process, and not merely a process of discipline and domination, we recover the intersubjective fantasies, the shared flights of imagination, by which people transcend what outsiders might call their marginality and open out subjective worlds of their own, some of them more deliberately hybrid than others, and some, exclusive of outsiders and, even in the subjects' own eyes, inward-looking to the point of obsession.

Moving from identity, to social memory, to our focus on subjectivity, one thing has been constant – our commitment to critical theory and comparative argument on the basis of fine contemporary cases, representing culturally nuanced understandings of everyday life as it is now being realised in specific parts of postcolonial Africa. Also writ large throughout the volumes is our lasting debt to the people of the post-colonies who made our insights possible by sharing their lives with us, whether as strangers come from America, Asia and Europe or as fellow Africans. In acknowledgment of our own debt, we dedicate this book to our postcolonial creditors in Africa, with our thanks and our hopes for a continuing twenty-first century dialogue.

## References

Afzal-Khan, Fawzia and Kalpana Seshadri-Crooks (eds.) (2000), *The Pre-Occupation of Postcolonial Studies*. Durham and London: Duke University Press.

Ahluwalia, Pal (in press), *Politics and Post-Colonial Theory: African Inflections*. London: Routledge.

Basu, Dipannita and Pnina Werbner (2001), 'Bootstrap Capitalism and the Culture Industries: A Critique of Invidious Comparisons in the Study of Ethnic Entrepreneurship'. *Ethnic and Racial Studies* 24 (2):236–62.

Comaroff, John L. and Jean Comaroff (1999), 'Introduction'. In John L. and Jean Comaroff (eds.) *Civil Society and the Political Imagination in Africa*. Chicago: Chicago University Press.

Durham, Deborah (1999), 'The Predicament of Dress: Polyvalency and the Ironies of a Cultural Identity'. *American Ethnologist* 26 (2):389–411.

Geschiere, Peter (1999), 'Globalization and the Power of Indeterminate Meaning: Witchcraft and Spirit Cults in Africa and East Asia'. In Birgit Meyer and Peter Geschiere (eds.), *Globalization and Identity*. Oxford: Blackwell.

Gluckman, Max (1949), 'The Village Headman in British Central Africa'. *Africa* 19:89–101.

Mamdani, Mahmood (1996), *Citizen and Subject*. Princeton: Princeton University Press.

Mbock, C. G. (ed.) (1996) *Cameroun: pluralisme culturel et convivialité*. Paris: Edition Nouvelle du Sud.

Mbembe, Achille (1992a), 'Provisional Notes on the Postcolony'. *Africa* 62 (1):3–37.

— (1992b), 'The Banality of Power and the Aesthetics of Vulgarity in the Postcolony'. *Public Culture* 4(2):1–30.

Mbembe, Achille and Janet Roitman (1995), 'Figures of the Subject in Times of Crisis'. *Public Culture* 7: 323–52.

Nkwi, P. N. and Francis Nyamnjoh (1997), *Regional Balance and National Integration in Cameroon: Lessons Learned and the Uncertain Future*. ASC/ICASSRT: Yaounde.

Nyamnjoh, Francis (1991), *Mind Searching*. Awka, Anambra State: Kucena Damian Nigeria Limited.

— (1999), 'Cameroon: A Country United by Ethnic Ambition and Difference'. *African Affairs* 98:101–18.

— (2001), 'Expectations of Modernity in Africa or a Future in a Rearview Mirror'. *Journal of Southern African Studies* 27:363–9.

Weiss, Brad (1999), 'The Barber in Pain: Consciousness, Affliction and Alterity in Urban East Africa'. Paper presented to the 15th *Satterthwaite Colloquium on Ritual and Religion*, Satterthwaite: University of Manchester, cited with permission.

— (2000), 'Thug Realism: Inhabiting Fantasy in Urban Tanzania'. Paper presented to the The Creekside Inn, cited with permission.

Werbner, Pnina (1996), '"Fun Spaces": On Identity and Social Empowerment among British Pakistanis'. *Theory, Culture and Society* 13 (4):53–80.

— (2001), *Imagined Diasporas among Manchester Muslims: The Public Performance of Pakistani Transnational Identity Politics*. Oxford: James Currey.

Werbner, Richard (1989), *Ritual Passage, Sacred Journey*. Washington, DC: Smithsonian Institution Press.

— (1996), 'Multiple Identities, Plural Arenas'. In Richard Werbner and Terence Ranger (eds.), *Postcolonial Identities in Africa*. London: Zed Books

— (1998), 'Beyond Oblivion'. In Richard Werbner (ed.), *Memory and the Postcolony*. London: Zed Books.

— (2000), 'The Minorities Debate and Cosmopolitan Ethnicity in Botswana'. Keynote Address, *Challenging Minorities, Difference and Tribal Citizenship*, 20 May, Gaborone: University of Botswana.

— (2001), 'Citizenship and the Politics of Recognition in Botswana', in Isaac Mazonde (ed.), *Minorities in the Millenium: Perspectives from Botswana*. Gaberone: University of Botswana and the International Centre for Contemporary Cultural Research.

— (in press), 'Truth-on-Balance: Knowing the Opaque Other in Wisdom Divination'. In Diane Ciekawy (ed.), *Witchcraft Dialogues: Anthropology, Philosophy and the Possibilities of Discovery*. Athens: Ohio University Press.

— (ed.) (forthcoming), 'Challenging Minorities, Difference and Tribal Citizenship'. Special Issue. *Journal of Southern African Studies*.

Whyte, Susan Reynolds (1997), *Questioning Misfortune*. Cambridge: Cambridge University Press.

# Part One

# Consciousness, Conscience and the Other

The Sultan, Maouana Madi, in possession of Nuriaty Tumbu,
Mayotte, August 1995
(J.S. SOLWAY)

# 1 ◎ Nuriaty, the Saint and the Sultan

## Virtuous Subject and Subjective Virtuoso of the Postmodern Colony

Michael Lambek

## Introduction: An Aristotelian Perspective on the Subject

Richard Werbner's original formulation, inviting contributions to *Post-colonial Subjectivities in Africa,* intriguingly conjured the notion of subjectivity as simultaneously about subjection to power, moral agency, and being the subject of one's own experience. This is a space where a number of ostensibly competing theories might be made to meet; I approach it by focusing on moral practice, in the conditions of and for acting with dignity and self-respect and making situated judgments. I draw from an Aristotelian perspective in which practical knowledge is understood not as detached from being or becoming, but as constitutive of them (Bernstein 1983: 146), yet seek to understand the way ambivalent subjects are able to make existential choices with respect to power. My subject here is a spirit medium who, subjected to power and history, nevertheless manages to constitute herself as a subject in her own right.[1]

With respect to the postcolonial, the locus is an anomalous one; Mayotte remains one of the few previously colonised places that is not exactly post-colonial, or rather, that has defined coloniality in an original, even post-modern way, in which the emphasis is on the second rather than the first morpheme of post*colonial*. Appropriated by France in 1841 and subjected to a harsh regime of sugar plantations through the early part of this century, followed by relatively benign neglect until the mid 1970s, Mayotte chose in vigorously contested referenda conducted in 1974 and 1976 not to sever its ties with France in order to join the emerging independent republic of the Comoros, of which it was certainly geographically and culturally a distinctive part (Lambek 1995, Vérin 1994). Mayotte received instead the status of Collectivité Territoriale, an ambiguous designation that in practice includes government by a French prefect alongside an elected local assembly and deputies to the French legislature. This is not the place to go into the complexities of the legal and political status or the lively local politics. Suffice it to say that the Mahorais (people of Mayotte) understood themselves to know what they were doing. And, despite the inevitable continuation of colonial attitudes on the part of the French, the Mahorais have been quite successful at getting what they thought they wanted.[2] Perhaps inevitably, they now want more and more.

Since 1976 Mayotte has undergone a striking transformation with respect to the economy, to social services, in particular education, and to the outlook of the population. Mayotte has been transformed into a post-traditional society in which subsistence rice cultivation has been entirely abandoned in favour of wage work and welfare benefits; in which a whole generation has been introduced to French schooling, some proceeding all the way through to the *baccalauréat*; in which people achieved social mobility and white collar jobs; and in which many inhabitants were able to relocate to La Réunion and even metropolitan France. Conversely, Mayotte has become a desirable location for outsiders: for metropolitan French seeking romantic escape in a tropical island that has an ever-increasing tourist infrastructure, supply of European amenities, and the security of the known; for desperately poor Comorians, especially Anjouanais, who often arrive on the beach at night and are willing to take employment on any terms; and for Malagasy from the Mahajanga region eagerly seeking work papers and drawing on old kinship connections to acquire French citizenship. Mayotte has become a local hub of movement and a whir of activity and opportunity. But in the background remain all those people who did not achieve the mobility, the education, the white collar jobs, the consumer items, and the respect that comes with them.

Originally despised for its political dependency and subsequently envied for its economic success (albeit relative and artificial), and certainly less buffeted by the effects of global economic forces than its neighbours, Mayotte has experienced rapid transition, a transition to which Nuriaty, the woman at the centre of this chapter, stands as moral witness. Yet this transition was something generally desired. When neighbouring Madagascar marks independence day by means of French custom (military parades, food, *bises*), the Malagasy are celebrating not only independence from

France but independence to be like France, to be another commensurable nation-state within the international order of nation-states. In this aspiration perhaps they are out of date. Mayotte, which is not only like France, but a part of France, stands as the first instance of a place that grasped the possibility of postcoloniality in the new global order for enhanced forms of connection and mobility.

## Situated Judgment and Practical Wisdom

To generalise about subjectivity risks engagement with the oxymoronic and so I turn to case history, a suitably Mancunian method that I have found indispensable. The story is that of Nuriaty Tumbu (a pseudonym). Modest in her range and abilities by comparison to some of the sophisticated spirit mediums I have since encountered in Madagascar, like them she is both a subjective virtuoso and virtuous subject.

The moral practice of spirit mediums in Mayotte and Madagascar, that is to say, their exercise of situated, yet imaginative judgment, is evident in at least three respects. The most obvious is the way that they demonstrate flexible role shifting, empathy and disinterestedness in their interactions with clients, each other, and their general 'public', both from within and outside states of active possession (Lambek 1993: 371ff.). The second is the way mediums come to be possessed by particular spirits rather than others, thereby reproducing and initiating specific social relations and emphasising certain social connections over others (Lambek 1988; 1993: 320ff.). The third, on which I focus here, is the way that some mediums come to assume a kind of consciousness – and conscience – of history (Lambek 1998a, 1998b, nd a). Their virtuosity is evident in the skill with which they can shift between historically distinct subject positions; their virtue in their combination of social advocate and social critic, of exemplary monarch (since most spirits are former rulers) and exemplary political subject (evident in the submission of mediums to their spirits).

I began some time ago to trace generational continuity among mediums and spirits in Mayotte and thereby discovered a logic of practice inherent in succession to mediumship (Lambek 1988, 1993). Asking who comes to be possessed by which spirit turned out to be much more interesting than simply asking why some people rather than others become possessed. One of the central figures in my description of the dynamics of succession was a woman named Nuriaty, the eldest daughter of Tumbu and Mohedja, people with whom I had lived and worked for some time and who, among other things in their productive and well-rounded lives, have been active spirit mediums. Soon after her first marriage Nuriaty too began to acquire spirits. The first was a junior male carouser spirit who assisted her in differentiating herself from her parents, but he faded in significance as Nuriaty became possessed by the main senior spirit who also possessed her father. This occurred with her father's tacit acquiescence and perhaps even with his encouragement. Tumbu passed on his knowledge of curing and sorcery extraction and Nuriaty took up his therapeutic practice as he withdrew from it. Within Nuriaty the senior spirit continued to look after the welfare of the extended family. Nuriaty also began to be possessed by two of the spirits who possessed her mother.[3] Nuriaty's actions fitted my model of succession to mediumship very well, exemplifying a process that includes mutual identification, introjection, negotiation of issues of connection and separation, and ultimately, displacement, growth and reproduction which resonate both on deep psychological and on social levels (Lambek n.d. b).

Succession implies success and I expected that Nuriaty would continue to expand her role as host to the main spirit who had possessed her father. However Nuriaty's career has not developed as either I or her parents had anticipated. I was disconcerted to find on a trip to Mayotte in 1995 that Nuriaty was no longer an active medium of any of the family spirits. Social change had destroyed the whole pattern, I assumed, and indeed the changes in Mayotte were enormous. But not quite so. What had happened was that Nuriaty's moral horizons had shifted.

Nuriaty is a warm, jovial, and slightly aggressive woman whom I have known since 1975 when, as a mother of three sons, she seemed much older than me, although in reality she is approximately my age. She likes to eat well, pays relatively little attention to her appearance, and unlike most people in the village of Lombeni in 1995, still lived in a wattle and daub thatch-roofed house. She has been married six times, but over the course of her adult life her investment in relations with her spirits has come to supersede any dependence on living male partners. One of her sons died at a young age and since then, to her great sadness, she has had no full-term pregnancies. She has also raised a sister's daughter, a younger brother, and now the former's daughter.

It was her infertility that broke up the marriage that was otherwise the happiest. Her husband at the time had never been previously married and had no children of his own. After several years during which Nuriaty sought to give birth, he listened to his mother's advice to have children elsewhere and took the opportunity to follow the socially approved scenario which until then he had avoided, namely to marry a virgin. This was an expensive proposition; moreover the requirements had inflated enormously since Nuriaty herself had married as a virgin (Lambek 1983, Solway and Lambek n.d.). Thus, while she lived in great simplicity she knew her husband was putting aside most of his earnings towards gifts for the new bride. The husband decided that polygyny would be too difficult and so when the time was ripe he left Nuriaty. She understood the reasons and even attended the wedding, which included a lavish display of gifts – a sewing machine, 70 cloth wrappers, a watch, and several pieces of gold. Nuriaty herself contributed an item to add to the gifts he brought.[4]

The new wife, more than a decade younger than Nuriaty and her husband, was a school graduate with a clerical job. She had enough money to build a fashionable house of durable materials, something which was still beyond Nuriaty's grasp (she is counting on her grown sons to help her build). There had been no comparable opportunities for schooling when Nuriaty was young. Living in relative poverty or at least materially simpler conditions, she watched younger cousins and nieces gain white collar jobs and incomes and display the associated signs of material prosperity and physical ease.

When I arrived in 1995 Nuriaty began to tell me about a series of dreams in which she witnessed how a saint had left his tomb which was located on the adjacent beach. Sharif Bakar was from *Arabie*; according to legend his burial took place well before the founding of the village, possibly several centuries ago. His tomb had been the site of community sacrifices until a few years earlier. Recently the beach had become the destination of Sunday visitors from town, young people in large numbers who arrived in cars and motorcycles and who drank, played ball, caroused, and possibly urinated on the tomb. In Nuriaty's dreams, the saint and his wife (the first I had ever heard of her) withdrew in anger from the pollution.[5]

This is not the only account of abandonment or flight on the part of earlier inhabitants of Mayotte in response to transformations of the landscape and social mores. Some years earlier there had been an epidemic in which spirits fleeing from the clearing of the bush (in order to make a highway) in which they had lived angrily invaded people's houses at night. But Nuriaty's was the only story I know of to refer specifically to events originating at Lombeni, the community in which I worked. Moreover, in her dream, the saint did not simply quit his tomb. Nuriaty saw Maouana Madi, the Sultan of Mayotte prior to the French takeover in 1841, arrive in a boat to fetch him, in effect to rescue him.

Here is a paraphrase of her account:

> The day they cleared the bush from around the tomb [in order to create a football field] Nuriaty first had the dream. Sharif Bakar and his wife got up and left angrily. Maouana Madi came and said to Nuriaty, 'Let's fetch Sharif Bakar, he can't stay there.' Maouana Madi asked her to help; she's his helper. She saw both Maouana Madi and Ndramañavaka [leader of the Sakalava *trumba* spirits, former Sakalava king and ally of Maouana Madi, and the man who signed over Mayotte to the French] invite him to join them. A *vedette* came, filled with beautifully dressed people. They performed the Maulida Shengy [musical poem and dance in honour of the Prophet performed by women], then took the Saint and his wife with them in the launch [to the Sultan's own tomb on the other side of Mayotte]. They speak in Shimaore to Nuriaty. They are good, beautiful people, *ulu tsara*. Their smell is very sweet, *mañitry*. They left with gold, a golden armchair, *fauteuil dahabu* and gold clothes on the chair.[6] After they left she woke up. She has had the dream three times.

> The *vedettes* were sea-going motorised vessels, without sails. They were manned by Europeans, *vazaha*, not Arabs, but the sailors acted like Arabs and spoke Shimaore. If I knew Shimaore she would be able to give me lots of material. The saint and his wife looked and spoke like members of the Mahorais elite. They don't know Kibushy [the dialect of Malagasy we are speaking].

> The Saint has left for good. You can still do a *fatiha* [Muslim prayer] at the tomb, but the tomb is now empty. He and all the elders, *ulu be*, were angry at how the tomb was treated, used as the site of ball games,[7] picnics, etc. The elders couldn't put up with drunken picnics [as she speaks we hear trucks full of noisy people leaving the beach]. Sharif Bakar was angry to see his house used in this way, so he got up and left.

Nuriaty thus undertook to serve as a modest witness to the changes taking place in Mayotte and the violation of respect to elders and predecessors. But the fact that the Sultan included her in this scene had even greater significance. The second thing that had happened to Nuriaty (and was partly realised through the first) was that the Sultan, Maouana Madi, now possessed her. Not only that, but she was apparently the only recognised medium of Maouana Madi on the island, the previous medium, a woman who had lived in town (L'Abattoir) and whom Nuriaty had never met, having died some years previously.

This is astonishing on several grounds. First, Maouana Madi – and hence Nuriaty as his only medium – is a figure of 'national' importance. A ritual of island-wide import is held at his shrine on an annual basis. Maouana Madi signifies the unity and pre-colonial autonomy of Mayotte. He is recognised throughout the island and is granted greater honour than the Sakalava monarch with whom he interacts, replaying by means of spirit possession in the late twentieth century their alliance in the early nineteenth century that preceded and was implicated in French conquest. In effect, the relationship between Maouana Madi and his *trumba* counterpart, Ndramañavaka, stands for the social composition of Mayotte as a union of (a majority of) Muslim Shimaore speakers with (a significant minority of) originally non-Muslim Kibushy (Malagasy)-speaking Sakalava.[8] Nuriaty herself is a Kibushy speaker but Maouana Madi speaks in an old version of Shimaore. In the present Maouana Madi is sought out by important, sophisticated clients, including, Nuriaty said, the leaders of the dominant political movement (Mouvement Populaire Mahorais: MPM) that engineered Mayotte's present political status. Certain clients have urged Nuriaty to move to town, a request that she has so far forthrightly declined despite the fact that they have offered to buy her a house. Ironically, some of these clients she classifies as European, *vazaha*.

That Nuriaty has become the sole and legitimate medium of Maouana Madi is also astonishing because she is a Malagasy (Kibushy) speaker and was raised in a village of Malagasy speakers, in modest circumstances. Her family roots are Malagasy, Comorian and East African – everywhere but amongst the Shimaore elite who are identified as the true indigenous inhabitants of Mayotte with the longest-standing rights on and to the island.[9] She has, moreover, had virtually no connection with such people and no grounding in their historical traditions. Nevertheless, when Nuriaty is in trance Maouana Madi speaks in an old dialect of Shimaore.

Perhaps most astonishing , once Maouana Madi had risen in Nuriaty and his identity had been confirmed following Nuriaty's participation at the annual ritual at the central shrine, the Sultan announced that he found the presence of Nuriaty's other spirits polluting and he wished for them to leave her. Someone of his stature – and there is no one higher in Mayotte – should not have to put up with their company. These spirits, the cumulative result of Nuriaty's possession activities to that date, who had formed the substantive connection with her parents, had looked after her family, and had served as the carefully cultivated basis of her career, agreed not to rise in her any longer.[10] Nuriaty still performed as a curer but only by means of Maouana Madi. That meant she gave up entirely participating in the possession ceremonies of other villagers. Once a devoted carouser at spirit ceremonies, she now merely observed from the sidelines. Moreover, at the urging of the Sultan, Nuriaty took up regular Muslim prayer.[11]

It was an act of some courage for Nuriaty to shift from the spirits of her parents, who provided her a stable, highly connected identity and a modest means for earning a living as a curer, to a spirit whose significance is island-wide and whose appearance transformed her into a player in the public arena, opening up a whole new set of clients and demands, of relations and sources of respect, but also of pitfalls. No one in her family or her community had had this spirit; no one expected her to get it. Her mother, an accomplished spirit medium, was as astonished and as bemused as I was. Moreover, it was the spirit himself who took the definitive step of asking all the other spirits whom she had acquired over the past 20 years to move aside.

In effect, Nuriaty has shifted from constructing herself to making history. Nuriaty plunged from a highly connected position on the family and village scene to a central yet precarious position on the island stage.[12] Why did this happen? In conversation and daily action Nuriaty had come to express a degree of resentment that I had not noticed when she was younger.[13] One can speak of Nuriaty's personal setbacks, her relative deprivation. However her acts cannot be described as mainly selfish or instrumental. In part she may be declaring the decline of a kin- and village-based mode of solidarity and mutual support, yet she also gave up practices that had afforded her a good deal of pleasure and security. She had devoted much energy to developing mature relationships with her previous spirits and had been comfortably established with them. In abandoning them in her mid-forties she made a leap into the unknown, took a tremendous risk.

Despite its edge of grandiosity, Nuriaty's act was not a direct expression of envy or an attack upon those more fortunate. Instead, she viewed her situation as a product of 'the times' and it was to historical forces she turned for meaning and for redress. It is clear from her dreams and from the identity of her new spirit that her concerns were not merely personal ones. They had to do with the disturbing effects of rapid social change on the entire community, the withdrawal of previous icons of authority and their displacement by new sources of knowledge, wealth, power, prestige, and pleasure, a process which left not only Nuriaty but large numbers of villagers, especially women of her age, out in the cold. Especially acute, for people of this last cohort not to receive French schooling, was the way that people a few years or more younger had displaced and rendered them marginal. Her personal situation, made more poignant by her ex-husband's new marriage, was by no means unusual; Nuriaty's experience indexed that of a whole generation. It had become, as Nuriaty's next younger sister put it, a 'papaya world' (*dunia papay*) in which, as on a papaya tree, the smaller, younger fruit rest above the larger ones.

More than this, the community sentiment once expressed in reverence to the saint was now dissipated as the village itself was increasingly permeated and fragmented by external forces and eroded by internal divisions of wealth, consumption, and class.[14] By 1995 a large number of village residents worked elsewhere during the week. And on weekends their beach was invaded by privileged and disrespectful picnickers. Moreover, while the sacrifice at the saint's tomb had been to pray for rain, it was, as another villager pointed out, no longer necessary since the rice-growing community I had observed in 1975 had 20 years later not a single family who still cultivated rice.

If the saint has withdrawn from his tomb, Nuriaty was there as a witness. And if the saint was abetted by Maouana Madi, who was justifiably outraged at the treatment of his comrade, so too was it Maouana Madi who brought Nuriaty as a witness. Despite the retreat of the Saint, the Sultan has shown his determination to persevere, as manifested by his appearance in Nuriaty. Behind her acts, ostensibly passive and obviously drawing on a 'mimetic faculty' and strong powers of identification, desire, and fantasy, clearly are will, commitment, and moral imagination. The Sultan is concerned with maintaining the dignity of the Saint, and Nuriaty is concerned about respect not only for the Sultan, but dignity for herself and her peers. Nuriaty likewise acknowledges that the locus of significant political action has shifted definitively from the village to the island-wide scene.

## Nuriaty's Historical Consciousness and Conscientious Intervention

What Nuriaty offers is not just a representation or unmediated expression of problems, but both a consciousness of the historical process and a conscientious intervention in that process. To serve as a witness is not to be passive. The Saint's tomb did not simply sink into oblivion; its passing was marked and articulated in a meaningful scenario as the Saint and his wife withdrew in dignity, accompanied by the celebratory strains of the Maulida.

As Maouana Madi, Nuriaty goes further. The Sultan comes to escort the saint from his polluted environs, and thereby acquiesces to change, but knowingly and on his own terms. And while the Saint abandons the community, acknowledging, in effect, its abandonment of him, the Sultan does the reverse, moving into the community and into Nuriaty herself. The particularity of the village is thus transcended by 'national' (island) identification, but this time on terms that Nuriaty sets.

It is interesting to note that the dream does not polarise Europeans and Muslims or modernity and tradition. The vessel is motorised, referred to as a *vedette*, and the sailors are said to be European although they act like Arabs. The image is one of affluent gentility. The opposition governing Nuriaty's thought is not that characteristic of so much contemporary social scientific discourse, between ancestral and colonial, or local and global, resistance and power, but between responsible and irresponsible practice, right and wrong action.

In addition, Nuriaty's position is not one of simple conservatism. She is not averse to change *per se* so much as to the way in which the past has been forgotten and, in effect, violated. Dressed in his glistening white Muslim garb,[15] the Sultan himself quietly pointed out to me how he had long served [in his previous medium] the interests of the Mouvement Mahorais, guiding the leaders in their [ostensibly secular] campaign to intensify French presence on the island.[16] MPM party leaders continued to consult with the Sultan before [hotly contested] elections and major decisions and to inform him of the arrival of political leaders from the Metropole. 'The land has changed,' pronounced the Sultan, 'so we all change. We all agree now to follow France. But before any major political event they have to inform the rightful masters of the land, *tompin tany*. It is right that the politicians come here when they need something, as they did before the last election, yet they remain ungrateful for their victories.' He was angry, but admitted, 'What can [we] elders, *ulu be* do? Elders are treated like garbage, *ulu be pringa* [literally the weeds at the edge of the village where garbage is dumped and children defecate].' Some visitors do bring a small gift[17] and the Sultan insists that he continue to be informed of political needs: 'They [the living political leaders, the people of Mayotte] are my responsibility, *re' tarimiku.*' He added that he did not discriminate between political parties and would assist all comers so long as they did not advocate union with the other Comoros Islands.

The spirit's viewpoint is composed of several intertwined strands. It is a nationalist stance, one that plays up the internal unity of Mayotte and its opposition to the neighbouring islands. Yet while the sentiment is modern in this respect and by no means opposed to the current policy of increased integration into the French state, it remains at arm's length from that policy, evincing a deep suspicion on moral grounds of some of the effects of the permeation of Mayotte by French values. It also draws on the picture of competition and warfare among the pre-colonial Sultans and fear of the rulers of the larger and more powerful islands. Nuriaty emphasises Islam as the basis for both the unity and continuity of Mayotte, albeit by means of an idiom, spirit possession, that has often been opposed by Islam. Hers is a picture of a traditionalist Islam, unlike the more recently arrived reformist and transnationalist strains that provide the basis for another kind of political response to French influence.

These ideological strands are condensed in the authoritative figure of the Sultan and his place in history. The Sultan insists on his own continuing relevance, on the importance, characteristic of Malagasy societies more generally, of gaining ancestral authorisation for present-day actions and choices (Bloch 1971, 1986, Edkvist 1997, Middleton 1999), of recognising what I would call the sanctification of the present by the past. It is here that there is increasing disjuncture with the modernist leadership who, insofar as they affirm their identity by means of Islam, turn to a more transnationalist version.

## Beyond Embodiment in Poiesis and Virtuous Practice

Most anthropological readings of Nuriaty's practice would divide along theoretical interests in psychological motivation – desire or resentment – and political action – power or resistance. Both of these arguments rest ultimately on some idea of perceived self-interest and in that sense are similar to each other rather than real alternatives, though they appear to be grounded in opposed theoretical positions. I do not dispute them, but alone neither of them captures what I find of greatest significance. Drawing from an Aristotelian perspective,[18] I would emphasise the following. First, with respect to the content of her dream narrative and her performances as the Sultan she engages in a virtuoso poiesis (crafting) of history, complete with plot, character, scene and so on. This of course draws on existing forms and remains within a particular genre. Second, with respect to her judicious, situated interventions with and as the Sultan, including having and recounting her dreams, her practice is a virtuous one. Hers are acts of dignity and indignation, of courage, of imagination, of concern and respect for herself and for others, of recognising the indebtedness of the present to the past, of integrity. She speaks for collective values, for what, in her understanding, makes life meaningful and fruitful. Her means are traditional; her end is human flourishing (eudaimonia). Her acts are an expression of who she is, not a calculation or manipulation of external knowledge. And while clearly her practice is embodied, embodiment as a paradigm does not cover the case.

If we were restricted to the terms of Plato's opposition between poetry and philosophy, between mimetic engagement and detached contemplation (Lambek 2000), Nuriaty's practice would incline to the mimetic pole. Yet clearly this too is insufficient; Nuriaty exhibits a consciousness of her historical situation and skilfully applies local knowledge to it – acting within the traditional terms of spirit possession, yet saying something of relevance to the present by its means. Moreover, she is making a practical intervention – in both her personal circumstances and in the history of her society. She is exercising judgment over the situation; she is addressing the contingent by means of values which transcend it; she is articulating a vision of historical action; she is acting with reason for the good. All this falls within the scope of what Aristotle terms phronesis (Aristotle 1976).

What Nuriaty shows us is neither detached contemplative reason nor fully impassioned identification alone but practical wisdom, that is, the understanding of how to make sense of the particular, the judgment involved in the timing, in the specific incarnation, in the articulation of the dreams, and so on. The judgment is confirmed to the degree her actions are acknowledged by others as fitting and to the degree that it brings her a degree of equanimity or happiness and her fellow subjects an increased consciousness of history and the place of their own agency within it. We can speak of what she has done not as rational or irrational, accurate or inaccurate, clear or mystified, critically radical or blindly conservative, but (in Aristotelian terms) as elegant or clumsy, wise or foolish, courageous or cowardly, dignified or undignified, virtuous or incontinent.

I do not mean to idealise Nuriaty or to suggest that she or anyone else does not act out of mixed emotions or does not harbour internal conflicts. I worry that she is over her head.[19] But to argue that people are political, desirous, or ambivalent subjects does not preclude them from being moral subjects, living virtuously or seeking the means by which they may do so.[20] As Gluckman (1963) observed, most societies hold an image of persons as reasonable and upright. Moreover, as Mauss (1966) recognised, that people act from self-interest does not prevent them from acting simultaneously with disinterest. Similarly for Aristotle, virtuous action is not selfless, but rather straddles the mean between self-interest and self-abnegation. Nuriaty herself put it this way: 'The senior spirits, *lulu maventy* are angry that all the sacred spots (places of pilgrimage), *ziara* are being destroyed. [As a result,] people with spirits (mediums) suffer. The spirits come and cry in our sleep.'

What may remain troubling for such an analysis is the fact that Nuriaty did not claim her choices; they claimed her. The spirits came and cried in her sleep. Her knowledge stemmed from dreams and her acts were carried out via the dissociation of spirit possession. But the act of entering a dissociated state is not itself a dissociated act. The question is, what were her relations to her possession and her dreams, to the Sultan and the Saint? Was Nuriaty simply their blind servant; or conversely, was she their instrumental manipulator? It should be obvious that I reject both these alternatives, seeing rather the expression of her cultivated subjective disposition by means of an available cultural idiom and scenarios. Spirit possession entails the disavowal of agency; but that should not prevent us from understanding it as neither more nor less spontaneous or calculated than any other act. It is a complex intertwining of action and passion. The knowledge Nuriaty brings to possession is composed both of a techne, of the skill of knowing how to speak in possession or as a Sultan, and of phronesis, of knowing how to make significant and timely interventions. She is able to distribute, deploy, and subsume agency. Although she could stand back and talk wryly in a common-sense and fairly objective way about her circumstances and the changes she had witnessed, the Sultan gave her an additional and more powerful vehicle with which to realise her concerns, to both embody and objectify them, to render them available to herself and others, and to dignify and authorise them. Mediumship expanded both her agency and her moral horizons.

Agency is a tricky concept. Leave it out and you have a determinist or abstract model, put it in and you risk instrumentalism, the bourgeois subject, the idealised idealistic individual, etc.[21] But we can see how agents are always partly constructed through their acts – constituted through acts of acknowledgment, witnessing, engagement, commitment, refusal and consent. In assuming responsibility and rendering themselves subject to specific liturgical, political, and discursive regimes and orders, people simultaneously lay claim to and accept the terms through which their subsequent acts will be judged (Rappaport 1999). People are agents insofar as they choose to subject themselves, to perform and conform accordingly, to accept responsibility, and to acknowledge their commitments. Agency here transcends the idea of a lone, heroic individual ostensibly independent of her acts and conscious of them as objects.

In their combination of action and passion and in their explicit denial of their tacit agency in choosing or permitting themselves to be possessed by particular spirits, and then in following out the consequences of such possession, spirit mediums like Nuriaty speak to universal aspects of moral practice. The success of Nuriaty's practice may be clarified by, and perhaps help illuminate, Zizek's argument (drawing on Elster's *Sour Grapes*) that respect and dignity cannot be successfully 'planned in advance or assumed by means of a conscious decision' (1991: 76). 'If I consciously try to appear dignified or to arouse respect, the result is ridiculous; the impression I make, instead, is that of a miserable impersonator. The basic paradox of these states is that although they are what matters most, they elude us as soon as we make them the immediate aim of our activity. The only way to bring them about is not to center our activity on them but to pursue other goals and hope that they will come about "by themselves". Although they do pertain to our activity, they are ultimately perceived as something that belongs to us on account of what we are and not on account of what we do' (1991:77).

I do not wish to deny that fantasy played a role, that Nuriaty's history was largely imagined. Imagined, however, is not to be confused with imaginary, nor is private fantasy to be confused with that which can be rendered public and socially meaningful (Obeyesekere 1981). Nuriaty did not invent an idiosyncratic response to circumstance, rather she deployed the means to address circumstance imaginatively, yet in such a way that made sense to those around her. She took up the ball that had been dropped with the death of the former medium. The nature of moral practice has been compared to producing narrative (Harpham 1995: 403; cf. Steedly 1993) and we can see that Nuriaty's practice was simultaneously a poiesis – a self-poiesis and a poiesis, a crafting, of history (Lambek 1998a). At the same time, as Zizek points out, the subject can never determine the way she appears or provokes transference in others (Zizek 1991:77).[22]

Nuriaty is not a prophet, she is not extraordinary. She is, rather, a good citizen and a *mensch*, an exemplary political subject, engaged with the past and future of her society. She lacks the self-confidence to be an *übermensch*, but then *übermenschen* are not always the best citizens. Nuriaty is doing what she can. It is the ends and means at her disposal, the unity of means and ends in her practice, and in people like her, that ought to be among the central topics of a postcolonial anthropology.

## Conclusion

I have characterised Nuriaty's practice in terms of historical consciousness. But it is clear that in taking on the burden of history, in witnessing the heroes of the past crying in her sleep and withdrawing in anger from their tombs, and in carrying on despite her impoverished material circumstances and despite the lack of recognition from contemporary political leaders, Nuriaty does more than display a heightened consciousness of history; she embodies an historical conscience. This is precisely the space where the political, moral, and personal threads of subjectivity, originally conjured by Werbner, are intertwined.

The portrait I have painted and the mood I have evoked are very different from the frantic sense of loss visible elsewhere in facets of the African memory crisis (Werbner 1998), the witchcraft epidemic in South Africa (Comaroff and Comaroff 1999) or Kinshasa (de Boeck, personal communication), or, for that matter, in the epidemic of accusations of Satanism and recovered memories of sexual abuse in North America and northern Europe (Comaroff 1997, Lambek 1997, Antze and Lambek, eds 1996, LaFontaine 1997) in which ancestral and parental figures are violently rejected in response, perhaps, to what is understood as their absence, their impotence, or their withdrawal of protection. Spirit mediums like Nuriaty capture a particular moment in the process of change, seen from a particular angle; the internalisation of an ancestor (or as here, an historical precursor) in the very act of withdrawal and thereby a kind of transfer of the ancestor from the public, external scene to the internal one. In so doing, the medium allows herself to be subjected by the ancestor, but equally to be empowered and enlightened, to become a subject. It is the obverse of projection, and the obverse of witchcraft. There are flashes of bravado; a rustle of anger at the inverted and inequitable papaya world in which dignity for some is hard to come by; an undertone of knowing sadness.

In that same slow, deliberate way, Nuriaty's elegy to the receding past comes to possess my own ethnography of Mayotte.

## Notes

1 The research, writing, and delivery of this chapter have been supported by grants from the Social Sciences and Humanities Research Council of Canada. I thank especially my collaborator Jacqueline Solway for her substantive contributions to the chapter but absolve her of responsibility for the final interpretation. I am also greatly indebted to Nuriaty Tumbu and her family and regret the use of pseudonyms. A portion of Nuriaty's story, placed within a broader theoretical frame, was presented in a lecture commemorating Roy Rappaport delivered at the University of Michigan, 15 April 1998; later versions were delivered at Trent University, at the Manchester conference, and at the Divinity School, University of Chicago. I thank the audiences at each occasion, especially Heike Behrend, Jonathan Benthall, Richard Fardon, Ray Kelly, Saba Mahmood, Marshall Sahlins, Paul Stoller and Dick Werbner for their interventions. An earlier version of the chapter appeared in *Anthropology Today* 16(2):7–12, April 2000.

2 Perhaps Mayotte awaits its Frantz Fanon.

3 They had not held their ceremonies or had the opportunity to announce their names before they were displaced.

4 Much of this was described to me by Nuriaty's ex-mother-in-law who wished to both justify her own actions and to praise Nuriaty.

5 As another medium – who thought she had heard a rumour to the effect that the saint had left his tomb – put it, the saint was undoubtedly sad to have the sound of Islamic recitation replaced by pop music from the radio.

6 'Good people' are here described as Muslims able to indulge in the outward signs of piety – beautiful clothes and scent, an elegance characteristic of the epoch of Muslim hegemony.

7 Football (soccer) was, in fact, a major means by which the French attempted to reorient and discipline youth and promote a civil rather than a Muslim identity.

8 All the Malagasy-speaking villagers in Mayotte, including Ndramañavaka himself in the first half of the nineteenth century, had converted to Islam by the early twentieth century.

9 Her primary caretaker, her father's mother, still knew an East African language (KiMrima, possibly Makua), indicative of indentured labour origins and possible subservience to the elite. It is, of course, not uncommon for people at the bottom or the margins to become the spirit mediums or diviners of the elite, but what has puzzled me is the source of Nuriaty's knowledge.

10 The most important of these, the spirit whom Nuriaty shared with her father, continued occasionally to advise her in her sleep. The others, she said, left outright. Nuriaty emphasised the Sultan's objection to the non-Islamic practices of the other spirits, especially the drink and the noise, whereas her father pointed out that the Sultan is a king and kings rule singly.

11 Regular prayer was commonly taken up by older and post-menopausal women. On the complex links between Islam and spirit possession in Mayotte, see Lambek 1993.

12 This is not to suggest that her day-to-day life has changed much. In 1995 she was still embroiled in the daily affairs of her parents' extended family and lived extremely modestly.

13 To my wife, who had also known her a decade earlier, she appeared harder, her warmth coloured by a streak of bitterness (J. Solway, personal communication).

14 In addition, the security of uneducated women had declined radically. With rising domestic costs, declining subsistence production and female immigration, local women were increasingly vulnerable to abandonment by their spouses and found it harder to

support their children. For the different sorts of difficulties faced by youths educated under the French system, see Vidal 1994.

15 The Sultan sported a spotless white shirt, long waist wrap, cloth belt, lacy scarf, fez-like red hat, and staff. The items were very expensive; some were purchased by Nuriaty and her husband, others were gifts from devotees of the Sultan. He also consumes rose water, betel nut and a drink made of powdered sandalwood, all long out of fashion in Mayotte.

16 See Lambek 1995 and Lambek and Breslar 1986 for brief accounts of aspects of this campaign and the referendum.

17 Clients should remunerate spirit mediums with gifts (*ishima*) rather than payment; the amount is up to the donor (Lambek 1993: 95–98, 361) and is an index of respect. While Nuriaty may anticipate that the Sultan will receive larger gifts from wealthy politicians than her other spirits received from village supplicants, she cannot be sure of this. Moreover, any indications of greed would immediately undermine the authority of the medium. Hence, while not irrelevant, material considerations are unlikely to be central in Nuriaty's shift in practice.

18 I am referring to *The Poetics* (Aristotle 1947) and *The Ethics* (Aristotle 1976). For an elaboration of the theoretical argument concerning the general value of an Aristotelian perspective, see Lambek 2000; for substantiation with respect to poiesis, see Lambek 1998a. Beattie (1977) provides an earlier, somewhat more literal treatment of spirit mediumship as theatre, as does Leiris (1958).

19 Moreover, things are changing so fast in Mayotte that she may become unable to attract and retain the degree of social respect necessary for her own self-respect.

20 That we place so much emphasis on the political may say more about us than about the subjects of our ethnography. Might we be living a vicarious political struggle; might the aporias of our own attempts to construct a viable politics not lead us to project yet another burden upon our subjects elsewhere?

21 Richard Fardon admonished in his comments on this chapter that agency ought to remain a question rather than an answer.

22 He illustrates the point by means of the *femme fatale* of film noir who through no action of her own other than her presence 'brings about the moral decay of all men around her' (Žižek 1991:77).

# References

Antze, Paul and Michael Lambek (eds.) (1996), *Tense Past: Cultural Essays in Trauma and Memory*. New York: Routledge.

Aristotle (1947), *Poetics*. In Richard McKeon (ed.) *Introduction to Aristotle*. New York: Random House.

— (1976), *Ethics*. (Ed.) J. A. K. Thomson, trans. Rev. Hugh Tredennick. Harmondsworth: Penguin.

Beattie, John (1977), 'Spirit Mediumship as Theatre'. *Royal Anthropological Institute News* 20 (June).

Bernstein, Richard (1983), *Beyond Objectivism and Relativism: Science, Hermeneutics, and Praxis*. Philadelphia: University of Pennsylvania Press.

Bloch, Maurice (1971), *Placing the Dead: Tombs, Ancestral Villages, and Kinship Organization in Madagascar*. London: Seminar Press.

— (1986), *From Blessing to Violence: History and Ideology in the Circumcision Ritual of the Merina of Madagascar*. Cambridge: CUP.

Comaroff, Jean (1997), 'Consuming Passions: Child Abuse, Fetishism, and "The New World Order"'. *Culture* 17: 7–19.

Comaroff, Jean and John L. Comaroff (1999), 'Occult Economies and the Violence of Abstraction: Notes from the South African Postcolony'. Max Gluckman Memorial Lecture, 1998. *American Ethnologist* 26(2): 279–303.

Edkvist, Ingela (1997), *The Performance of Tradition: An Ethnography of the Hira Gasy Popular Theatre in Madagascar*. Uppsala: Almqvist and Wiksell.

Gluckman, Max (1963), 'The Reasonable Man in Barotse Law'. In *Order and Rebellion in Tribal Africa*. London: Cohen and West, pp. 178–206.

Harpham, Geoffrey Galt (1995), 'Ethics'. In F. Lentricchia and T. McLaughlin (eds.) *Critical Terms for Literary Study*. Chicago: University of Chicago Press.

LaFontaine, Jean (1997), *Speak of the Devil: Allegations of Satanic Child Abuse in Contemporary England*. Cambridge: Cambridge University Press.

Lambek, Michael (1983), 'Virgin Marriage and the Autonomy of Women in Mayotte'. *Signs* 9 (2): 264–81.

— (1988), 'Spirit Possession, Spirit Succession: Aspects of Social Continuity among Malagasy Speakers in Mayotte'. *American Ethnologist* 15 (4): 710–31.

— (1993), *Knowledge and Practice in Mayotte: Local Discourses of Islam, Sorcery, and Spirit Possession*. Toronto: University of Toronto Press.

— (1995), 'Choking on the Quran and Other Consuming Parables from the Western Indian Ocean Front'. In Wendy James (ed.) *The Pursuit of Certainty*. ASA Monographs, London: Routledge, pp. 252–75.

— (1997), 'Monstrous Desires and Moral Disquiet: Reflections on Jean Comaroff's Consuming Passions: Child Abuse, Fetishism, and "The New World Order"'. *Culture* 17: 19–25.

— (1998a), 'The Sakalava Poiesis of History: Realizing the Past through Spirit Possession in Madagascar'. *American Ethnologist* 25 (2): 106–27.

— (1998b), 'Body and Mind in Mind, Body and Mind in Body: Some Anthropological Interventions in a Long Conversation'. In M. Lambek and A. Strathern (eds.) *Bodies and Persons: Comparative Perspectives from Africa and Melanesia*. Cambridge: CUP. pp. 103–23.

— (2000), 'The Anthropology of Religion and the Quarrel between Poetry and Philosophy'. *Current Anthropology* 41 (3): 309–20.

— (n.d. a), 'Memory in a Maussian Universe'. Paper presented at the conference 'Frontiers of Memory'. London, 18 September 1999.

— (n.d. b), 'Fantasy in Practice: Projection and Introjection. Or, the Witch and the Spirit Medium'. Paper presented at the symposium 'The Repressed and Its Come Backs': Anthropology in the Shadows of Modernity'. Amsterdam School for Social Science Research. Amsterdam, 11 June 1999.

Lambek, Michael and Jon Breslar (1986), 'Ritual and Social Change: The Case of Funerals in Mayotte'. In Conrad Kottak, Jean-Aimé Rakotoarisoa, Aidan Southall and Pierre Vérin (eds.) *Madagascar: Society and History*. Durham, NC: Carolina Academic Press.

Leiris, Michel (1958), *La Possession et ses aspects théâtraux chez les Ethiopiens de Gondar*. Paris: Plon.

Mauss, Marcel (1966), *The Gift*. Trans. Ian Cunnison. London: Routledge and Kegan Paul.

Middleton, Karen (ed.) (1999), *Ancestors, Power and History in Madagascar*. Leiden: Brill.

Obeyesekere, Gananath (1981), *Medusa's Hair: An Essay on Personal Symbols and Religious Experience*. Chicago: University of Chicago Press.

Rappaport, Roy A. (1999), *Religion and Ritual in the Making of Humanity*. Cambridge: Cambridge University Press.

Solway, Jacqueline and Michael Lambek (n.d.), '"There Are No More Virgins": Towards the History of an African System of Marriage'. Paper presented at the 1996 annual meeting of the American Anthropological Association.

Steedly, Mary Margaret (1993), *Hanging Without a Rope*. Princeton: Princeton University Press.

Vérin, Pierre (1994), *Les Comores*. Paris: Karthala.

Vidal, Jean-Michel (1994), 'Adolescence in Mayotte: History, Change and Paradoxes. An Anthropoclinical Study of Identity'. Doctoral dissertation (in French), Université de Montréal.

Werbner, Richard (ed.) (1998), *Memory and the Postcolony*. London: Zed Books.

Zizek, Slavoj (1991), *Looking Awry: An Introduction to Jacques Lacan through Popular Culture*. Cambridge, MA: MIT Press.

# 2 ◎ 'I Am Like a Movie Star in My Street'

## Photographic Self-Creation in Postcolonial Kenya

Heike Behrend

## Introduction

In the last few years, together with some friends and colleagues, I have been working to open up a new field of research and knowledge having as its subject the photographs Africans have produced and continue to produce for Africans, and their discourses and practices in relation to photography (Behrend 1998; Behrend 1999, 2000a, 2000b; Behrend and Wendl 1998). In contrast to the images Westerners have taken from Africans, the production, circulation and consumption of these pictures have been largely controlled by Africans. As most of these photographs are portraits, they allow us to reconstruct a history of self-representation and self-creation from colonial times to the present.

In this chapter, however, as well as using the photographs made by Africans for Africans to generate knowledge about their self-images, I am also interested in the photographic practices which allow people to relate to themselves as well as to others. Media like photography offer a new mode of objectification and, at the same time, transform human beings into subjects. In my chapter I want to show how in postcolonial times in Kenya the medium of photography is used as a technique of the self, as a means to objectify and at the same time to subjectify the photographed person. I will discuss an example of local self-creation by global interaction and global media of a young man, Peter Mwasunguchi in Mombasa, an obsessive consumer of photography.[1]

## A Short History of Photography in East Africa

Only a few months after photography was invented in Europe (in 1839), the new medium of technical reproduction reached Africa. However, the first studios in Zanzibar and Mombasa were established by Indians (from Goa), who for centuries had formed their own diasporas at the coast. Since the 1860s they have brought their own photographic conventions to East Africa, deeply influencing local photographic styles. Thus Western hegemony in photographic practices at the East African coast was decentred from the beginning, and countered by Indian artistic traditions that had developed at the courts of the maharajas and in urban spaces. A short time later, Europeans also opened studios at the coast. From there, photography spread into the hinterland. In the 1910s and 1920s nearly all towns in Kenya owned studios in which Africans learned photographic techniques, although mostly in subordinate positions.

Despite strong resistance at the beginning to the new medium, it was soon appropriated, routinised, commercialised and integrated into various local practices. Whereas in the early years commercial studio photography was limited mainly to the urban spaces, the colonial state soon adopted this new technique for control and surveillance and demanded that its subjects in the rural areas, too, be photographed for identification purposes. Thus, the colonial state enforced an alliance between photography, surveillance and identification. While in the commercial studios customers were offered the possibility of creating various identities, to play with a wide range of self-images and illusions, the photographic images the state demanded became objectified as documents and fell into the domain of truth production. Like the 'blueprints' or fingerprints that accompanied the IDs of colonised Africans in Kenya, photography's indexicality served as a sort of trace to guarantee the identity of the image and the photographed person.

When I started collecting photographs and doing research on photographic practices in Kenya in 1993,[2] I was surprised to discover how deeply this originally Western technique of reproduction had become integrated into African everyday life, especially as portrait photography. Women and men of all social classes made use of it as a mass-produced commodity. Women who had a new dress, a new hairstyle or a new boyfriend would go to the photographer and take a picture. Sometimes, women or men who felt lonely or sad went to the photographer to get a picture because doing this cheered them up; thus, in this context, the practice of photography became some sort of cure or therapy. Young body builders would regularly take pictures to document the development of their muscles. Social events, feasts, and rites of passage were photographed and gave evidence of a person's social network and his or her biography. Photographs were integrated into the cult of the dead, especially in Central and Western Kenya. They were also used in practices of healing and harming in Islamic and 'pagan' contexts as well as in (independent) Christian churches. Furthermore, photographs were sent to relatives and friends in foreign countries who had not been able to participate at the festivities, while the migrant workers abroad sent their portraits to compensate for their absences.

The photographic images were stored in albums which were shown to visitors and guests as a way of introducing oneself. In addition, they were often displayed – framed and fixed on the walls of saloon or sitting room. Thus, while photography was integrated into already existing traditions, it also occupied new spaces, shaping in new ways memories, constructions of personhood, biographies and, last not least, subjectivities.

## Portraiture

As already mentioned, African photography was established, above all, in the domain of portraiture, whereas landscape or still life photography never really evolved as genres. While photography in Europe in the nineteenth century developed its realist discourse in strong opposition to the art of painting, in Africa photography could establish itself in a space that was not occupied by painting. Whereas portrait photography in Africa was partly integrated into already existing sculptural and performative art traditions and conventions, it strongly influenced portrait painting, an art form that came into existence in Africa only recently. In contrast to the West, in Africa it was photography that forcibly shaped the conventions of portrait painting.

In Africa, the art of portraiture has a long history that comprises a large spectrum of naturalistic as well as abstract portraits. Often the boundaries between a portrait and other forms of representation were blurred: when pots, chairs, houses and masks represented persons, for example, or when spirit mediums who were possessed by the spirits of the dead became 'living portraits' of the deceased person. As Fritz Kramer has shown (1987), abstract and naturalistic representations did not exclude each other, but could exist in one region beside each other as complementary options. Often it was the category of the social person that determined the abstract or naturalistic code. Social persons with high status and prestige, like kings and chiefs, were represented in a more abstract, idealising way, the posture being balanced, symmetrical and 'cool', their faces resembling timeless masks. Non-persons like strangers and slaves, on the other hand, were pictured in an often brutal realistic code, asymmetrical, unbalanced, and 'hot', with faces that unveiled their age, sorrow and suffering. Thus a realism, corresponding to photographic realism, existed as one possible option in African portraiture. It was not often used, however, because as an extreme form of representation it seemed dangerous (Thompson 1974:26).

The appropriation of photography into local practices, thus, did not produce a discontinuity, a completely new realistic way of representation, but instead only reinforced what in some artistic styles was already being practised. The specific realism or indexicality of photography did not prevent the new technique from being widely appropriated.[3] While, as I have tried to show, various forms of portraits existed in precolonial times, it is photography as a mass-produced commodity that – like money – in some domains developed its own autonomy and created decisive discontinuities. It opened up a new field of production, circulation and consumption of mass-produced images which allowed one to relate in a new way to one's self and to the Other.

## Photographic Self-Creation

The creation of the self is a complex process of interaction of multiple practices of identification external or internal to a subject, an elaborate game of mirrors (cf. Friedman 1993). Unfortunately, little work has been done in anthropology on personal singularity and social multiplicity as social and cultural values. We know very little of local concepts of individuation (Guyer and Belinga 1995). Spirit possession and masquerades have been interpreted as cultural practices offering individuals the possibility of differentiating themselves from others (Kramer 1987). For example, *ikenga* carvings among the Igbo in Nigeria centred on the male individual and represented the person as a particular individuum, contrasting his own personal achievements with those which can be ascribed to hereditary qualities or to some other external source (Boston 1977:14). A man's *ikenga* ceased to exist when the owner died; the formal rule that the carving should be split and thrown away shows how strongly the carving was linked with the idea of individual development and attainment rather than with the nexus of qualities that the Igbo attribute to lineage membership (*ibid.*:84). In the *ikenga* carving we find an example of local self-evaluation, a kind of materialised double of the successful person which had to be cared for, had to be fed by sacrifices, etcetera. In the course of the owner's life cycle, various items were added to the carving: a successful hunter, for example, might incorporate a leopard's jawbone and the skull of a bushcow. The *ikenga* then represented the accumulation of success as well as the new composition of the represented person – the quantitative as well as the qualitative changes in a man's life – in one double, in one carving or representation. Thus the statue allowed a man a reflexive attitude towards himself; however, it did not so much serve to produce self-knowledge as give visual representation to the social success and prestige of its owner.

While during a man's life he owned only one *ikenga* carving and in a way celebrated his uniqueness, photography allows women and men to produce and own many permanent portraits that can be stored and used to remember persons and events. Thus, through photography, a person can gain various self-images which give evidence more of his multiplicity rather than his or her uniqueness.

The photographic image, because it is a sort of mirror, is the only space in which the photographed person is subject and object at the same time (Barthes 1981). There is a fundamental schism between the subject that perceives and the image that looks back at him, because that image, in which he or she is captured, is seen from the vantage of another (Krauss 1985). Thus, a photographic portrait allows a person to see herself or himself mediated by the gaze of another.

A series of portraits give – on one side – evidence of the unsteady and changing state of selfhood in different cultural contexts as well as the problematics of self-creation in their relation to issues of power (Battaglia 1995:1f). On the other side, the images promote an additional awarenes of self, self-examination that may extend to self-problematization. The photographs serve as a site to begin to relate to oneself as a subject of aesthetic experience (Hunter 1992:348 cited in Battaglia 1995:87).

## A 'Cult' of Anti-Elegance: Hip Hop in Mombasa

In March 1998 in Mombasa, I met Peter Mwasunguchi, a young man of 18 years. Peter and his friends came from the ranks of those largely excluded from social and economic opportunities. They formed an oppositional subculture and contested the institutions and norms of African and Western societies which frustrated their aspirations for wealth and status (cf. MacGaffey and Bazenguissa-Ganga 2000). In a song Peter composed, he expressed his critical attitude to and deep frustrations with the religious and political establishments in Mombasa as well as his intense feelings of insecurity. I quote this song at full length to give an insight into the growing sense of loss and rupture that characterises the postcolonial world of Peter and his friends:

*Hi soyo sawa*
*kwawo hi ni sawawa*
*mungu aware nini?*
*ila gunia la chawa*
*sasa twaripo: tafuta pasop*
*twataka kusafiri kikafiri*
*popoie tutafika hata Southafrica*
*Nyumbani tumechoka twazidi…*
*Polisi watusaka twaonekana vibaka*
*kwasababu hatuna kazi au sababu ya mavazi*

It is not good
They do not care
What shall God give you?
But a sack full of lice
Now we tell you: search for the passport
We want to travel, little non-believer
We will reach everywhere, even South Africa
At home, we are fed up
The police are after us, we appear as branded
because we have no work nor decent clothes.

Peter was one of the regular customers of the photographer Maina Hutchinson with whom I had developed an intense working relationship. Maina Hutchinson had told me before that this young man was obsessed with fashion and photography and that he had very precise ideas about how to present himself before the camera. While often the photographers guide their customers in how to pose, Peter authored the production of his portraits. He would bring Afro-American magazines and chose some styles and poses as a model that he wanted to imitate on the photograph. His photographs give evidence not only of an obsessive self-representation, but also of an idiosyncratic attempt at photographic self-creation.

'I AM A SUPERSTAR'

He formed part of a youth culture in Mombasa that was strongly oriented towards African-American rap and hip hop,[4] admiring artists and groups such as Snoop Doggy Dog, Ice Cube, Craig Mark or Mark Ten. Peter also rapped; a few times he had been given the chance to sing rap songs in the night clubs of Mombasa. Like the *sapeurs* of Kinshasa and Brazzaville – *les hommes les plus élégants du monde* – Peter and his friends developed a transnational 'cult of clothes' (Gandoulou 1984, 1989; Friedman 1992, 1993; MacGaffey and Bazenguissa-Ganga 2000). Both the *sapeurs* and Peter's group positioned themselves in a global arena informed by the interactions between locally specific practices of self-creation and the dynamics of global processes. Although Peter and his friends did not – like the *sapeurs* – undergo a transcultural rite of passage, they nevertheless were obsessed with fashion that was produced outside Kenya. They established a hierarchy of firms and labels, including, for example, Pelepele and Faubourg,

'COOL'

but also Gucci and Armani, and competed among themselves and with other groups. Although Peter's mother worked as a tailor, he insisted that he wanted only ready-made clothes. In addition, Peter and his friends adamantly refused the cheap imitations of sports shoes, for example, that were offered in Mombasa's shops. Copies, even when excellent, caused a deadly reaction when recognised. It had to be the 'real thing' (cf. Friedman 1990:117–18). This, however, contrasts with the hip hop fashions in the United States, where fake Gucci and other designer emblems are patch-stitched to jackets, pants, wallets, and sneakers, and fake Gucci-covered b-boys and b-girls brush past Fifth Avenue ladies adorned with the 'real thing', thereby mocking them (Rose 1994:38).

While the *sapeurs* displayed their elegance following the conventions of famous, successful Western and Asian designers, the African-American youth in the ghettos, as well as Peter and his friends in Mombasa, opposed

'SMALL IS BORING'

these rules of elegance by wearing oversized pants and shirts, showing the underclothes, with heavy boots prepared for streetfighting, thus displaying an 'I don't care' attitude – although, of course, they took great care to look careless. Like their African-American counterparts and the *sapeurs*, they were engaged in a never-ending battle for status, prestige, power and group adoration in which the consumption of clothing and photography was of eminent importance.

While the generation of Peter's parents never really held the African-American culture in the USA in esteem, because they saw African Americans as former slaves, it seems that the young generation of Peter and his age mates changed this more or less negative view into a positive one, taking the urban rap and hip hop scenes of the African-American ghettos as their model. By choosing African-American culture as their example they differentiated themselves from their parent's generation and opposed the

'GET AWAY'

old colonial European hegemony. While the *sapeurs*, when they travel to Paris to buy their designer clothes, still follow French colonial and neo-colonial hegemonies, Peter and his friends instead established an Africa-centred transatlantic alliance, thus occupying a space that not only picked up the transcontinental thread of slavery but also dehegemonized the (white) West.

In addition, they were developing a transcultural, global subjectivity that strongly opposed ideas of local African ethnicity and traditions. Since the postcolonial government in Kenya under Arap Moi is one of the most repressive in Africa, actively engaged in organizing outbreaks of violence along ethnic lines,[5] this absence has to be interpreted as some sort of resistance to the state. While the dominant discourse led by the political and religious establishments is largely based on ethnicity and (religious) traditions (cf. Moore 1998), Peter and his friends – in strong opposition –

marked a radical rupture by deciding to define themselves as modern and 'American'. As in rites of spirit possession by alien spirits, they chose their Other outside of Kenya and Africa, far away in the United States of America.

Peter had seven sisters. One of them was married in the USA. With her, he established a transcontinental exchange system. He sent her money and detailed instructions to buy for him certain trousers, shirts and shoes from this or that firm. When the parcel – the cargo – arrived, he would dress in the new clothes. 'I am like a movie star in my street,' Peter said, proudly displaying his imported plumage. For a few days, he would parade his spectacular new appearance and increase his self-esteem by displaying his visibly transformed self. Then he would go to the photographer, most often to Maina Hutchinson, and ask him to take a picture. After this, he sold the clothes to his friends, sent the money to his sister in the USA with new instructions to buy certain clothes ... and began a new cycle of buying, receiving, displaying, photographing and selling. In this exchange system, it was photography that created the conditions for the system's perpetuation. As already mentioned, Peter and his friends formed part of a subculture in which they attempted to live life to the full on their own terms, to improve the conditions of their existence and to achieve status through ostentatious consumption of clothes and photographs (cf. MacGaffey and Bazenguissa-Ganga 2000:7). Because they were too poor to accumulate clothes, but instead had first to sell to be able to buy new ones, photographs became the substitute for these 'lost' clothes. Peter could sell his new clothes because the photographs gave evidence of what had been; they authenticated the existence of Peter's various appearances. The photographs still existed, conferring on the events a kind of immortality and importance they would never have otherwise enjoyed (Sontag 1977:11).

## Poses

Peter did not only sell his clothes, but he also exchanged poses. He invented new poses, and when they pleased his friend, they asked him: 'Give me a pose.' This he did in exchange for a 'copy', a photograph. And it was with these 'copies' that he filled his album with photographs of his friends. In a way, his position resembled that of a big man, forming the centre of a network of clientship and exchange.

The poses Peter and his friends displayed formed part of a highly

'I ONLY LIKE MY TWO FRIENDS'

'I AM ALONE'

complex rhetorical culture, partly taken over from the African-American culture, and partly locally produced.

I think it is possible to relate some of these poses to the 'freeze' in break-dance in a double way. While in conventional disco music, the primary duty of the DJ was to merge one song's conclusion into the next song's introduction as smoothly as possible, the new style in contrast focused on the break points, to highlight and extend the breaks between songs and give the dancers the opportunity to execute highly sophisticated, acrobatic movements that stressed the rupture in the musical break (Rose 1994:47). As the new dance was routinised, breaking began to centre on the freeze, an improvised pose or movement that ruptured or 'broke the beat' (*ibid.*). In the freeze, the dancer also took on an alternative identity, as superhero, business man, elderly or injured person, or female pin-up; or he would directly challenge an opponent, presenting his behind, holding his nose or grabbing his genitals to suggest bad odour or sexual domination. The freeze

'ENOUGH FOR MY POCKET'          'I GOT THE POWER'

pose was an element of surprise, a little shock, that formed a challenge to the next dancer to outdo the previous pose (*ibid*.:48). It seems probable to me that the freeze pose is an ironic adoption or imitation of the photographic process itself, repeating in another (this time performative) medium the moment when the photographer pushes the trigger and the person photographed has to freeze. By freezing their pose, the dancers transform themselves in advance into an image. It was Roland Barthes who characterised the moment of being photographed as a moment of dispossession, of objectification and death (1981:13ff.). The freeze represents that very subtle moment when the photographed is neither subject nor object, but a subject that feels he is becoming an object, when he invariably suffers from a sensation of inauthenticity and sometimes of imposture (*ibid*.). Thus, I suggest, the freeze pose in breakdance can be seen as an attempt to single out, reflect and comment in performative action on this special moment in the process of producing a photograph when the photographed person is

'PEACE IN MY HEART'

turned into an object and put at the mercy, at the disposal of others. Peter and his friends not only danced the freezing, but also took pictures of it, thus establishing an image repertoire of themselves and of the frozen gazes of the others.

## Photography and Memory

When in 1859 Oliver Wendell Holmes dubbed the new invention of photography a 'mirror with a memory', he recognised photography's capacities in a prophetic way. In recent years, a scientific discourse has emerged in which memory has become a major idiom in the construction of identity, both individual and collective, and a site of struggle as well as identification (Antze and Lambek 1996: vii). Memories are never simply records of the past, but interpretive reconstructions that bear the imprint of local narrative conventions, cultural assumptions, discursive formations and practices, and the social context of recall and commemoration (*ibid.*: vii); and they also bear the imprint of the media that externalise and increasingly objectify memory (*ibid.*: xvii).

In the West, memorialising the achievements of individuals as members of families as well as of other groups is the earliest popular use of photography (Sontag 1977:8). Through photographs, stored in an album, persons and families construct a portrait chronicle of themselves, a portable kit of images that bears witness to their connectedness (*ibid.*). Photography became a rite of family life as well as of initiation into other social groups (*ibid.*). Furthermore, photographic portraits provide the possibility of constructing individual biographies in new ways and, as already mentioned, of exploring the unsteady and changing state of selfhood.

In Western discourse, on the one hand, the photographs stored in albums are seen as an upholding of memory, a manifestation of identity, continuity and stability. On the other hand, however, photographs are also interpreted as images of the past which hinder or even destroy remembrance and become substitutes for experience (Barthes 1981, Anders 1983). In this discourse, photographs do not initiate a process of remembering, but instead fix and provide the subject with an alien self-image that blocks memory and conceals as much as it reveals (cf. Kolesch 1995:210). I will not enter here the debate on photography, writing and arbitrary and non-abitrary memory, because the photographs presented here serve not so much to produce non-arbitrary remembering as to uphold memory on a more mnemo-technical level, as a means of reconstructing the 'that-has-been' (Barthes 1981:77).

Peter stored the photographs in four albums. One, by far the biggest, was reserved for photographs showing himself alone in different poses, always with new clothes. In this personal archive, he celebrated himself in hundreds of different versions. In this album, his biography was constructed as an open series of outfits and poses, not kept in any chronological order. His biography did not appear as a gradual linear development through time, but as an accumulation of various images without any attempt to classify or order them.

While the first album centred on himself, the second album showed photographs of himself and his male friends, thus giving evidence of his social connectedness. The third album was exclusively reserved for pictures of his friends, while the last album was filled with photographs of his girl-friends. Thus, the albums formed a gendered hierarchy, clearly putting Peter on top, followed by his friends, with his girlfriends ranked last, thus giving expression to the dominant male-centred gender discourse of the East African coast. The photographs in Peter's albums focused upon his own generation and completely excluded his family.

As far as I could find out, the photographs in all four albums were stored there only for a short time because most images were given away as presents, as gifts and counter-gifts – picked by admirers, circulating among friends and relatives, being stored in their albums for a short time, before again being given away. Thus the albums did not form a fixed archive so much as a flexible, changing place of accumulation, always reflecting a network of changing social relations.

The albums also served as the site where the ostentatious display of indi-vidual reputation and status gained permanent visibility and objectification.

While, as already mentioned, the clothes had to be sold out of economic necessity, the albums accumulated all the images of moments of success, of 'shining' and of intense satisfaction. Thus, in a way, the albums became the site of and, at the same time, the substitute for festive occasions[6] which Peter and his friends could not afford to celebrate.

The photos in the albums did not have captions. They were not fixed in space and time, nor were their meanings guided by a text. Thus, Peter did not try to control the process of interpretation (Edwards 1992:11). Instead, the pictures were open to interpretation and generated new variations of narratives when, every few days, Peter and his friends came together to look at the photographs in the various albums. Then they discussed, commented on and criticised the photographed persons, their clothes, poses, chosen backdrops, etcetera. By doing so they related to their visualised bodies and thereby continously subjectified as well as objectified their subjectivities. However, their goal was not so much to reach an inner state of being, of happiness, purity or immortality, but to gain power and prestige through the consumption and ostentatious display of commodities and poses. Although Peter and his friends did not examine their souls but, instead, the surface of their visualised bodies, I still adhere to the thesis that portrait photography is a technique of the self, because through photo-graphic portraits a new sort of watchfulness and awareness towards the self is produced. In the act of taking a picture as well as through consuming photographs the experience of the self gains more intensity and expansion (Foucault 1993). A new field of perception is opened up and reflected upon – in narratives, but also in performative actions such as the 'freeze' – that far transcends the field of perception created, for example, by *ikenga* carvings.

The impact of this reflexivity mediated by photographs on self-definition is difficult to assess because besides photography there are also other media – like TV, cinema and video – which interact in shaping subjectivities. I would not dare to say, for example, that the dominant *ikonomanie* (Anders 1983:108) and the huge number of self-images owned by many people produces a more narcissistic personality.

In conclusion, I would like to argue that out of feelings of deprivation, frustration and a deep sense of loss – as expressed, for example, in Peter's song – he and his friends in the photographs created images of themselves as others that compensate for their suffering. They turned photography into a wish-fulfilling machine. Peter told me that when looking at his pictures his friends said that these images were so beautiful that they could not be Kenyan. In postcolonial times, heaven is not situated in Kenya but far away in the United States. As in rituals of possession by alien spirits, the medium of photography provides images of the successful transformation into the desired other, in this case, the 'American'.

However, this American is not the rich yuppie but the poor African-American young men and women from the ghettos who express their specific experience of violence, oppression and marginalisation and offer a discourse of protest and resistance. Thus, Peter and his friends appropriated not only clothes and poses but also a critical and reflexive attitude towards their own social and political situation in Mombasa that far transcends the potential of protest and rebellion actualised through the embodiment by alien spirits.

When I returned to Mombasa in April 2000 to talk to various photographers and also to meet Peter Mwasunguchi, he could not be found. Maina Hutchinson, the photographer who took most of his pictures told me that he had not seen Peter for more than a year. He had asked some of Peter's friends but they also did not know where Peter was. They said that he had got lost. Maybe he went to his sister in the United States to live in consumer heaven where all the spectacular clothes came from.

## Notes

1 I would like to thank Peter Mwasunguchi who kindly talked to me about his love of photographs and who gave me his portraits for publication. In addition, I am grateful to Dick Werbner for his critical and helpful remarks, and to Reinhard Klein-Arendt for helping me to translate Peter's songs.

2 I want to thank the German Research Foundation who kindly funded my research.

3 However, I think it was not by chance that photographs also became integrated into practices of healing and harming. Like hair, fingernails or other parts of the body, they were – probably because of photography's indexicality – identified as a part of the photographed person (Behrend 2000c).

4 Hip hop culture and rap music bring together some of the most complex social, cultural and political issues in contemporary American society. It began in the mid-1970s in the South Bronx of New York City as part of hip hop, an African-American and African-Caribbean youth culture that combined graffiti, breakdancing and rap music (Rose 1994:2). Young men and a few women produced combinations of the ever-changing black urban slang with musical, television, film, cartoon, gang culture, karate, and certain technical innovations (*ibid.*: xvi). Their rap tales refer to black cultural figures and rituals, and to mainstream film, video and television characters, thus reformulating and subverting bits and pieces of the dominant visual culture and relating them to their specific experiences of violence, marginalisation and oppression in their black neighbourhoods and ghettos. At

the same time, the stories and ideas articulated in rap lyrics invoke and revise stylistic and thematic elements that are part of a number of black cultural storytelling forms, most prominently toasting, preaching, boasting and the blues (*ibid.*:3). Rap has followed the patterns of other black popular musical traditions – blues, jazz, early rock'n'roll – in that at the outset it was emphatically rejected by black as well as white middle-class listeners. At the end of the 1980s, rap music became mainstream and has been a substantial success also with white teenagers. It has also spread and expanded to Europe, Asia and Africa.

5 In Mombasa in August 1997, before the elections in December, some politicians organised armed gangs (with the help of Hutu Interhamwe members from Rwanda) to stir up violence between residents and migrant workers along ethnic lines. However, most of the residents of Mombasa did not respond to the invitation to create a sort of 'Rwanda' in Kenya. Instead of killing migrant workers, I was told, some of them even offered their assistance in protecting these people.

6 Over a long period, festive occasions on the East African coast constituted what Marcel Mauss termed 'total social phenomena' in which kinship, economics, politics and rituals became deeply entangled. High rank was – and to a certain extent still is – intimately linked with values of ostentation in dress and adornment, competitive dance and composition of verses by rival poets, as well as the lavish distribution of food and other gifts (Glassman 1995:147). Gifts of imported luxury commodities – swords, sacks of rice and above all cloth – were manipulated to challenge a rival who when humiliated had to organise another feast and display even more aggressive generosity to outdo his rival (*ibid.*:167). With the recent economic decline of the East African coast (and other parts of Africa) these feasts have almost disappeared, although to a certain extent weddings today serve as a site for the ostentatious display of wealth and status, in which photography plays an important part.

# References

Anders, Günter (1983), 'Ikonomanie'. In Wolfgang Kemp (ed.), *Theorie der Fotografie III*. Munich: Schirmer/Mosel.

Antze, Pauk and Michael Lambek (eds.) (1996), *Tense Past. Cultural Essays in Trauma and Memory*. New York: Routledge.

Barthes, Roland (1981), *Camera Lucida*. New York: Hill and Wang.

Battaglia, Debora (ed.) (1995), *Rhetorics of Self-Making*. Berkeley, Los Angeles, London: University of California Press.

Behrend, Heike (1998), 'Love à la Hollywood and Bombay. Kenyan Postcolonial Studio Photography'. *Paideuma* 44:139–53.

— (1999), 'Fotografie als Wunschmaschine'. In *Porträt Afrika*. Berlin: Haus der Kulturen der Welt.

— (2000a), 'Imagined Journeys. The Likoni Ferry Photographers in Mombasa/Kenya'. In Chris Pinney and Nicolas Peterson (eds.) *Photography's Other Histories*. Durham: Duke University Press.

— (2000b), '"Feeling Global": The Likoni Ferry Photographers in Mombasa, Kenya'. *African Arts* 33 (3):70–77.

— (2000c), 'Fotozauber: Fotografien, ihre Ermächtigung und Verwandlung in kenianischen Heilungspraktiken'. In Gisela Ecker and Susanne Scholz (eds.) *Umordnungen der Dinge*. Königstein: Ulrike Helmer Verlag.

Behrend, Heike and Tobias Wendl (eds.) (1998), *Snap Me One. Studiofotografen in Afrika*. Munich: Prestel.

Boston, John (1977), *Ikenga Figures among the north-west Igbo and Igala*. Lagos and London: Ethnographica in association with Federal Department of Antiquities.

Edwards, Elizabeth (ed.) (1992), *Anthropology and Photography*. New Haven and London: Yale University Press.

Foucault, Michel (1993), 'Technologien des Selbst'. In Luther H. Martin, Huck Gutman and Patrick H. Hutton (eds.) *Technologien des Selbst*. Frankfurt: Fischer.

Friedman, Jonathan (1990), 'The Political Economy of Elegance'. *Culture and History* 7:101–25.

— (1993, 1990), 'Being in the World: Globalization and Localization'. In Mike Featherstone (ed.) *Global Culture*. London, Newbury, New Delhi: Sage Publications.

Gandoulou, Justin Daniel (1984), *Entre Paris et Bacongo*. Paris: Harmattan.

— (1989), *Dandies à Bacongo. Le culte de l'élégance dans la société Congolaise contemporaine*. Paris: Centre Georges Pompidou.

Glassman, Jonathan (1995), *Feasts and Riots. Revelry, Rebellion and Popular Consciousness on the Swahili Coast, 1856–1888*. Portsmouth, London, Nairobi, Dar es Salaam: Heinemann, James Currey *et al.*

Guyer, Jane and Samuel M. Eno Belinga (1995), 'Wealth in People as Wealth in Knowledge: Accumulation and Composition in Equatorial Africa'. *Journal of African History* 36: 91–120.

Hunter, Ian (1992), 'Aesthetics and Cultural Studies'. In Lawrence Grossberg, Cary Nelson, and Paula Treichler (eds.) *Cultural Studies*. New York: Routledge.

Kolesch, Doris (1995), 'Vom Schreiben und Lesen der Photographie – Bildlichkeit, Textualität und Erinnerung bei Marguerite Duras und Roland Barthes'. *Poetica*, 27, 1–2:187–214.

Kramer, Fritz (1987), *Der Rote Fez*. Frankfurt: Athenäum.

Krauss, Rosalind (1985), 'Corpus Delicti'. In Rosalind Krauss and Jane Livingston (eds.) *L'Amour Fou. Photography and Surrealism*. Washington, New York: Abbeville Press.

MacGaffey, Jane and Remi Bazenguissa-Ganga (2000*)*, *Transnational Traders on the Margins of the Law*. Oxford and Bloomington: Indiana University Press.

Moore, Sally Falk (1998), 'Systematic Judicial and Extra-Judicial Injustice: Preparations for Future Accountability'. In Richard Werbner (ed.) *Memory and the Postcolony*. London: Zed Books.

Rose, T. (1994), *Black Noise. Rap Music and Black Culture in Contemporary America*. Hanover and London: University Press of New England.

Sontag, Susan (1977), *On Photography*. London: Penguin Books.

Thompson, Robert Faris (1974), *African Art in Motion, Icon and Act*, Los Angeles, Berkeley, London: University of California Press.

# 3 ◎ The Making and Unmaking of Consciousness

## Two Strategies for Survival in a Sudanese Borderland

Akira Okazaki

Regional comparisons of subjectivities are rare in postcolonial studies. Although much has been forcefully debated about resistance to domination by the marginalised and the dispossessed, far too little has been said about the different subjectivities they create even when they live under similar conditions of subjugation within the same region of postcolonial Africa. There is a critical need to show how and why people create alternative postcolonial subjectivities through strategic action in a single extreme region. I have in mind the kind of postcolonial region where everyone faces endemic civil war, exacerbated by the legacy of a colonial policy of 'divide and rule', a region where no one can fully escape from severe discrimination, marginalisation and exploitation by outsiders. This chapter meets that critical challenge for comparative analysis of subjugation, forms of consciousness and strategies for subjectivity.

My approach is through documenting how peoples in such a region form subjectivities of their own which are alternative, the region being the ill-defined borderland between Northern and Southern Sudan, where Nuba and Gamk live. Both Nuba and Gamk have been oppressed by outsiders, mainly by Northern Sudanese but sometimes also by Southern Sudanese. Both have borne the brunt of an ill-advised World Bank policy. As a direct consequence, both have been exploited by multinational private investors in environmentally destructive mechanised farm projects, implemented by confiscating the land of numerous Nuba and Gamk farmers. Yet each people has found a distinctive strategy, using one form of consciousness or another. For the Nuba, cultural consciousness comes in and through armed resistance to domination. By contrast, the Gamk resort to ritual rather than political violence, and what they rely on as a strategic subjectivity for survival is dream consciousness.

I am aware that 'dream consciousness' is liable to conjure up misleading ideas, taking us back to the individual subject and private experience, apart from social situations. Lest I be misunderstood about dreaming, and appear to fall into an individualist illusion about the actual force of the subjective in resistance, I must stress, from the very start, that Gamk dreaming is far from merely personal or subjective experience, but a social and intersubjective activity in which many people participate. In this way, dreams are involved in their historical, economic, political, religious and therapeutic processes. Dreams among Gamk are the stuff of everyday social life.

## The Politics of Subjectivity

The issues this comparative analysis raises disclose how problematic established conceptualisations of resistance actually are. The exposed weakness is critical because it stands in the way of our theoretical understanding of the relations between power and the management of forms of consciousness. I discuss alternative forms of consciousness, which open out the remarkable potential for survival in an endangered life world.[1] Here, my own argument addresses closely the question of agency, both political and moral, and I take account of the contribution made by intersubjective dreaming not merely to the consciousness of subjects but also to their conscience, to their subjectivity as moral beings who perceive the moral ambiguities of their social lives.

In my view, it is necessary to put the issues in a broader context, from the very start, in order to explore the distinctiveness of postcolonial subjectivities. This broader context of modern politics brings the notion of self-determination itself into question. It is no longer simply a matter of the individual's exercise of free will but of participation in the process of subjugation or, in Butler's sense, 'subjection'. Following Foucault, Butler argues: '"Subjection" signifies the process of becoming subordinated by power as well as the process of becoming a subject' (1997:2). Similar arguments are put from various perspectives. Dillon has argued in relation to the notion of freedom:

> Modern politics is the politics of subjectivity. Self-determination becomes the violent determination of the self when it assumes – takes on, or presupposes – the subjectivism of modern politics. The violence of the determination to secure self-determination [...] puts in question the way in which human freedom and identity are understood and pursued politically (1997: 162).

From an 'ecofeminist' perspective, Maria Mies, in her article 'Self-determination: The End of a Utopia?', criticises the concept of self-determination for being too Eurocentric (as well as bourgeois- and male-centric). She argues that the concept presupposes the free and autonomous subject stemming from the Enlightenment, and she denounces the European notions of 'liberation' and 'free subject' as being based upon the suppression of non-Europeans and the colonisation of nature and women (1993). Likewise, from a politically informed historical perspective, Greenblatt, in his discussion of 'Renaissance self-fashioning', also argues that the desire for self-fashioning is implicated in early colonialist desires to control the Other: 'Autonomy is an issue but not the sole or even the central issue: the power to impose a shape upon oneself is an aspect of the more general power to control identity – that of others at least as often as one's own' (1980:1).

Whether it is the violent determination of the self or the Eurocentric notion of self-determination or self-fashioning, the point is that the very existence of desires for imposing a shape upon oneself as well as others has something to do with 'the more general power to control identity'. So it is not surprising that both colonial administrators and anthropologists are implicated in the formation of subjects. Majima (2000) examines in detail the way subjects were formed by colonial power (in French West Africa during the period of Vichy) and also the way postcolonial subjects (as the subject of resistance) have been described (or 'discovered') by 'neoliberal' anthropologists for the last two decades.[2] Certainly, he admits the difference between racism among colonial administrators and liberalism among anthropologists, but he points out similarities between these two ways of forming subjects, especially in terms of their attention to the body, of the individualisation of local people, and of the objectification of subjects by transplanting the concept of the subject from outside.

This suggests that the issue of postcolonial subjectivities in Africa cannot properly be addressed without taking into consideration the problem of subjectivities among Europeans. For instance, if there is a tendency for the latter to 'restore a pristine notion of the subject, derived from some classical liberal-humanist formulation, whose agency is always and only opposed to power' (Butler 1997:17), the courageous and self-constituting aspects of postcolonial subjects will tend to be highlighted. This is the situation within which O'Hanlon, in her article 'Recovering the Subject: Subaltern Studies and Histories of Resistance in Colonial South Asia', had to warn: 'We must also bear in mind the siren attractions of the idea of the self-constituting human subject, in a political culture in which the free and autonomous individual represents the highest value' (1988:197). Furthermore, Grossberg (1996) points out the self-fulfilling nature of the argument over subjectivity, and says 'subjectivity is only possible in the places constructed by the coloniser. In fact, Spivak (1988) seems to argue that subjectivity is itself a western category…' (Grossberg 1996:96).

Therefore, it should be difficult to talk about subjectivity as if it is a universal category. So Nikolas Rose rightly argues:

> the impassioned anthropologist now seeks to retrieve the self from the welter of its social and cultural determinations, and from the relativism that this implies (e.g., Cohen 1994). But despite such endeavors, it has proved impossible convincingly to reuniversalise and renaturalise this image of the person as a stable, self-conscious, self-identical center of agency. (Rose 1998:5)

Foucault considers that 'the historical hegemony of the juridical subject' (Butler 1997:101) has been created partly by the universalisation of this kind of stable, self-conscious, self-identical individual subject, and he describes this type of modern power structure as the 'political double bind', which is the 'simultaneous individualisation and totalisation' (Foucault 1982:216).[3] On this basis of problematising our very category of subjectivity and thus bringing our arguments about postcolonial subjectivities into a more historical perspective, we can now turn to our comparative analysis of the Sudan borderland cases, first the Nuba and then the Gamk.

## Cultural Consciousness among the Nuba[4]

Living in the Nuba Mountains almost in the centre of Sudan, and administratively within South Kordofan, a province of Northern Sudan, the Nuba have 'a position of the greatest ambiguity' (Baumann 1987:7), relative to the North–South divide of Sudan – they are now in the borderland claimed by both sides in the current civil war. The term 'Nuba' is an alien blanket label, 'applied by Arabic-speaking intruders to all the African hill dwellers of the region' (*ibid.*:9), a population numbering about 1,300,000. Nuba are not a homogeneous people, but are composed of numerous groups, speaking different languages often unrelated to each other. In fact, 'until recently, many Nuba villagers had no conception of the wider community of the Nuba as a whole' (African Rights 1995:11). Moreover, there is a diversity of religious faiths – Islam, Christianity and local African religions – among the Nuba people. But '[w]hat is common to virtually all Nuba groups, is a history of enmity and strife with precisely those populations [intruders]' (Baumann 1987:9). It is this common history as well as the 'common experience of discrimination and repression that created a unified Nuba identity' (African Rights 1995).

The war in the Nuba Mountains began in July 1985 with an isolated raid by an SPLA (Sudan People's Liberation Army) unit on a cattle camp for Baggara Arab nomads. The war intensified with the arrival of the SPLA Division in 1989. By that time a number of Nuba youths had joined the

SPLA. In addition to the experience of discrimination in education and workplaces, the confiscation of Nuba farmland by the government's Mechanised Farming Corporation (which was also financed by the World Bank and European and Arab private investors) impelled the Nuba to take up arms to fight against the oppressive government.

However, this did not happen suddenly. Modern political movements among the Nuba people began during the 1950s. The first Nuba political party, the General Union of the Nuba Mountains (GUN), was organised in 1963 and the party contested parliamentary elections in the 1960s with some success. But politics remained dominated by a cartel of Northern families. In 1969, disillusioned Nuba politicians took part in a coup plot and went into exile. The party ceased to be active in the 1970s. Then, a group of Nuba students formed a new clandestine organisation called Komolo (which means "youth" in Miri, a Nuba language) (African Rights 1995:55–6).[5] A number of cells have been created throughout the Nuba Mountain areas and beyond. The organisation encouraged its members to join the political organs of the government such as the Sudan Socialist Union, the Sudan Women's Union and People's Trade Unions in order, they said, to 'control from inside the work of these political organs' (Kuku 1998). It also created cells among the armed forces, the police, the security services and the prison service.

After the 1985 popular uprising, two Nuba parties were formed. The Sudan National Party (SNP) had aspirations to be a regional and national party, whereas another new party, that used the name GUN, shared with Komolo the agenda of forging a specific Nuba identity. But at that time the two parties, SNP and GUN, cooperated so closely that they 'were instrumental in creating a coalition known as Rural Solidarity, that embraced political organisations from all the marginalised areas of Sudan, including the South, Darfur, the Southern Blue Nile and the Beja Hills' (African Rights 1995:58). All this contributed to winning many seats in the elections to various organs such as popular committees, student unions and women's unions as well as in the elections to the regional and national assemblies, including a seat in Greater Khartoum. Many of those elected were said to be Komolo members (Kuku 1998).

But Komolo laid greater emphasis on promoting Nuba identity than any other Nuba parties. Eventually, splits in the Nuba movement were becoming more evident. Some of the Komolo leaders, realising that there was no sign of a lasting solution to the issue of Nuba identity, opted to join the SPLA and took up arms (African Rights 1995:55–8).[6] Although many Komolo members were arrested or killed by the end of the 1980s for other reasons (fabricated by the security police), the authorities had not detected the existence of the organisation itself. By then, Komolo cells were active in facilitating the passage of SPLA recruits to the South or Ethiopia.

Now their activities are no longer secret. *Nafir* (Newsletter of the Nuba Mountains) published 'A Brief Introduction to the History of Komolo' by Izz el Din Kuku (1998), a former secretary of Komolo, which outlines the aims and activities of the organisation:

- to maintain the Nuba's culture and heritage and to make the Nuba culture widely known in all aspects of life;

- to fight and eradicate bad traditions in Nuba society which have led to dissoluteness and subservience;

- to encourage creativity and whatever is good in society, especially traditions which reflect authenticity and love of the land;

- to recruit Nuba students, teachers, civil servants and other employees who believe in the cause of the Nuba Mountains to contribute to the political movement and rescue its people from injustice and oppression;

- to collect contributions from its members in order to help students who could not continue their study, support those fined by the court while carrying out the organization's duty by providing them with lawyers, and, if a member was imprisoned, support his family;

- to establish a library which contains all the books concerned with Black and African literature and liberation movements across the world;

- to develop Nuba literature;

- to issue a cultural and artistic magazine which explains the Nuba people's customs, traditions and cultures, to enable the members to be more aware of all the traditions of the people;

- to encourage exhibitions at the universities and colleges and in foreign countries, including displaying photographs, pottery, antiquities and introducing the geography and history of the Nuba Mountains and its tribes, traditions and culture;

- to spread cultural awareness and to fight against tribalism and religious extremism among the Nuba;

- to encourage marriage among Komolo members so as to eradicate social differences among the Nuba themselves.

This is a powerful declaration of their self/cultural consciousness. Although the Komolo organisation itself ceased to exist, its members joined the SPLA. In the SPLA-controlled (or 'liberated') area of the Nuba Mountains, their consciousness has been promoted even further. They began establishing 'a full array of civil institutions':

> The civil administration has been expanded, the judiciary improved, schools and clinics opened, a relief organisation created (based entirely on self-help), customary laws reformed, and a religious dialogue conference convened. This is an unprecedented political renaissance, begun and developed without any external input whatsoever. There is a new pride in Nuba identity, and a renewed determination to resist domination.... (African Rights 1995:9; see also *Nafir* for details of many other innovative social reform projects).

What is more remarkable is the fact that all this has been done at the height of the government's scorched-earth policies or, to use the regime's term, *jihad* (holy war) and *fatwa* against the Nuba people. Consequently, the Nuba people have been brought to the brink of extinction or 'genocide' (African Rights 1995:1–3, 137–275). This suggests that, although – or, probably, because – they are confronted with enormous dangers and the threat of powerful subjugation, their self/cultural consciousness is even more strongly promoted. Now let me turn to the case of the Gamk.

## Dream Consciousness among the Gamk[7]

The Gamk people (45,000) live in the Ingessana Hills located in a more eastern part of the border region than the Nuba Mountains. Here in this eastern part, slave raids by Northern Sudanese groups (including groups based on the Ethio-Sudan borderlands) were rampant until well into this century (James 1968). Even today the Northern Sudanese traders exploit the people and resources of the Hills, and large herds of Northern pastoralist groups seasonally invade the Gamk villagers' farmlands. These intruders regard the Gamk villagers as 'unbelievers' or infidels and often treat them as second-class citizens. Recently, the Hills have become battlefields of the (second) civil war. Many villages in the Hills were attacked and plundered by Southern guerrillas (probably one of the SPLA splinter groups). So the Gamk have now been exposed to violence from both sides.

The Gamk people, like many other groups in the borderlands, have been subjected to severe discrimination, humiliation, exploitation and marginal-isation. However, rather than taking up arms against their oppressors, the Gamk lower their profile for survival. Obviously, their anxieties and sufferings are grave, and deeply felt. But they have a forceful way of their own to deal with such problems. They insist that dreams can reveal to them potential threats from various kinds of power within and beyond the Hills, so that people can take precautions against imminent dangers. Dreams are thus of great concern to the villagers. In fact, while I had no special interest in dreams when I began my fieldwork, my field notes were rather disproportionately filled with data on their dreams, such as discussions about dreams among the villagers themselves and the social action taken due to dreams, including healing rituals and communal ritual fights against intruders.[8] It was, therefore, apparent that, if dreams were not adequately dealt with, I would fail to understand an important aspect of their social life and, especially for the present discussion, their way of fighting against power.

There are serious dream cases concerning 'demons' (*naangk*). The Gamk insist that these demons have increased recently. These demons are concerned with a variety of people's experiences, such as daily contact with high-handed Northern Sudanese merchants and government officials, exploitative mechanised farm labour, the seductions of luxury goods or alien women/men, attacks by guerrillas and so on. In other words, the 'demon' in Gamk is a form of invisible power operating in the border region.[9] Most of the healing rituals and communal fights take place when people are visited by dreams and realise that there is a problem that may have dire consequences. Then, people intensively discuss the problem and crosscheck many dreams that have visited other villagers. In this process, dreams also act as a touchstone for people to reflect on past experiences and present concerns, all of which will, in turn, be woven together into a shared narrative. And finally, according to such dream narratives, healing rituals are carried out.

What is important for the present discussion is the fact that dreaming enables people to make sense of their complex political situation in the borderlands so that people can transform their social situation by ritual means (healing rituals, communal ritual fights) and overcome the uncertainties and hardships of life in the borderlands. In this sense, their attention to dreams, or dream consciousness, is a vital means for survival. In fact, unlike the Nuba people, the Gamk neither declare their own self/cultural consciousness nor stand up to powerful dominators in broad daylight. But they are able, in dreams and subsequently by rituals, to put up a strong 'resistance' to these demons, which are in fact power in disguise. The question, then, is whether it is possible to call such a practice 'resistance', or whether resistance should presuppose agency. I shall return to this point later.

Another important point is that dream consciousness is valuable to the Gamk for dealing with internal affairs as well as external affairs. That is, dreams help people to realise what are, first, latent social problems within their own community, such as frictions or splits among themselves, and, second, their own moral ambiguities or ambivalence, such as negligence of duty or contradictory allegiances within themselves. Then, by the dream work of correlation – by perceiving the relations between these social and moral issues revealed in dreams – people often try to identify the problem that may be corrupting them.[10] In this sense, their attention to dreams can also be considered a practice creative of the conscience of the people themselves. With respect to the question of subjectivity, Gamk dream consciousness, therefore, presupposes the complexity of subjectivity – complex in the sense that one cannot represent oneself simply by self-consciousness.

## Self/Cultural Consciousness: Creativity and Vulnerability

We have seen that the Nuba make use of self/cultural consciousness and take up arms in order to fight against domination, whereas the Gamk make use of dream consciousness and carry out rituals.[11] Now let me examine more closely the issue of self/cultural consciousness among the Nuba.

The Komolo's declaration, quoted above, indicates that the notion of culture used by the Nuba is different from the one that has usually been used, at least until recently, by anthropologists. For example, the Nuba want 'to maintain the Nuba's culture and heritage, to develop Nuba literature, to issue a cultural and artistic magazine which explains the Nuba people's custom, traditions and cultures, and to enable the members to be more aware of all the traditions of the people'. This kind of cultural consciousness may easily be dismissed as an essentialist view of culture. But the Nuba's notion of culture is somewhat similar to the one that has recently been discussed in various ways: 'the politicisation of culture' (Wright 1998), 'the appropriation of culture' (Clifford 1988), 'the objectification of culture' (Handler 1984) or 'the invention of culture' (Wagner 1980). This kind of strategic use of 'culture' by disadvantaged indigenous peoples is nowadays seen as an important part of their struggle for physical, economic and political survival (Wright 1998; see also, for example, Turner 1991 for the case of the Kayapo and Clifford 1988 for the case of Indians in Mashpee). In fact, in order to make out a strong case for land or natural resources, for instance, the claim to have a distinctive culture is often of vital importance in the court. Therefore, it may well be called the strategic essentialisation of culture.

Importantly, the Nuba use the term 'culture' or 'tradition' not only in an essentialised form but also in a creative or hybrid form, as indicated in the declaration:

> [They want] to fight and eradicate bad traditions in Nuba society which have led to dissoluteness and subservience; to spread cultural awareness and to fight against tribalism and religious extremism among the Nuba; to encourage creativity and whatever is good in society, especially traditions which reflect authenticity and love of the land.

When we talk about 'the invention of tradition' (Hobsbawm and Ranger 1983), 'invented' traditions are distinguished from 'authentic' ones, although such a distinction may be problematic in certain contexts. On the other hand, the Nuba appear to regard authenticity merely as an element of their invented hybrid culture. This suggests something of the situation within which culture must inevitably be seen as at once authentic/essential and hybrid/creative. In fact, as mentioned earlier, the term 'Nuba' can only be used 'creatively', to signify a new identity (a newly united group), because, until recently, the 'Nuba' didn't exist except in the form of highly hetero-geneous groups. Hence, to promote a new cultural identity calls for creative essentialism.

For the promotion of cultural consciousness, the Nuba exploit whatever is available to them. The well-known (and controversial) photographs of the naked Nuba people taken by Leni Riefenstahl (published as 'The Last of the Nuba' and 'People of Kau') are probably the most 'authentic/creative/essentialist' representations of the 'Nuba' in the world. She has been accused of having 'paid for young women and men to undress, participate in bracelet fighting and undergo scarification' while 'she chased away the elders and the dressed', and of making 'her fortune out of simple people who were photo-graphed for no reason other than her commercial enterprise' (Shurkian 1997). Nevertheless, her photographs of the naked Nuba people seem to be appreciated by the people themselves (see a photograph of three Nuba women admiring Riefenstahl's 'People of Kau' in *Nafir* 1997, No. 2). I have also noticed that her predecessor George Rodger's photographs of the naked Nuba were proudly displayed at Nuba Campaign Exhibitions in the United Kingdom in the 1990s. Recently his famous picture of a naked Nuba wrestler (which fascinated Riefenstahl and impelled this 60-year-old woman to visit the Nuba Mountains) has been chosen as the cover photograph of the book *The Right to be Nuba*, published by the International Nuba Coordination Centre (Rahhal 2000). These photographs have no doubt helped, or perhaps even provoked, the Nuba people to objectify themselves and their culture; needless to say, self-consciousness involves self-objectification.

But the irony is that the anti-nakedness campaign mounted by the government in the 1970s after President Nimeiri saw Leni Riefenstahl's pictures (Shurkian 1997) seems to have created an historically irreversible form of self-consciousness in the Nuba Mountains:

> two generations ago, public nudity or semi-nudity was the norm for many Nuba. Clothing was adopted through social pressures, but today all Nuba have accepted that being fully clothed is an absolute requirement of modernity, and almost all people feel ashamed to appear in public without 'proper' clothing. (African Rights 1995:19; see also Baumann 1987:47–8)

Despite, or probably because of, this irreversible change, the Nuba now use these photographs even more enthusiastically. It is easy to criticise them for not representing their realistic and hybrid 'modern' ways of life, and instead essentialising their 'traditional' images. But Riefenstahl's essentialisation of Nuba culture and Nuba's own essentialisation by using her or Rodger's photographs are quite different in intention; while in Riefenstahl's case it may be for the 'work of art' (see her response to Shurkian's article, Riefenstahl 2000), in the case of the Nuba, it is for promoting self/cultural consciousness and uniting people in order to resist domination.

But there are dangers in essentialism and self/cultural consciousness. It may be argued that essentialism presupposes cultural homogeneity within a community and therefore, at the same time, suppresses diversity within it (Gilroy 1993). The danger is that essentialised self/cultural consciousness invites attacks, as David Parkin suggests in general terms:

> to have such marked self-consciousness, whether individual or group, is also to have fears for its preservation and a sense of vulnerability. Raised now to the level of an essence ... the possibility that this self can be appropriated by others, or can simply atrophy, is a final loss that no amount of redefinition could reverse. The very consciousness of selfhood here creates its vulnerability. (Parkin 1991:161)

The Nuba leaders (especially those in the 'liberated' area) are careful not to present the people simply as a homogeneous group. As declared also in Komolo's aims, they are said to fight against tribalism and religious extremism among the Nuba. They have even declared that they are trying to construct 'a tolerant society where Muslims and Christians live together peacefully and where law and justice prevail' (*Nafir*, 1995, No. 2). Whether they have achieved these aims or not, highly self/cultural conscious subjects have nevertheless been formed in the Nuba Mountains. In concluding the article on Komolo, its former secretary wrote: 'The Nuba Mountains can now be seen more clearly on the map of the world.' But, I am afraid, the 'Nuba' have now become more likely to vanish than ever, precisely because of their very consciousness of themselves as the 'Nuba'. In fact, as mentioned earlier, the people of the Nuba Mountains have been brought to the brink of extinction by the Northern regime. Importantly, unlike those who 'fight' in the court by strategically employing essentialised culture, the Nuba people are fighting on the real battlefield, desperately, against the odds.

## Self-Determination: 'Divide and Rule' in Disguise?

Another danger is that essentialised self/cultural consciousness not only suppresses internal diversity but also creates dissenting groups and makes reconciliation between them very difficult. In fact, the real problem is not so much how to construct a religiously tolerant society as how to reconcile a long-standing dispute among the Nuba. As mentioned earlier, there has been a deep cleavage between those who wish to express Nuba identity and those who tend to assimilate to Northern Sudanese. Politically, therefore, the latter tend to support non-ethnic but regional or national parties.

This cleavage affects not only Nuba politicians but also ordinary Nuba people. For example, most Nuba judicial officers are said to deny their ethnic roots and behave like Arabs, so much so that they have never been helpful to ordinary Nuba people (African Rights 1995:46). A more serious problem is the case of the Nuba soldiers who are sent to battlefields in the Nuba Mountains in order to fight against their 'brothers'; in short, the problem of 'institutionalised fratricide' (*ibid.*:146–59). In fact, the government army units operating in the Nuba Mountains consist of many Nuba soldiers. They become soldiers because of poverty or, often, because of forced conscription.

However, the fact is that not only politicians and soldiers but also the whole Nuba people are virtually divided. Among the estimated total Nuba population of 1,300,000, only 200,000 people (15 per cent) live in the areas 'liberated' by the SPLA, whereas 1,000,000 people (77 per cent) live in (or are displaced to) the areas controlled by the government (including so-called 'peace camps') (*ibid.*:12–13), and probably 100,000 people (8 per cent) are working as migrant labourers outside the Nuba Mountains. Of course, we should not take these figures as reflecting the Nuba people's genuine decisions. The SPLA-controlled areas are not only dangerous because of frequent attacks and even aerial bombings, making it difficult to work in the fields, but also completely excluded from humanitarian programmes. On the other hand, because the government deliberately creates hunger by appropriating aid foods from abroad and ruining Nuba fields, many people have to flee to 'peace camps', unaware that these are like prisons. In these 'peace camps' people receive meagre assistance on the condition of total submission. Numerous atrocities (rape, detention, torture, forced labour and forced Islamisation) committed by the regime have been witnessed (*ibid.*: 206–75). Nevertheless, the ordinary Nuba people are unable to leave the camps because of hunger. I believe that, if not forced in such a way, the majority of the people would remain ambivalent and undecided about whether or not to follow those who prefer to assimilate to Northern culture.

Of course, the Northern regime is fully responsible for their atrocious tactics. But this cleavage is originally a product of the British colonial policy of 'divide and rule', and its patronising and discriminatory administrative system. In order to demonstrate this, let me briefly describe what happened in the borderlands during the period of the Anglo-Egyptian rule.

The border regions gave to the British the dilemma of whether the peoples of the regions as a whole should be 'preserved' and isolated from Arab influence or assimilated (on unequal terms) with the North (*ibid.*:17). The Closed District Order declared in 1922 seems to have intended at first to protect people from 'possible exploitation by the Arabs (as traditional slave hunters)' (A. Ibrahim 1985:42). Apart from trading, a particular emphasis was placed on language and education. The colonial regime tried to isolate the peoples of the regions from Arabicisation in the hope that they would eventually be assimilated to the educational policy of the Southern Sudan (see James 1988:257). But, in practice, the policy resulted in the isolation of these peoples from the educational systems of both Northern and Southern Sudan. Thus, the peoples of the border regions were cut adrift, their future uncertain. Furthermore, economically this policy prevented people from participating in the rapidly changing situation of the region until the abolition of the policy in 1947. In sum, the policy ended up favouring the Arabs, by giving them better education, more economic opportunities, and better representation in the centres of power.

Another important fact is that the colonial government played a game of 'divide and rule' even within the Nuba Mountains. The policy operated efficiently to divide the Nuba groups against each other. For instance, the Nyima who live at the northern extremity of the Nuba Mountains came to play a prominent role in this game, as they still do. Since then, the Nyima have provided a disproportionately high number of educated Nuba. They were encouraged to play a role as the elite, and then they were co-opted as a 'Nuba' leadership that could represent, and control, the other Nuba groups. The tendency of the Nyima elite to cooperate with the government remains strong to this day (African Rights 1995:34).

A similar policy of 'divide and rule' was introduced into other communities in the border regions, including the Gamk. This resulted in dividing people into two: those who collaborate with and prefer to assimilate to Northerners, and those who remain oppressed and sceptical about the government. More important, this seems even to create a cleavage within a person. This is why a Nuba writer had to ask himself about 'the dual identity of the Nuba':

> Are the Nuba people and the Nuba Mountains part of the North? Or do they belong to the South? Or are they a nation with an independent and distinctive identity? ... Now let's ask a serious question.... Are we Arabs? If so, why are we rejected by the Arabs? Why don't the Arabs accept our Arabism then? Are we African? If so, why do the Africans say to us "Go away, you Arabs"? Why do they reject us in any African gathering?
> [On the other hand] ... both of them (the Northern and the Southern

forces) now speak on behalf of the Nuba: 'You belong to us, you are part of us and your cause is ours.' Brothers in the Nuba Mountains, for how long are we going to live in this duality? (*Nafir*, 1998, No. 3)

People began talking about self-determination. Some have remained optimistic about this. But the question is whether self-determination helps people in the border region to get out of their long-standing predicament or whether it is merely another form of the political technology of 'divide and rule' which helps only powerful groups. Let me briefly describe how the idea of self-determination has emerged and what kinds of problems are involved.

At first, the SPLA took up arms to fight for a united, democratic and secular Sudan. But as the war has continued these aims have faded. In 1991, the SPLA were weakened by the fall of the Ethiopian regime as well as by their own factional conflicts. In such a situation, secessionist ideas of separating the South from the North emerged for the first time. In 1992, the Nasir faction of the SPLA proposed a referendum. This campaign for self-determination proposed not only to ask the Southern Sudanese peoples whether they wished to remain united with the North or to form a new independent Southern Sudan, but also to ask the peoples of the border regions, such as South Kordofan, Darfur and Blue Nile, whether they wished to be incorporated into an independent Southern Sudan.

There are a number of problems involved in this proposal. First, it is given in the form of a double bind in which the peoples of the border regions can only choose whether to remain as second-class citizens under an exploitative regime (North) or to become members of an entirely devastated part of the Sudan (South) as the most marginalised groups among other politically strong Southern groups. Second, it is quite likely that the vote will split into two, given the deep cleavage mentioned above. Such a situation would definitely make people in the region more vulnerable to outside political manipulation. The act of self-determination would then only create more problems than it solves. Third, during the interim period before the referendum, a special administrative (and probably also peace-keeping) arrangement between North and South is necessary. But, if such an arrangement can be established properly, there would have been no need for people to vote in a referendum in the first place. In other words, it is almost impossible to imagine that a referendum could be properly (fairly and without violence) executed. Fourth, the idea of self-determination itself presupposes that the situation is an 'inevitable' historical process in which these 'marginal' (or 'indecisive') communities existing on the continuum between North and South are 'destined' to be absorbed into (or otherwise destroyed by) economically, politically and culturally more powerful groups.

Thus it tends to exclude the right to refuse self-determination or to remain undecided.

As suggested by the African Rights group, 'the shallowness of the debate on "self-determination"' among politicians is obvious:

> For most Sudanese politicians and international diplomats, 'self-determination' is just an event, such as a referendum, which decides who is to rule which area. For the Nuba who are practising self-determination, it is a political process of self-enfranchisement. The Nuba certainly have a long way to go: but they have started. (African Rights 1995: vii)

Indeed, the Nuba, at least those in the 'liberated' areas, have already demonstrated their courage, 'their heroism, their extraordinary resilience, and the strength of their communal values' (*ibid.*: 340).

However, for those who remain in the government-controlled areas, self-determination is, in practice, no more than the official order that is forced on them. Importantly, they are the majority (77 per cent) of the Nuba people. This is also the case with most of the peoples in the border region, including the Gamk. The problem is that the media tend to highlight those who are practising self-determination as a process of 'self-enfranchisement', not the 'undecided' silent majority. Moreover, the referendum will make their shifting identities fixed, implicit cleavages in their community explicit, and ill-defined boundaries definite. Thus, having an effect similar to that produced by cultural essentialism, self-determination will serve to create self/cultural consciousness and clearly demarcated communities. Obviously, this will help powerful groups (whether the government or the rebels or international agencies) to rule people. This is why I suggest that self-determination is part of the modern political technologies that include the divide-and-rule technology used by the colonial power. But this view is hardly new in itself. Decades ago, in his article 'The illusion of tribe' (1970), Southall demonstrated that such self/cultural consciousness was often first created by colonial administrators.[12] Rather, the point I want to emphasise is that, although self-determination may appear to be the individual's exercise of free will, it is in fact the process of subjugation or 'subjection' in Butler's sense; that is, 'the process of becoming subordinated by power as well as the process of becoming a subject' (1997: 2). This is also the case with the process of self-determination among the Nuba that may well be 'a political process of self-enfranchisement'. In other words, seen in terms of the politics of subjectivity discussed earlier, the formation of a subject, even a 'free' subject, is a process of modern politics.

## Resistance to Identity: Power and the Question of Agency

I have tried to show how the formation of the subject in subjugation or 'subjection' takes place in the colonial and postcolonial contexts. Now let me examine the question I raised earlier. Should resistance presuppose agency? I have shown that the Gamk put up a strong 'resistance', in dreams and subsequently by rituals, to the demons that are in fact power in disguise. But is it possible to call such a practice 'resistance'?[13] Or is the notion of 'resistance' itself not implicated in modern power structures? Then, as in the case of subjectivity, is resistance only possible in the places constructed by modern power? O'Hanlon argues:

> The very dichotomy between domination and resistance, as we currently conceive it, bears all the marks of dominant discourse, in its insistence that resistance itself should necessarily take the virile form of a deliberate and violent onslaught. Rejecting this, we should look for resistances of a different kind: dispersed in fields we do not conventionally associate with the political.... (1988:233)

Whereas resistance among the Nuba people may take a virile form, that of the Gamk is indeed of a different kind. We tend to call such a practice 'survival' rather than 'resistance'. But Scott has discussed diverse forms of 'resistance' (1985). Brown, agreeing with Scott, draws attention to 'a variety of subversive forms which do not readily yield up their meanings' (1999:14). Thus, 'resistance' in dreams and rituals among the Gamk appears to be such a subversive form. But Scott and Brown still try to read agency into resistance. For them, resistance is a practice that 'creates and preserves spaces of autonomy and agency' (*ibid.*). So they retain 'resistance' (and perhaps also themselves) within the places constructed by modern power after all. In fact, it is not easy to maintain 'resistance' outside the places constructed by modern power because of the nature of subjection:

> What does it mean, then, that the subject, defended by some as a presupposition of agency, is also understood to be an effect of subjection? Such a formulation suggests that in the act of opposing subordination, the subject reiterates its subjection. (Butler 1997:11)

However, Nikolas Rose discusses resistance without agency:

> One no more needs a theory of agency to account for resistance than one needs an epistemology to account for the production of truth effects. Human beings are not the unified subjects of some coherent regime of government that produces persons in the form in which it dreams. On the contrary, they live their lives in a constant movement across different practices that subjectify them in different ways. (1998:35)[14]

Here, to deny agency does not necessarily mean to have a determinist view, but rather to accept the fragmentary and shifting nature of human experience. On the other hand, to call for agency may mean to accept 'the unified subjects of some coherent regime of government'. In fact, unlike Nuba self-consciousness that produces 'unified subjects', Gamk dream consciousness presupposes, as I have mentioned, the complexity of subjectivity – complex in the sense that one cannot represent oneself simply by self-consciousness. This is why dream consciousness helps people to understand and accept the contradictory nature of their experiences such as shifting or overlapping identities, ambiguous political allegiances and even stories of defected soldiers. Dreams show, for example, that a pious Muslim Gamk man has to keep a pig just in case his ancestor should need it. Through such a dream, he can realise that his clear-cut identity as a Muslim was in fact no more than the identity imposed by power upon his complex subjectivities and overlapping identities. In other words, this kind of resistance in dreams or, we may say, a tacit resistance to identity can at least temporarily unmake what power made in relation to the subject, such as self-consciousness and clear-cut identity.[15] In this sense, to remain ambiguous, ambivalent and shifting, or 'shifty', can be a powerful means of resisting the regime that tries to produce 'unified subjects'.

In addition, dreams not only reveal one's complex subjectivities hidden behind clear-cut identity but also unmask power in disguise. Dreams reveal that what was taken for granted when one was conscious is not true by showing that the trader one met during the day, for instance, was not a human but a demon that is power in disguise. Charles Taylor has noted that 'a modern system of power … is both more all-penetrating and much more insidious than previous forms. Its strength lies partly in the fact that it is not seen as power, but as science, or fulfilment, even "liberation"' (1986:69). Probably, many other masks for power are in circulation today. It may be more difficult to unmask them than a 'liberal' mask. In any case, it is quite difficult to uncover this by means of 'conscious efforts', which are part of liberal discourse.

Likewise, the Gamk insist that power is not seen as power but as a merchant with luxurious goods or as a respectable Muslim man. But it is not very difficult for them to uncover this, because dreams enable them to realise that these people are demons that are in fact power in disguise. Dream consciousness opens out a remarkable potential for resistance.[16]

## Notes

1 By 'alternative forms of consciousness' I do not mean the notion of 'altered states of consciousness' extensively discussed in the 1970s (e.g., Bourguignon 1972).

2 'Neoliberals' Majima mentions are, for example, anthropologists such as Comaroff 1985, Stoller 1989, Werbner and Ranger (eds.) 1996, Werbner (ed.) 1998, and political scientists Harbeson *et al.* (eds.) 1994.

3 It is suggested that in his later years Foucault himself may have repudiated such an anti-liberalist view of subject because he paid more attention to the issue of 'the care of the self' (e.g., Hall 1996:10–13). But, while Hall and others tried to interpret later enigmatic Foucault, he himself made it clear that 'the care of the self' is itself a part of the discourse at the time, not practice of 'free agency' in our sense (see an interview with Foucault in Bernauer and Rasmussen 1988).

4 Unlike the Gamk case, my study on the Nuba people is based upon literature such as Gerd Baumann's ethnographic monograph on the Miri/Nuba: *National Integration and Local Integrity,* a book titled *Facing Genocide* published by African Rights, and numerous articles in the newsletter *Nafir.* Please refer to these references for more details of the history and social formation of the Nuba Mountains.

5 I am not sure whether it was established in 1972 (*Nafir* 1998) or in 1977 (African Rights 1995).

6 There were other reasons why the Nuba resorted to arms. These include the fact that in 1985 the Baggara (Arab) militia, created by the government, began looting, burning and killing those who resisted being looted, and the policy of eliminating the educated and community leaders on the pretext of SPLA presence.

7 Fieldwork among the Gamk was conducted intermittently between 1981 and 1991. For more details of the history of the Gamk people and the social significance of dreams among them, see Okazaki 1997.

8 See Okazaki 1992 for details.

9 Recently, a number of reports of similar 'demon' or 'spirit' stories, which could be considered as a form of response to social changes, the emergence of new powers or the introduction of new consumer goods, have been published: e.g., stories about pacts made with the Devil in the new capitalist economic system in Colombia and Bolivia (Taussig 1980); stories about a new spirit of desire which kills those it loves among the Giriama working on the Kenyan coast where the tourist industry is expanding (Parkin 1991); or the spread of new stories about satanic riches in Christian Ghana (Meyer 1994) (see Parkin 1993 for more examples).

10 Elsewhere, I described in detail the kind of 'soul-searching' cases that occurred (1) after Gamk villages were attacked by guerrillas (Okazaki 1992) and (2) when a man exploited communally owned baobab fruit for his own ends (Okazaki 1997).

11 Here I do not suggest that armed resistance and ritual action are incompatible with each other (see, for example, Lan 1985 for the collaboration between spirit mediums and armed guerrillas in Zimbabwe). But, while Nuba 'priests' seem to have played an important role in the past, even using dreams (Baumann 1987:122), I am, so far, unable to find any evidence that they are consulted by Nuba SPLA resistance fighters. On the other hand, to my knowledge, the number of Gamk SPLA resistance fighters is extremely small compared to the Nuba.

12 Parkin, referring to the same paper by Southall (1970), writes, 'The self-consciousness of these newly discrete and demarcated cultures, which were previously often no more than clusters of overlapping identities, was often first created by colonial administrators who wanted the convenience of ruling neatly bounded units' (Parkin 1991:161).

13 This is the question raised by Richard Wilson in a conference discussion of this chapter. I

thank him for his comments. See also his review of the conference (Wilson 1999).

14 A similar account was given by an ethnographer: 'I suggest that the Giriama construct their notions of personhood, not by first referring to the intrinsic self-determining features of a human agent, but the other way round, by outlining what they see as the parameters and possibilities of human movement and expression. That is to say, they refer not to a particular "I", but to the spirits, ancestors, relatives and clan which situate an individual. They define the moving centre, so to speak, by describing its constantly shifting environment' (Parkin 1991:205).

15 Moreover, we may suggest that this kind of resistance is quite common, as Lacanian psychoanalyst Jacqueline Rose says: 'The unconscious constantly reveals the "failure" of identity.... It appears not only in the symptom, but also in dreams, in slips of the tongue and in forms of sexual pleasure which are pushed to the sidelines of the norm.... [T]here is a resistance to identity at the very heart of psychic life' (1987:90–91, quoted in Butler 1997).

16 But such an alternative form of consciousness as Gamk dream consciousness is not unique at all in Sudan. There are a variety of forms, which have opened out the potential for resisting power, for revealing secrets of the world, for understanding moral ambiguities and conscience or for dealing with affliction. For example, prophecy (Johnson 1994), spirit possession as a 'mute' resistance (Boddy 1989), and divination for dealing with foreign powers (James 1988).

# References

African Rights (1995), *Facing Genocide: The Nuba of Sudan*. London: African Rights.

Baumann, Gerd (1987), *National Integration and Local Integrity: The Miri of the Nuba Mountains in the Sudan*. Oxford: Clarendon Press.

Bernauer, J. and D. Rasmussen (eds.) (1988), *The Final Foucault*. Cambridge Mass: MIT Press.

Boddy, Janice (1989), *Wombs and Alien Spirits: Women, Men, and the Zar Cult in Northern Sudan*. Wisconsin: University of Wisconsin Press.

Bourguignon, Erika (1972), 'Dreams and Altered States of Consciousness in Anthropological Research'. In F. Hsu (ed.) *Psychological Anthropology*. Cambridge Mass: Schenkman

Brown, K. S. (1999), 'Marginal Narratives and Shifty Natives: Ironic Ethnography as Anti-Nationalist Discourse'. *Anthropology Today* 15(1):13–16.

Butler, Judith (1997), *The Psychic Life of Power: Theories in Subjection*. Stanford: Stanford University Press.

Clifford, James (1988), *The Predicament of Culture: Twentieth-Century Ethnography, Literature, and Art*. London: Harvard University Press.

Cohen, A. P. (1994), *Self Consciousness: An Alternative Anthropology of Identity*. London: Routledge.

Comaroff, Jean (1985), *Body of Power, Spirit of Resistance: The Culture and History of a South African People*. Chicago: Chicago University Press.

Dillon, Michael (1997), 'Otherwise than Self-Determination: The Mortal Freedom of Oedipus Asphaleos'. In Hent de Uries and Samuel Weber (eds.) *Violence, Identity, and Self-Determination*. Stanford: Stanford University Press.

Foucault, Michel (1982(86)), 'The Subject and Power'. I. H. Dreyfus and P. Rabinow (eds) *Michel Foucault: Beyond Structuralism and Hermeneutics*. Chicago: University of Chicago Press.

Gilroy, Paul (1993), *The Black Atlantic*. Cambridge Mass: Harvard University Press.

Greenblatt, Stephen (1980), *Renaissance Self-Fashioning*. Chicago: University of Chicago Press.

Grossberg, Lawrence (1996), 'Identity and Cultural Studies – Is That AllThere Is?' In S. Hall and Paul duGay (eds.) *Questions of Cultural Identity*. London: Sage Publications.

Hall, Stuart (1996), 'Introduction: Who needs "Identity?"' In S. Hall and Paul duGay (eds.) *Questions of Cultural Identity*. London: Sage Publications.

Handler, R. (1984), 'On Sociocultural Discontinuity: Nationalism and Cultural Objectification in Quebec'. *Current Anthropology* 25(1):55–71.

Harbeson, J.W. *et al.* (eds.) (1994), *Civil Society and the State in Africa*. Colorado: Lynne Rienner Publishers.

Hobsbawm, E. and T. Ranger (eds.) (1983), *The Invention of Tradition*. Cambridge: Cambridge University Press.

James, Wendy (1968), 'A Crisis in Uduk History'. *Sudan Notes and Records* 44:17–44.

— (1988) *The Listening Ebony: Moral Knowledge, Religion, and Power among the Uduk of Sudan*. Oxford: Clarendon Press.

Johnson, Douglas (1994), *Nuer Prophets: A History of Prophecy from the Upper Nile in the Nineteenth and Twentieth Centuries*. Oxford: Clarendon Press.

Kuku, Izz el Din (1998), 'A Brief Introduction to the History of Komolo'. *Nafir* 3(4):8–10.

Lan, David (1985), *Guns and Rain: Guerrillas and Spirit Mediums in Zimbabwe*. London: James Currey.

Majima, Ichiro (2000), 'Rekisi-Shutai No Kouchiku-Gijutu To Jinruigaku (La technique de formation des sujets historiques et l'anthropologie)'. *Minzokugaku-Kenkyu* (The Japanese Journal of Ethnology) 64(4): 450–73.

Meyer, Birgit (1994), ' "Delivered from the Powers of Darkness": Confessions about Satanic Riches in Christian Ghana'. Tenth Satterthwaite Colloquium on African Religion and Ritual.

Mies, Maria (1993), 'Self-Determination: The End of a Utopia?' In M. Mies and V. Shiva (eds.) *Ecofeminism*. London: Zed Books Ltd.

*Nafir* (The Newsletter of the Nuba Mountains, Sudan). International Nuba Coordination Centre

O'Hanlon, Rosalind (1988), 'Recovering the Subject: Subaltern Studies and Histories of Resistance in Colonial South Asia'. *Modern Asian Studies* 22(1): 189–224.

Okazaki, Akira (1992), 'A Gamk Anti-"Dingi" Ritual: The Imagination of Power among a "Pre-Nilotic" People'. *Journal of Religion in Africa* 22(1): 66–77.

— (1997), 'Open Shadow: Dreams, Histories and Selves in a Borderland Village in Sudan'. PhD dissertation, University of London.

Parkin, David (1991), *Sacred Void: Spatial Images of Work and Ritual among the Giriama of Kenya*. Cambridge: Cambridge University Press.

— (1993). 'Nemi in the Modern World: Return of the Exotic'. *Man* 28:1–21.

Rahhal, Suleiman Musa (2001), *The Right to be the Nuba: The Story of a Sudanese People's Struggle for Survival*. International Nuba Coordination Centre. The Red Sea Press.

Riefenstahl, Leni (2000), 'A Response to Shurkian's Article'. *Nafir* 5(4):9–10.

Rose, Jacqueline (1987), *Sexuality in the Field of Vision*. London: Verso.

Rose, Nikolas (1998), *Inventing Our Selves: Psychology, Power, and Personhood*. Cambridge: Cambridge University Press.

Scott, James (1985), *Weapons of the Weak: The Everyday Forms of Peasant Resistance*. New Haven: Yale University Press.

Shurkian, Omer M. (1997), 'Leni in the House the Nuba Built'. *Nafir* 3(2):12.

Southall, A. W. (1970), 'The Illusion of Tribe'. *Journal of Asian and African Studies* 5(1–2):28–50.

Spivak, Gayatri Chakravorty (1988), 'Can the Subaltern Speak?' In C. Nelson and L. Grossberg (eds.) *Marxism and the Interpretation of Culture*. Urbana: University of Illinois Press.

Stoller, Paul (1989), *Fusion of the Worlds: An Ethnography of Possession among the Songhay of Niger*. Chicago: University of Chicago Press.

Taussig, Michael (1980), *The Devil and Commodity Fetishism in South America*. Chapel Hill: University of North Carolina Press.

Taylor, Charles (1986), 'Foucault on Freedom and Truth'. In D.C. Hoy (ed.) *Foucault: A Critical Reader*. Oxford: Basil Blackwell.

Turner, Terence (1991), 'Representing, Resisting, Rethinking'. In G. Stocking Jr (ed.) *Colonial Situations*. Madison: University of Wisconsin Press.

Wagner, Roy (1980), *The Invention of Culture*. Chicago: University of Chicago Press.

Werbner, R. and T. Ranger (eds.) (1996), *Postcolonial Identities in Africa*. London: Zed Books Ltd.

Werbner, Richard (ed.) (1998), *Memory and the Postcolony: African Anthropology and the Critique of Power*. London: Zed Books Ltd.

Wilson, Richard (1999), '(A Review of) Visions and Voices'. *Anthropology Today* 15(6):20–21.

Wright, Susan (1998), 'The Politicization of "Culture"'. *Anthropology Today* 14(1):7–15.

# 4 ◎ Gendered Violence and the Militarisation of Ethnicity

## A Case Study from South Sudan

Sharon Elaine Hutchinson
Jok Madut Jok

Cynthia Enloe has argued that processes of militarisation – equated with an increased focus on, toleration of and motivation for violence – occur through 'the gendered workings of power' (Enloe 1995: 26).[1] Whether guided by imperialist, nationalist or ethno-nationalist agendas, processes of militarisation require the mobilisation and, often, intensification of gendered identities. In her words: 'Militarisation … simply won't work unless men will accept certain norms of masculinity and women will abide by certain structures of femininity.' She and other feminist scholars have shown how military movements worldwide strive to inculcate a kind of hyper-masculinity in their recruits, associated with demonstrations of aggressive-ness, competitiveness and the censure of emotional expression. Women can reinforce and resist this masculinised and militarised mentality in complex and contradictory ways. However, all-too-often women's attempts to participate in the war effort, whether as combatants or non-combatants, are brutally turned against them.

While men's responsibilities for protecting unarmed women and children are commonly invoked during the early phases of mobilisation, they often become twisted with time into justifications for the targeting of these vulnerable groups within the 'enemy' population. Consequently, what may have begun as extremely fluid and situationally contingent constructions of group boundaries become 'primordially' charged enough for opposed military groups to turn their guns against each other's entire populations. This transformation may be fostered and manipulated from the 'outside'. However, it is primarily the ways internal military leaders conceptualise the defence and appeal to their constituencies to join the war effort that magnify the powers men hold over women. More often than not, processes of militarisation increase women's vulnerabilities to violence and rape, at the hands not only of enemy troops but also of their own male 'protectors'.

Here we develop these issues in the context of the rapid polarisation and militarisation of Nuer and Dinka ethnic identities during the 1991–9 period of Sudan's continuing civil war.[2] We attempt to identify the specific historical conditions that led to the abrupt, post-1991 abandonment of ethical restraints on gendered violence previously honoured by generations of Nuer and Dinka combatants. In the process, we link the problematic of militarisation and gendered violence to a distinctive turn in their post-colonial subjectivities, showing how Nuer men and women, in particular, have begun to reject a 'performative' concept of ethnicity in favour of a more 'primodialist' concept based on procreative metaphors of shared blood. This wartime shift of perspective, we argue, has contributed not only to a dramatic escalation in the viciousness of Nuer/Dinka violence but, more uniquely, to a major reformulation of the relationship between gender and ethnicity in their eyes.

At the start of Sudan's second civil war (1983–present), the Dinka and Nuer were heavily intermarried and bound together by both a common ancestry and a shared agro-pastoralist economy. The colonial structures imposed upon them by the Anglo-Egyptian condominium government (1898–1955) had minimised direct competition between them for political power. At that time, skirmishes between them were infrequent and short-lived, being generally limited to spear-fights rooted in competition over cattle, dry-season grazing grounds, fishing pools and other coveted economic resources. Following Sudan's independence in 1956, successive Khartoum regimes have occasionally played Dinka and Nuer political leaders against one another in the interests of maintaining Northern political hegemony. However, it was not until after the renewal of full-scale civil war in 1983 and the collapse of Southern military unity in 1991 that rural Nuer and Dinka communities of the South succumbed to national- and regional-level programmes of divide and rule. These tragic developments, in combination with the wartime dissemination of massive numbers of guns, have forced ordinary Nuer and Dinka civilians to rethink the social and spiritual ramifications of acts of homicide. Intra- and inter-ethnic struggles over the safeguarding of reproduction and of inviolate persons have steadily mounted, as gun-wielding Nuer and Dinka youths have shed all feelings of personal accountability for homicides carried out under the orders of their military superiors. The end result has been a hardening of this once flexible inter-ethnic divide – a profound shift in people's moral reasoning and personal consciousness that has had especially devastating consequences for unarmed women and children.

## The Historical Setting

Ever since leadership struggles within the Sudan People's Liberation Army (SPLA) split the movement into two warring Southern factions in 1991, rural Nuer (*Nei ti naath*) and Dinka (*Jieng*) communities in the South have been grappling with an expanding regional subculture of militarism and ethnicised violence. These two groups have supplied the bulk of the guerrilla forces fighting since 1983 to overthrow a Northern-dominated, national, Islamic state government in Khartoum. Since 1991, however, their homelands have also provided the major battlefield for escalating military confrontations among Southern Sudanese themselves (Human Rights Watch 1999 and 2002, Johnson 1998, Jok and Hutchinson 1999, Nyaba 1997). These struggles have coalesced around two main figures: Dr John Garang, a Bor Dinka and long-standing commander-in-chief of the SPLA, and Dr Riek Machar, a Dok Nuer, who formed the break-away SPLA-Nasir faction following his botched coup attempt against Garang in August 1991. Initially, 'the two doctors' divided over the question of whether or not the SPLA should abandon its declared aim of creating a 'united, democratic, secular Sudan' in favour of 'self-determination' or 'political independence' for the South. Machar and other disgruntled SPLA officers also accused Garang of heavy-handedness, Dinka favouritism and dictatorship in running the movement. It was not long, however, before questions of 'nationalism' gave way to a more basic drive for self-preservation. Both Garang and Machar reached for the 'ethnic' card. What followed were years of increasingly anarchic South-on-South violence that has destroyed hundreds of Dinka and Nuer communities throughout the Western Upper Nile, Bahr-el-Ghazal and Jonglei provinces. This tragic turn of events has made prospects for peace in Sudan more elusive than ever.

After months of intense South-on-South fighting, mostly targeting the civilian population along ethnic lines, this military situation began to stalemate in late 1992. Garang's, predominantly Dinka, SPLA-Mainstream (or SPLA-Torit) forces controlled most of the Bahr-el-Ghazal and Equatoria, while Machar's overwhelmingly Nuer SPLA–Nasir forces held most of the countryside in the Upper Nile. Outbreaks of inter-ethnic violence, however, have continued unabated.

The Khartoum government, of course, has actively fanned the flames of this South-on-South violence as part of a broader strategy aimed at waging a proxy war against Garang and the SPLA–Mainstream and at gaining control over the vast oil wealth of the South.[3] The split also made it much easier for government propagandists to portray 'the problem of the South' as one generated by internal tendencies toward 'tribalism' rather than by the government's discriminatory policies.

As the Southern military stalemate dragged on, Machar's faction grew steadily weaker, owing to internal power struggles and to recurrent defections to the sides of both Garang and the government. The growing instability of Machar's command was reflected in, among other things, a series of political make-overs in which SPLA–Nasir was reorganised as the SPLA–United in 1993 and then as the Southern Sudan Independence Movement/Army (SSIM/A) in 1994. Finding himself without access to the international frontier, and thus without a reliable means of resupplying his troops in the Upper Nile, Machar was drawn deeper and deeper into the government's net. What apparently began as early as 1992 as a secret arms alliance with the Khartoum government was gradually transformed into a full-fledged 'peace agreement' in 1997. This infamous April 1997 accord committed Machar and other Southern signatories to grafting their remaining SSIM/A forces onto the national army as the Southern Sudan Defence Forces (SSDF) in order to coordinate future assaults on Garang and the SPLA–Mainstream. This agreement also required Machar to recognise 'Islam and custom' as the overarching principles to which all national legislation must conform. In exchange for what many Southern Sudanese viewed as little more than unconditional surrender to the National Islamic Front government in Khartoum, Machar received a vaguely-worded promise that Southern Sudanese 'rights of self-determination' would be recognised in a Southerner-wide referendum to be held after an 'interim period' of four – or more – years.

The April 1997 'peace agreement', however, brought anything but renewed peace to Nuer regions nominally under Machar's control. By mid-1998, ordinary Nuer villagers were growing alarmed at the increasingly obvious intentions of the Khartoum government to exploit the unbounded 'interim period' set forth in the agreement for the strategic deployment of

Northern troops in formerly 'liberated' Nuer regions and, more disturbingly, for the rapid extraction of previously untapped Southern oil reserves in the Western Upper Nile. Both government objectives were being pursued by fomenting political rivalries and armed confrontations between allied Nuer (and Dinka) SSDF officers (Human Rights Watch 1999 and 2002).

The immediate life circumstances of rural Nuer and Dinka civilians have continued to spiral downwards in 2000, as a deeply fragmented and increasingly predatory Southern military elite faces the prospect of permanently losing control of the estimated 1.2 billion barrels of proven oil reserves in the Western Upper Nile to a consortium of international petroleum companies (Human Rights Watch 1999 and 2002). Aided by thousands of imported Chinese labourers, the Sudanese government completed the construction of a 1,110-km oil pipeline from Bentiu to Port Sudan in December 1998, designed to pump Southern crude directly from the Western Upper Nile Province to newly constructed oil refineries and export terminals in the far North. What's more, the government of Sudan has begun to channel the profits from this 1.6-billion-dollar oil development scheme into the domestic development of arms factories in order to bolster its 18-year siege of the South and other politically marginalised regions of Sudan (Human Rights Watch 1999 and 2002).

Whatever currents of optimism currently flow through the hearts of Nuer and Dinka civilians revolve primarily around recent steps taken by Dinka and Nuer civilian and religious leaders to end the vicious cycle of Nuer–Dinka violence sparked off by the 1991 leadership split in the SPLA. Rupturing a seven-year stranglehold on inter-ethnic communications imposed by rival Southern military factions, scores of prominent Dinka and Nuer chiefs gathered first in Lokichokkio, Kenya, during June 1998 and, later, in Wunlit, Bahr-el-Ghazal during February–March 1999 in order to forge a grassroots peace agreement aimed at ending 'this nasty little war that the educated [Southern military elite] makes us fight!' With financial and logistical support garnered from the New Sudan Council of Churches, these peace workshops (both of which one of us, Sharon Hutchinson, attended) have succeeded in greatly reducing tensions between Nuer and Dinka communities located on the west bank of the White Nile.[4] They have also pressured Southern military leaders into investigating and restraining the cattle-raiding activities of some of their most abusive field commanders.[5]

Nevertheless, it remains to be seen whether or not this civilian drive for peace and reconciliation will triumph over intensifying government efforts to foment further mistrust and violence among rival Southern military leaders so as to extend its control over the oil zone. In 1998 the central government began to undermine Machar's position by funding the rival military exploits of a Bul Nuer warlord named Paulino Matiep Nhial. Matiep has taken the lead in recent years in driving Nuer civilians out of the Western Upper Nile. In June 1998 he destroyed Machar's home town of Ler. From there, he proceeded to clear a path for an extension of the oil pipeline southwards from Bentiu to Adok.

If nothing else, the government's lunge for the oil motivated renewed contact and cooperation between SPLA and SSDF field commanders on the ground, despite the continuing unwillingness of Garang and Machar to compromise their personal ambitions for the greater good of the South. In November 1999 there was a significant realignment of Nuer forces in which many groups abandoned the government's side to form a new, anti-government alliance, the Upper Nile Provisional Military Command Council (UNPMCC), which has remained independent from Garang. Of the estimated 70,500 Nuer civilians displaced from the Western Upper Nile (Unity State) between June 1998 and December 1999, many eventually found safe refuge among Dinka communities of the Bahr-el-Ghazal, owing in large part to the spirit of cooperation and non-violence generated by the Lokichokkio and Wunlit peace conferences.

At present, SPLA officers in the Bahr-el-Ghazal appear determined to seize the peace. In a public meeting held in northern Gogrial, Bahr-el-Ghazal, during June 1999, regional Dinka and Nuer SPLA officers explained to a gathering of Dinka and Nuer civilian and religious leaders the positive outcome of the Wunlit peace conference. One Dinka spiritual leader insisted, however, that he wanted to hear the word 'reconciliation' from the mouth of a visiting Nuer spiritual leader, rather from that of a Dinka SPLA officer. His request granted, he went on to propose a future conference of Dinka and Nuer spiritual leaders to foreswear any further hostilities. 'If we can achieve that and Nuer and Dinka spiritual leaders turn their spears against the North, the real enemy of our people,' he remarked, 'I am sure that the Islamic spirits cannot defeat the [united] power of our ancestral spirits.' Garang, however, has shown little interest in extending the peace beyond his home territory of Bor. Reportedly fearful that a successful reunion of the Dinka of the Bahr-el-Ghazal and the Western Nuer could undermine his command, Garang recently transferred several Dinka SPLA officers sympathetic to the peace away from the Bahr-el-Ghazal.

As of the time of writing, the April 1997 peace agreement appears to be a dead issue. Charging the Khartoum government with repeated violations of both the spirit and terms of the agreement, Machar resigned from the government in January 2000 and made his way back to Nairobi, where he is currently struggling to regain some of his former political prominence.

## The Shifting Ethics of Nuer and Dinka Warfare

Before this war and, indeed, up until the collapse of SPLA unity in 1991, Nuer and Dinka fighters did not intentionally kill women, children or elderly persons during violent confrontations among themselves. The purposeful slaying of a child, woman or elderly person was universally perceived not only as cowardly and reprehensible but, more importantly, as a direct affront against God as the ultimate guardian of human morality. Such acts were expected to provoke manifestations of divine anger in the form of severe illness, sudden death and/or other misfortunes visited on either the slayer or some member of his immediate family. Acts of homicide within each group, moreover, were governed by a complex set of cultural ethics and spiritual taboos aimed at ensuring the immediate identification and purification of the slayer and at the swift payment of bloodwealth cattle compensation to the family of the deceased. Regional codes of warfare ethics also precluded the burning of houses and the destruction of crops during Nuer–Dinka community confrontations. Cattle, of course, were fair game. But there was little interest in pursuing the vanquished after their cattle had been captured. Nevertheless, it was not uncommon in the past for Nuer and Dinka raiders to carry off young women and children to be absorbed as full members of their families.

The gradual unravelling of this regional ethical code of warfare during Sudan's present war represents the gravest threat to the future viability of Nuer and Dinka communities in the South today. While the recent targeting of Nuer and Dinka women and children has been provoked in part by the national army, it also represents a major turning point in relations between opposed Southern military leaders and their civilian constituencies. Although commonly portrayed in pro-government propaganda tracts as the release of 'ancient tribal hatreds' that have allegedly been simmering for years, the root cause of the post-1991 surge in Nuer–Dinka violence is more fluid and complex. First, processes of identity creation – whether defined in terms of ethnic, regional, racial, religious or national affiliations (to name those most pertinent to Sudan's unresolved civil war) – are always historically contingent and socially contested. As Liisa Malkki (1992:37; 1995) remarked: 'Identity is always mobile and processual, partly self-construction, partly categorisation by others, partly a condition, a status, a label, a weapon, a shield, a fund of memories … a creolised aggregate.' Second, Nuer and Dinka communities were never organised into neatly circumscribed 'tribes'. Rather, both groups held overlapping and sometimes competing loyalties to a wide spectrum of named social units, including patrilineal clusters, regional court systems, town groupings, temporary confederacies, and extended networks of cross-cutting kinship ties. Both groups had also intermarried for generations and continued to recognise their common ancestry through a variety of oral traditions and shared cultural practices.

During the early nineteenth century, breakaway Nuer groups began migrating out of their original homelands on the west bank of the White Nile into Dinka- and Anyuak-occupied lands further east. By the end of that century, these invading Nuer groups had reached the Ethiopian frontier, effectively tripling their original land base and assimilating tens of thousands of Dinka residents, captives and immigrants in the process. As one contemporary Nuer man laughingly summed up the results of this long-standing assimilation trend: 'There are no [real] Nuer. We are all Dinka!' Dinka creation myths also recognise a shared ancestry with the Nuer. Their historical division is attributed to a legendary struggle over two cows bestowed on them by God. As one contemporary Dinka elder explained: 'Because the cow is the only source of conflict between us, we have always considered it a conflict between brothers. And when brothers fight, they always know deep in their heart that they do not intend to kill each other. But what we don't understand is how we moved from brotherly fights to wars of elimination.'

In complex historical situations such as these, it is crucial to ask: in whose image and whose interests have these ethnic labels been most recently forged? And when and why did these two groups' politicised sense of their own identity become threaded through with pressures for their menfolk to take up arms? Discussing processes of militarisation more generally, Cynthia Enloe has argued that: '[m]ilitarisation occurs because some people's fears are allowed to be heard … while other people's fears are trivialised and silenced' (1995:26). Following her lead, it will be important to examine the myriad ways in which women have been implicated in the recent polarisation and militarisation of Nuer and Dinka ethnic identities.

## Duelling Stereotypes

Among the most powerful forces promoting continued violence between what have become the ethno-nationalist armies of John Garang and Riek Machar are mutual suspicion and ignorance. Direct channels of communication between these two factions were officially severed in 1991. Since that time a handful of self-serving Southern military commanders have repeatedly undercut civilian attempts to forge local peace agreements. While there is reason to hope that the 1999 Wunlit peace conference will continue to restrain inter-ethnic fighting along the turbulent Western Upper Nile/Eastern Bahr-el-Ghazal frontier, everyone knows that confrontation between opposed SPLA and SSDF forces may re-erupt at anytime. Moreover, the military situation in Dinka and Nuer areas east of the White Nile remains extremely volatile.

Having attempted to tap ideological currents on both sides of this bitter divide, we were amazed at how pervasive and yet superficial many of these mutual misunderstandings were. To our initial surprise, we found that contemporary Nuer and Dinka men and women often agreed with the behavioural generalisations drawn about them by their 'ethnic others'. What they rejected, however, was the negative motivational spin placed on these characteristics from outside. They also vehemently objected to the efforts of rival military leaders to exploit these stereotypes in their fight for regional power

So what are the common ethnic slurs that contemporary Nuer and Dinka men and women hurl at one another in their efforts to explain their rapidly deteriorating relations during the 1991–9 period? While some of these stereotypes were undoubtedly circulating long before this war began, others appeared to have been picked, reshaped and redeployed by Southern military leaders and warlords seeking to justify not only their political ambitions but their very existence in the eyes of those they claimed to protect.

When asked to describe how Nuer and Dinka differ, most Dinka men and women interviewed usually pointed first to the alleged 'unruliness' of

Nuer. From their perspective, Nuer 'egalitarianism' verges on chaos. There is, in fact, a widely held perception among Dinka soldiers and civilians alike that Nuer make both poorer leaders and poorer followers because they are 'too' democratic and 'too' impulsive. As one prominent member of the Dinka educated elite explained: 'The Nuer can be very difficult people to work with because they do not respect the authority of others. Every Nuer [man] thinks that he should be a leader. A Nuer [man] will not even show special respect to his own chiefs. Instead, he will talk to a chief just like he talks to everyone else. But with us, it is different. We, Dinka, know the importance of showing respect [to those in authority].' Especially in times of fighting and warfare, Nuer men were said to react first and ask questions later.

In contrast, many Dinka men characterised themselves as more 'discriminating' and 'reflective'. Whereas most Dinka men would hesitate to join a physical confrontation before investigating the underlying causes of the dispute, Nuer men – according to this stereotype – would readily leap to the defence of their closest situational allies. During the 1970s and 1980s, for example, young Nuer migrants in Khartoum won the admiration of many Dinka counterparts by rushing to the latter's defence in situations where individual confrontations with 'Arab' Northerners escalated into spontaneous street fights. One older Dinka man, who had witnessed several such incidents, said there were times when Nuer youth came to the defence of unrelated Dinka combatants, while other Dinka men stood by.

The 'down-side' of the unbridled willingness of Nuer men to respond to the battle cry relates, according to many Dinka interviewed, to matters of coordination and timing in warfare. During the first Sudanese civil war (1955–72), Dinka commanders within the Anyanya guerrilla movement often delayed informing their rank-and-file Nuer recruits of an impending military offensive until the day it was to begin. The expressed fear was that, if Nuer soldiers were told of a planned attack ahead of time, they would feel compelled to take action immediately. The underlying premise of these stories and stereotypes was, of course, that Dinka are better suited to the responsibilities of leadership than the admirably brave but notoriously impulsive Nuer.

Significantly, several leading Dinka politicians and military advisers claimed that Nuer themselves agreed with this assessment. They too, so it was said, recognised that Dinka make better leaders. In support of this claim, one prominent Dinka politician pointed to the frequency with which descendants of immigrant Dinka were elected as Nuer government chiefs. Another Dinka elder explained that it was common practice in mixed urban areas for disputes over the distribution of meat between individual Nuer men to be turned over to a Dinka third party, who would make the final cut. 'And that man's decision was always accepted,' he continued, 'because the Nuer realise that we, the Dinka, are a very fair people!'

Whatever its basis in history or fantasy, this widely expressed attitude certainly provided contemporary Dinka SPLA officers with a convenient rationale for restricting the ethnic scope of higher-level strategy sessions, should they have political motives for doing so. And it is precisely suspicions and counter-suspicions of this sort of exclusion from the central levers of power that have fuelled much of the mistrust and violence between the Dinka allies of John Garang and Nuer supporters of Riek Machar in recent years (Nyaba 1997).

Contemporary Nuer men and women, in contrast, invoked a different set of premises when characterising the Dinka and themselves. They usually stressed the alleged 'arrogance' and 'deceitfulness' of their Dinka rivals. 'The Dinka think that only they can lead!' Whereas many Dinka viewed Nuer 'egalitarianism' as quasi-militaristic, contemporary Nuer bitterly resented what they perceived to be the stubborn refusal of Dinka to treat them as equals. This long-standing complaint, which gained force during the political manoeuvring of Abel Alier and other Dinka members of the Southern Regional Assembly in Juba during the 1972–83 interlude between the civil wars, was aimed, more recently, at the autocratic leadership style of John Garang.

Ironically, what many contemporary Dinka cited as *prima facie* evidence of their superior leadership qualities – namely, the existence of many Nuer chiefs of Dinka descent – was held up by contemporary Nuer as positive evidence of their 'democratic spirit' and their 'openness' to the leadership potential of all Southern Sudanese. The problem, as far as Nuer men and women were concerned, was that this 'openness' to others was rarely reciprocated by Dinka. Whereas Nuer communities had expanded successfully over the past 200 years by assimilating thousands of Dinka immigrants and clients, they said that, no matter how many generations immigrant Nuer live in Dinka communities, they always remain to some degree marginalised outsiders who are excluded from local leadership positions.

In contrast, many Dinka portrayed the relative openness of Nuer communities to ethnic outsiders as both calculated and self-interested. Nuer welcome Dinka immigrants because they want to expand their communities and their military capacities for future cattle raids on non-Nuer. Other Dinka saw this Nuer trait as motivated by cultural arrogance. As one Dinka elder remarked: 'You could not live among Nuer with your identity as non-Nuer! They would not let you – and the quicker you behave like a Nuer, the faster you can be accorded full Nuer status.' The quasi-consensus among Dinka civilians and military officers alike was aptly summed up by one man who said: 'The Nuer are not really as hospitable as they claim. They just want everybody to be Nuer and they do not want Nuer to be absorbed by others. That is why they may live among Dinka for generations and still regard themselves as Nuer.'

Nuer feelings of resentment on the leadership question came out loud and clear at the peace workshop held in Lokichokkio in June 1998. While simultaneously condemning the years of irrational and self-destructive violence between Nuer and Dinka communities fostered by a self-serving military elite, one charismatic Nuer chief concluded his speech with a warning: 'If you are a Dinka, don't say that a Nuer cannot be a leader! Because if you do that, it is just like what the Arabs did [to all Southerners], after the English left: the Arabs refused to let us rule! And so, when you say to a Nuer that he cannot be a leader, that [attitude] is what we adamantly reject! If you are a Dinka or a Shilluk or from Juba [Equatoria], you can become a leader. But that is what the Arabs denied. That was the trick that the Arabs played on us [after the British left]. But is that not the attitude that started this whole war in the first place?!'

It is easy to see how the negative ramifications of these duelling stereotypes can reverberate up and down the entire Southern political and military hierarchies. These clashing perspectives and attitudes have also left people vulnerable to both external manipulation and internal division. In its long-standing efforts to mount a proxy war against Garang, the government of Sudan has repeatedly raised the spectre of 'Dinka domination' in an effort to lure alienated and ambitious Southern leaders into its military web. One does not need to know much about current governmental strategies of divide and rule to recognise the tremendous exploitative potential of these stereotypical contrasts in Dinka and Nuer attitudes of 'respect' and 'openness' toward each other's leaders. Perhaps more than anything else, these mutually reinforcing stereotypes have undermined Southern feelings of 'national' unity over the past decade.

## Evolving Nuer Concepts of Ethnicity

One key to understanding these tragic developments begins with an appreciation of contemporary differences in Nuer and Dinka understandings of the socio-physical bases of their ethnic identities. For reasons that date back to the early nineteenth century, Nuer today, as we have seen, regard themselves as more 'hospitable' to the assimilation of ethnic outsiders. Throughout their famous nineteenth-century expansion eastwards across the White Nile into Dinka and Anyuak-occupied lands (Evans-Pritchard 1940, Gough 1971, Kelly 1985), individual Nuer men competed with one another for positions of local leadership by gathering around themselves as many co-resident Dinka and Anyuak clients and supporters as possible. The enduring loyalty of these co-resident immigrants was secured, primarily, through the generous provision of Nuer cattle and Nuer wives. What underwrote the dramatic expansion of Nuer communities during the nineteenth century, in other words, was the rapidity and completeness with which Nuer could make ethnic outsiders feel like insiders.

Accordingly, what made someone 'Nuer' was primarily how he or she behaved. Language skills, a love of cattle, co-residence, community participation and moral conformity were all central in ways that biological parentage was not. In other words, past and present generations of Nuer have tended to view ethnic unities and distinctions in performative terms.

Contemporary Dinka, in contrast, stressed the overwhelming importance of human blood lines in determining who is and is not Dinka. The primordialist thrust of contemporary Dinka concepts of ethnic affinity makes eminent 'sense' when viewed in the light of their nineteenth-century experiences. Many Dinka men and women came under heavy pressure during that period to jettison their *Jieng* identity and to become *Naath*. One way Dinka could defend themselves against the sticky grasp of their Nuer neighbours was to reaffirm the fundamental indissolvability of their ethnic identity through the elaboration of blood-based metaphors of procreative descent. Whereas it remained common practice during the 1980s, for example, for descendants of immigrant Dinka to be accepted as Nuer government chiefs, the reverse scenario rarely, if ever, occurred. This was in part because most Dinka considered *Jieng* to be born, not made. Accordingly, heredity appears to have played a large role in determining chiefly succession patterns than it has among the Nuer.

Contemporary Nuer, on the other hand, have tended to treat their ethnic identity more like an 'honorific title', conferred together with the social approval of other community members. And just as Nuer believe that anyone can potentially become 'a real person' or 'a true human being' (*raam mi raan*) by conforming to certain behavioural norms, so, too, a person may be stripped of this status for major transgressions of those same norms. There was a case during the early 1980s, for instance, in which a Nuer man, who was born and raised by Nuer parents, scandalised the extended community by making an especially shocking rape attempt. People's immediate gut reaction was: 'No Nuer would do such a thing! That man must be a Dinka!'[6]

Since 1991, however, there appears to have been a gradual sealing off of this once permeable inter-ethnic divide. Whereas women and children were more likely to be kidnapped than slain by Nuer and Dinka cattle raiders in the past, the reverse is now true. Militarised segments on both sides of this ethnic divide have sought to rationalise their increasing viciousness as retaliation for abominations earlier experienced. However, there is more behind their conscious targeting of unarmed women and children. People's concepts of ethnicity themselves have been mutating. Nuer fighters, in particular, appear to have adopted a more primordialist, if not racialist, way of thinking about their ethnic 'essence' in recent years. And it is precisely this kind of thinking that can be twisted so easily into military justifications for the intentional killing of unarmed women and children belonging to other ethnic groups.

## Guns and the Military

Nevertheless, it is important to realise that local ethical codes of intra- and inter-ethnic warfare began unravelling long before the 1991 splitting of the SPLA. Throughout the first eight years of this war, Southern military leaders consciously sought to mute the significance of ethnic differences among their recruits. This was done not only to reduce ethnic tensions within their ranks and to engender deeper feelings of Southern nationalism but, also to ensure an effective chain of command. Since Southern youths were forcibly recruited by the national army as well as by the SPLA, members of the same ethnic group were often forced to face one another on the battlefield. Consequently, it was necessary for SPLA regional commanders to ensure that orders would be carried out without hesitation, even when those orders required their troops to kill members of their own ethnic groups. This in turn necessitated the dismantling – or, at least, situational suspension – of earlier ethical codes of local warfare.

During the late 1980s, Riek Machar, who was then reigning SPLA zonal commander of the Western Upper Nile, endeavoured to convince his rank-and-file recruits as well as local civilians that acts of inter-ethnic homicide carried out in the context of a 'government war' were devoid of the social and spiritual risks associated with those generated by more localised fighting and feuding. There was no need, he argued, for a slayer to purify himself of the 'embittered' blood of the slain. Nor was there any possibility of the family of the slain seeking bloodwealth cattle compensation from the slayer's family. In essence, Machar was arguing that the overarching political context of the present war should take precedence over the personal identities and social interrelations of the combatants in people's assessments of the social and spiritual ramifications of intra-ethnic homicide (see Hutchinson 1998 for a fuller discussion of these issues).

Furthermore, as guns burned deeper and deeper into regional patterns of warfare, many Nuer and Dinka began to wonder whether the spiritual and social consequences of intra-ethnic gun slayings were the same as those realised with spears. Whereas the power of a spear, they reasoned, issues directly from the bones and sinews of a person who hurls it, that of a gun is eerily internal to it. Unlike individually crafted spears, moreover, the source of a bullet lodged deep in someone's body is more difficult to trace. Often a fighter did not know for certain whether or not he had killed someone. And, as a result, acts of intra- and inter-ethnic homicide became increasingly 'secularised' and 'depersonalised' (cf. Hutchinson 1996).

The traumatic shift from spears to guns as the dominant weapon of Nuer and Dinka warfare during the early years of this war was magnified by the military's reliance on novel fighting tactics, such as recourse to surprise, night-time attacks, the burning of houses and the intentional destruction of local food supplies. Nevertheless, it was not until after the collapse of SPLA unity in 1991 that the killing of unarmed women and children became 'standard practice' between Nuer and Dinka combatants. God, it seems, was no longer watching.

## From Mobile Assets to Military Targets

In many ways, women and girls were less firmly rooted than men in the ethnic identities of Nuer and Dinka at the start of this war. This was because women and girls could potentially confer any ethnic identity on their children, depending upon who married them. Both groups are exogamic in the sense that women and girls may only be married by men who are, by definition, 'strangers' or 'outsiders'. Both groups also share a strong bias toward patrilineality, with most children taking on the lineage affiliations and ethnic identities of their fathers' rather than of their mothers' people. Third and finally, wives in both groups tend to take up residence in their husbands' homes after marriage. For all of these reasons, most Dinka and Nuer took the attitude before this war that 'A woman has no [fixed] cattle camp'. A woman could marry several men during her lifetime and produce heirs for all of them. Similarly, people stated that: 'A girl belongs to everyone' – meaning she was a potential marriage partner for all unrelated men.

Women's more ambiguous position at the crossroads of ethnic unities and distinctions afforded them considerable protection and social mobility at the start of this war. They were the points through which adversarial relations among men could be potentially defused and transformed into relations of affinity through marriage. For this reason, women and children were regarded as illegitimate targets of attack during inter- and intra-ethnic confrontations. There was, if fact, an elaborate ethical code among Nuer and Dinka that treated women and girls as 'points of safe refuge' for fleeing or wounded men. Prior to the widespread introduction of guns by the SPLA, it was common practice for western Nuer women to accompany their husbands, brothers and sons to the battlefield in order to protect and carry away the wounded. A woman could also protect a man who had fallen in battle by throwing herself over him, confident that advancing warriors from the other side would not dislodge her in order to finish him off. In their past discourse on war and courage, Nuer and Dinka alike believed than no man should waste his time pursuing another man so cowardly as to seek refuge among women and children, let alone killing women and children themselves. Similarly, any Nuer or Dinka warrior who retreated into someone's cattle byre or house was not pursued. These rules were firm and respected, since any breach of them would have caused the original conflict to spin rapidly out of control. Consequently, Nuer and Dinka men alike regarded the slaying of a women, child or elderly person during major inter-ethnic confrontations as, by definition, 'accidental'. The presumption was that no self-respecting Nuer or Dinka man would kill an unarmed woman or child on purpose. Such deaths placed the offending side at a moral disadvantage and usually resulted in a swift transfer of bloodwealth cattle to the family of the victim.

The gendered division of tasks in both groups was also one in which only men bore arms. Women and children, in contrast, were treated more like mobile assets and, as such, were sometimes kidnapped during major inter-ethnic confrontations. However, they were not intentionally slain. But following the widespread introduction of guns and of novel fighting techniques targeting entire cattle camps and civilian villages by the SPLA, Nuer and Dinka women and children were thrown willy-nilly onto the front lines. The SPLA did not promote the taking of war captives. Their limited food supplies and mobility requirements militated against this. And thus, in an area of recurrent starvation caused by the intentional destruction of the 'enemy's' support base, rival Southern military leaders recast women and children as legitimate targets of ethnic annihilation.

As Garang and Machar squared off, their troops, sometimes under orders and sometimes on their own initiative, began to slit the throats or otherwise slaughter women and children encountered during their cattle camp raids. This spiral of Nuer/Dinka 'vengeance' attacks soon spun out of control. In the process, women's potential for resolving conflicts through inter-ethnic marriages was politically marginalised, if not negated entirely.

More important for our purposes, the purposeful killing of women and children necessitated a major reformulation of presumed socio-physical roots of ethnic affiliations, particular for Nuer combatants. The rationale for killing a Dinka child entailed the assumption, whether implicit or explicit, that the child would mature into a 'Dinka' child. That child's ethnic identity, in other words, was presumed to be fixed at birth. The idea that a Dinka child could potentially become a 'Nuer' or vice versa was thus lost in a fury of 'revenge attacks'.

Of course, Dinka soldiers had long held the view that 'a Nuer is always a Nuer'. And since Nuer were killing Dinka children, the possibility of being regarded as cowardly for killing a child was quickly forgotten by them, especially since firearms were being used.

## Guns and Masculinity

Long before the split, the SPLA had attempted to instill in its recruits an ideology of hyper-masculinity, which glorified the raw power of guns. Recruits were told that the only thing that had separated the South from the political reigns of power in the past was a lack of guns. Backed by the raw 'masculine' power of the gun, anything was possible – a theme clearly reflected in the 'graduation song' allegedly taught to all SPLA trainees prior to the split on the conferral of their first rifles:

> Even your father, give him a bullet!
> Even your mother, give her a bullet!
> Your gun is your food, your gun is your wife.

Similarly, the SPLA's emphasis on male bonding was such that relationships with women and the family were increasingly devalued and displaced. For example, Hutchinson heard reports of a disturbing incident that occurred during the mid-1990s in which a beautiful young girl, who had been carried off by ex-SPLA soldiers loyal to the Dinka warlord, Kerebino Kuanyin Bol, became the source of a heated argument. Three different soldiers all wanted to claim her as their consort. After summoning the three men and the girl and hearing their respective arguments, the commander allegedly settled the dispute once and for all. Pulling out his revolver he shot the girl between the eyes and declared that no woman would be permitted to cause dissension in his ranks. The three soldiers allegedly shrugged off the incident. But the logic of the commander was clear: the girl's life meant nothing in the context of troop solidarity and discipline.

A growing sense of entitlement to the domestic and sexual services of related and unrelated women also pervaded this hyper-masculinised and militarised world view. Just as Dinka and Nuer men saw themselves as responsible for maintaining the war front so, too, they reasoned that women should be active in keeping up 'the reproductive front'. Pressure for women to disregard the weaning taboo (which prohibits their having sexual relations during lactation) steadily mounted, as husbands and lovers on short, unpredictable military leaves returned home determined to con-ceive another child. Similarly, women were pressured by husbands and in-laws to reduce the 'fallow period' between pregnancies by weaning their infants earlier. Whereas before the start of the war infants were usually suckled for eighteen months or more, many contemporary Dinka and Nuer men now argue that a period of nine months is optimal. And because most Nuer and Dinka women did not feel free to refuse their husbands or lovers sexual access for fear of a beating, they were increasingly forced to make choices that no woman should have to make. 'How can I take the risk of another pregnancy and childbirth when I can't even feed the children I already have?' 'Should I attempt to abort, knowing how many other women have died or become infertile in the process?' 'How would my husband and his family react if they discovered I had aborted "their" child?' 'Who will care for my children, if I die?' 'Will God punish me for these thoughts?' (Jok 1999). The agony of these reproductive dilemmas weighed down heavily on Nuer and Dinka women alike. These were not communities that had accumulated generations of experience in medicinally or physically provoking abortions. It is thus hardly surprising that the frequency of maternal deaths attributed to 'excessive bleeding' appears to have risen in both regions during the course of this war.

To these feminine hardships must be added the ever-present dangers of rape and of the forceful commandeering of scarce household resources by gun-toting men. Nearly every Nuer and Dinka woman we encountered had experienced threatening demands by armed men for the immediate provision of cooked or stored food, portage services and/or sexual access. Satisfying these unpredictable and, often, recurrent demands severely limited the energies and resources these women were able to devote to their children.

Nevertheless, women were more than passive victims of these militarising trends. Many Nuer and Dinka women actively reinforced this militarised mentality by encouraging their brothers, husbands and sons to join the military or to participate as civilians in collective cattle raids and vengeance attacks on neighbouring ethnic groups. For example, there was a bitter debate raging in 1996 in the Western Upper Nile between two Nuer women, Rebecca Nyanciew and Elizabeth Nyawana Lam. These women were the elected heads of the women's unions of the Bul and Leek Nuer, respectively. The issue these two women debated was whether or not Nuer military forces should resort to the killing of Dinka women and children during their cattle raids. Rebecca was an outspoken advocate of 'an eye for an eye'. Dinka soldiers had killed Nuer children, so Nuer soldiers should do the same. Elizabeth vehemently objected. No woman with breasts and a womb for bearing children, she argued, should support the killing of women and children under any circumstances, regardless of whatever atrocities Dinka soldiers had committed in the past.

This debate, which radiated throughout local military units and the wider civilian population, took a dramatic turn during the following year. Rebecca was arrested, beaten and jailed for her alleged role in 'fanning' (*kuothe*) the flames of intra-ethnic violence between Bul and Leek Nuer during the mid-1990s (discussed below). Elizabeth was pivotal in this outcome. Rebecca, who reportedly lost a pregnancy as a result of the beating, was later 'pardoned', released and brought to Khartoum under orders from Riek Machar.

Women were also capable of banding together to restrain eruptions of inter-community violence, especially those in which local military units were not directly involved. For example, there was a series of mixed spear/gun battles that erupted between the Bul and Leek Nuer in late 1995 which were successfully quelled by Elizabeth Nyawana Lam, in her capacity as the elected head of the Leek Nuer women's union. Elizabeth Nyawana had already gained a reputation by that time for extraordinary courage. In fact she had been trained and had served in SPLA fights against 'the Arabs' during the early years of the war. She ended this particular confrontation by ordering all Bul and Leek Nuer women who ran to the battle scene with their men to return home immediately. Before the outbreak of the current civil war it was standard practice, as was noted, for western Nuer women to accompany their brothers, husbands and sons to the battlefield, where they took responsibility for protecting and carrying away the wounded. Without the assurance of these feminine protections, Nuer fighters on both sides of the confrontation decided to withdraw as well.

Although these feminine support systems were increasingly undermined by the wartime dissemination of guns, Nuer and Dinka women retained considerable influence over patterns of inter-community violence through their well-recognised abilities 'to shame' their husbands, brothers and sons into either participating or not in specific military campaigns. As one young Nuer woman explained:

> Men say that 'women are women' but men do a lot of listening to us! Women are good at persuasion; we can convince men in a quiet way. Men pretend not to be listening but it [the woman's message] is already recorded!

Understanding the myriad ways in which Nuer and Dinka women have contributed to regional processes of militarisation may open up novel possibilities for 'rolling back' these same processes. This, at least, is our hope. Perhaps it would be possible to convince individual Southern field commanders that respecting earlier ethical restraints on the killing of women and children, even if pursued unilaterally, would be politically and military advantageous in the long run. For example, there was a series of major clashes during 1997 and 1998 between the Murle and Lou Nuer. At one point, a group of Murle raiders slit the throats of several Nuer children they came across. Although Murle raiders had often kidnapped small numbers of Nuer children in the past, the purposeful killing of women and children had never before occurred between these two ethnic groups. Incensed by this blatant transgression of established fighting norms, Lou Nuer organised a counter raid. Although Lou Nuer raiders discussed the possibility of killing Murle women and children, they decided not to respond in kind. After successfully driving off the defenders of their Murle target, the Lou Nuer men grabbed sticks and beat the Murle women and youth left behind. The women were reportedly told that 'next time' they would be killed unless their Murle men stopped killing Nuer women and children during their cattle raids. This strategy proved remarkably effective. Under pressure from these women, the Murle initiated peace negotiations with the Lou Nuer and, shortly thereafter, returned nearly two dozen Nuer children carried off in earlier cattle raids.

## Conclusions

As local codes of inter- and intra-ethnic warfare have twisted and collapsed beneath the weight of AK-47 rifles and the heavy blows of rival Southern military leaders, ordinary Nuer and Dinka men and women have been forced to reassess the social bases of their personal and collective security. And of the many thorny issues requiring rethinking, one of the most fundamental and far-reaching concerned the nature, significance and scope of their ethnic affiliations. On the one hand, this war has witnessed the violent rise of ethno-nationalist ideologies on previously unimaginable scales within both groups. On the other hand, whatever sense of ethnic unity these groups fostered in the context of continuing political rivalries between John Garang and Riek Machar has been repeatedly shattered from within. Break-away warlords intent on carving out their own domains of military dominance have fractured and destroyed countless local communities.

While the former fluidity of Nuer and Dinka ethnic identities may be traced back to the early 1800s and earlier, contemporary Nuer men and women, in particular, have moved away from a performative concept of their ethnic oneness to a more closed and fixed primordialist concept based on procreative metaphors of shared human blood. This perspectival drift has contributed, as we have seen, not only to a deepening of the Nuer–Dinka divide but, more tragically, to a negating of women's and children's former status as immune from intentional attack.

Women's more fluid and ambiguous position at the margins of ethnic unities and distinctions has thus been turned against them during this war. What was formerly a source of both social protection and social mobility for women has become a dual liability. From a perspective internal to Nuer and Dinka social networks, women continue to be regarded less fully as persons, or complete human beings, than their militarily active menfolk. If anything, women's status as independent agents in men's eyes appears to have declined in the context of militarised glorifications of the raw masculine power of guns. The irony is that, despite the hyper-masculinised military subculture, Nuer men – like their Dinka counterparts – have become less and less capable of fulfilling their most important social role as the protectors of their immediate families, homesteads and herds. This failure has provoked what might be called a 'crisis of masculinity' – a crisis that manifested itself in rising rates of domestic violence and sexual abuse against women. As the primary agents of cultural and individual continuity, women have come under heavy pressure to conceive and procreate, even in situations that threaten their physical well-being and their nurturing responsibilities toward their children. And thus, women's involvement in the civil war effort and, in particular, their roles in keeping up 'the procreative front' have become increasingly burdensome.

With respect to Nuer–Dinka violence, women's position on the margins of ethnic difference has been increasingly overshadowed by an externally imposed perception of ethnic rigidity. In the eyes of both Nuer and Dinka assailants, unarmed women and children belonging to the opposite ethnic group have been redefined from that of mobile assets to targets of ethnic annihilation. The vast majority of civil war victims have been defenceless women and children – an historical trend that, tragically, mirrors late-twentieth-century patterns of militarised violence across the globe. This chapter has underscored the importance of a 'primordialist' turn in Nuer concepts of ethnicity – propelled in large part by Northern military strategies of divide and rule – as pivotal in the emergence of this trend in Southern Sudan. Let us hope that the atmosphere of inter-ethnic peace created by the 1999 Wunlit peace conference will continue to reawaken Nuer and Dinka men and women to the historical fluidity and permeability of their ethnic identities for the greater good of the South.

Further research on these kinds of transformations in Sudan and in other war-torn regions of Africa and beyond will be of critical importance in deepening our understanding of how processes of militarisation have reshaped postcolonial subjectivities worldwide. However, such research poses very real challenges. Beside the unavoidable hardships and dangers experienced by any researcher working under conditions of full-scale civil war, there are the risks of having one's findings manipulated and misused to fan the hostilities. In carrying out field research in Southern Sudan, both of us have risked alienating local military leaders through our continual critiques. Yet we depend on their tolerance, if not support, in gaining continued access to the field. We have thus struggled with issues of objectivity and self-censorship. But throughout the process of doing fieldwork, we have been guided by one overarching goal: to expose the growing brutality experienced by the most vulnerable elements of Sudan's unfinished war, the defenceless women and children of the South.

## Notes

1 This chapter is an expanded and revised version of a single-authored piece entitled 'Nuer Ethnicity Militarized' published in 2000 in *Anthropology Today* 16(3): 6–13. Hutchinson wishes to thank the editors of that journal for permission to republish it here in modified form.

2 This chapter draws on many years of intensive field research in Nuer (Hutchinson) and Dinka (Jok) regions of Southern Sudan. Our collaborative field investigations have been supported most recently by joint grants from the Harry F. Guggenheim Foundation during 1998/9 and 1999/2000. We are deeply grateful for this support.

3 As early as 1986, the government of Sudan had begun arming several Northern Baggara Arabs groups in Kordofan and Darfur and had encouraged them to raid deep into Nuer and Dinka regions of the Western Upper Nile and Northern Bahr-el-Ghazal provinces (Salih and Harir 1994, Human Rights Watch 1999). Trained in counter-insurgency methods, these Northern Baggara raiders ignored long-standing regional codes of warfare and began killing Nuer and Dinka men, women and children indiscriminately during their dry-season incursions for cattle and slaves. Despite the massive displacements and devastating losses of life caused by these Baggara raids, the government of Sudan failed to gain sufficient control over Southern oil fields to promote their exploitation until after the 1991 collapse of SPLA unity.

4 A subsequent 'People to People's Peace Conference' held in Liliir during May 2000 was

reportedly far less successful in reducing inter- and intra-ethnic tensions on the east bank of the White Nile.

5 Although the SPLA–Mainstream had succeeded in brokering a truce between the Nuer groups bordering Garang's home region of Bor during the mid-1990s, Garang has thus far demonstrated little interest in extending this peace to other Nuer and Dinka areas.

6 Such statements should not be taken at face value but, rather, form part of a broader inter-ethnic 'humour', meant to convey what one group considered to be the peculiar weaknesses and strengths of the other.

# References

Enloe, Cynthia (1995), 'Feminism, Nationalism and Militarism: Wariness Without Paralysis?' In Constance R. Sutton (ed.) *Feminism, Nationalism, and Militarism*. Washington, DC: Association of Feminist Anthropology and the American Anthropological Association.

Evans-Pritchard, E. E. (1940), *The Nuer: A Description of the Modes of Livelihood aand Political Institutions of a Nilotic People*. Oxford: Clarendon Press.

Gough, Kathleen (1971), 'Nuer Kinship: A Re-examination', in T. O. Beidelman (ed.), *The Translation of Culture: Essays to E.E. Evans-Pritchard*. London: Tavistock Publications.

Human Rights Watch (1999), *Famine in Sudan, 1998: The Human Rights Causes*. New York: Human Rights Watch.

— (2002), *Sudan, Oil and Human Rights*. New York: Human Rights Watch.

Hutchinson, Sharon (1996), *Nuer Dilemmas: Coping with Money, War and the State*. Berkeley: University of California Press.

— (1998), 'Death, Memory and the Politics of Legitimation: Nuer Experiences of the Continuing Second Civil War'. In Richard Werbner (ed.) *Memory and the Postcolony: African Anthropology and the Critique of Power*. London: Zed Books.

Johnson, Douglas (1998), 'The Sudan People's Liberation Army and the Problem of Factionalism'. In C. Clapman (ed.) *African Guerrillas*, pp. 53–72. Oxford: James Currey.

Jok, Jok Madut (1999), 'Militarism, Gender and Reproductive Suffering: The Case of Abortion in Western Dinka'. *Africa* 69(2): 194–212.

Jok, Jok Madut and Sharon Hutchinson (1999), 'Sudan's Prolonged Second Civil War and the Militarization of Nuer and Dinka Ethnic Identities'. *African Studies Review* 42(2):125–45.

Kelly, Raymond (1985), *The Nuer Conquest: The Structure and Development of an Expansionist System*. Ann Arbor: University of Michigan Press.

Malkki, Liisa (1992), 'National Geographic: The Rooting of Peoples and the Territorialization of National Identity among Scholars and Refugees'. *Cultural Anthropology* 7(1):24–44.

— (1995), 'From "Refugee Studies" to the National Order of Things'. *Annual Review of Anthropology* 24:495–523.

Nyaba, P. A. (1997), *The Politics of Liberation in South Sudan: An Insider's View*. Kampala: Fountain Publishers.

Salih, M. A. Mohamed and Sharif Harir (1994), 'Tribal Militias: The Genesis of National Disintegration'. In Sharif Harir and Terje Tvedt (eds.) *Short Cut to Decay: The Case of Sudan*. Uppsala: Nordiska Afrikainstitute.

# Part Two⊙

# Uncertainties, Subjection and Subjunctivity

# 5 ◎ 'A Child Is One Person's Only in the Womb'

## Domestication, Agency and Subjectivity in the Cameroonian Grassfields[1]

Francis B. Nyamnjoh

I see agency not in terms of dependence or independence, but inter-dependence and intersubjectivity. Too much of the theory of agency merely asks about the empowerment of the individual and the extent to which individuals are creators or creatures of the social structures wherein they operate (cf. Cohen 1987; Davies 1991; Giddens 1993:705–731). Hence the central question is neglected: how are individuals able to be who they are – agents – through relationships with others? The same holds for communities. Here the question is: how do communities as corporate bodies articulate and defend collective or group interests in a world of hegemonies of all kinds? The reality is that modernity and globalisation are bazaars to which many are attracted, but few rewarded or given clear-cut choices. As this reality dawns on individuals and groups the world over, the need for alternative channels of fulfilment and protection imposes on marginalised groups and individuals. Agency in this sense is open to individuals and groups alike, and discussions of it must go beyond the empowerment of the individual alone to show how the quest for individual fulfilment negotiates *conviviality* with collective interests which may include but are not limited to their cultural dimensions.

Very broadly, conviviality involves different or competing agentive forces which need a negotiated understanding. In the most familiar sense, an individual, a group of people, or an atmosphere is said to be convivial when festive, gay and sociable. It suggests good company where enmity and gloom have no place, and where an individual or group can legitimately afford to be merry. In a convivial setting, one can risk a glass too many and be hilarious in extreme, without fear of being taken advantage of, because one knows that one is in fellowship, that one is secure, that one is part of a whole imbued with the spirit of togetherness, interpenetration, interdependence

111

and intersubjectivity. Conviviality thus stresses empowerment for individuals and groups alike, and not the marginalisation of the one by or for the other. My own usage builds on the notion of *convivialité culturelle* as it is used in Cameroon. In June 1995 Charly Gabriel Mbock and the Interdisciplinary Office for Social and Cultural Research (AGIREC), which he headed, organised a colloquium on how interdependence or harmonious coexistence could be encouraged in a multicultural Cameroon threatened by political, religious, ethnic and economic differences and inequalities. For three days, academics, politicians, journalists, writers, the clergy and others explored the imperatives of conviviality in Cameroon, especially in the wake of the genocide in Rwanda. The outcome was a book (Mbock 1996) and further academic interest in what keeps Cameroon united despite its internal contradictions and differences (cf. Nkwi and Nyamnjoh 1997; Nyamnjoh 1999). United by diversity, Cameroon constantly needs to balance the tensions of a triple colonial heritage and other multiple identities that have made of it 'Africa in miniature' (Mbock 1996) and, also, a paradise of paradoxes. Influences from different historical sources have been creatively synthesised into a new reality that is less one of autonomy or dependence than interconnectedness, an interconnectedness that starts in the home and extends into the world at large.

The Cameroon case reveals the need for a fresh theoretical space for agency and subjectivity, addressing not only individual rights and freedoms, but also the interests of communal and cultural solidarities (the interests of which are more than just the composite of many individual interests). This reality, in the case of Africa, is a 'mix between the individual legacy of liberalism and collectivist legacy of ethnicity' (von Lieres 1999:143); a marriage, in other words, of the bifurcation between 'citizens' and 'subjects' as highlighted by Mamdani (1996; 1998), in acknowledgement of individuals and groups who live their lives both as citizens and subjects. Ferguson talks of a 'full house' of cultural styles which, as a strategy of survival, combines the local and the cosmopolitan in the same space (Ferguson 1999:82–122). It is survival strategy, especially given the constraining reality of Africa being at the fringes of global consumer capitalism. This fringe location provokes or reinforces survival strategies, having 'no fixed divide between self and other', and also an interconnectedness marked by continuous centrifugal and centripetal pressures within and among nations 'to assert and elaborate particular identities' or 'to create broader, more universalistic alliances' for strategic purposes (P. Werbner 1997a:248–9). The context is one in which individuals and groups are more than contingent hybrids, where the fascination with boundaries and belonging makes the experience of hybridity 'disturbing and shocking for some' and 'revelatory' for others

(P. Werbner 1997b:22), and where marginality limits action and creativity for both individuals and groups. In this postcolonial African context, discussions of agency and subjectivity must be informed by the reality on the ground of the creative quest for survival. The same is true of the creole/pidgin/hybrid reality depicted in Karin Barber's *Readings in African Popular Culture* (1997). This calls for hybrid/pidgin/creole ideas of agency and subjectivity, but it also calls for new notions of community and conviviality.

This chapter on domestication, agency and subjectivity in the Bamenda grassfields of Cameroon draws from widely shared but changing notions of personhood in Bum, and from my personal experiences as someone without an identity in the conventional sense of belonging to a bounded unit that is culturally and geographically specific. I hate to admit the idea of an identity crisis, for this presupposes fixed identities essential to each and everyone of us.[2] Yet the stubborn insistence on *Identity* (in singular and with a capital I), even among academics, has impaired understanding of the interconnectedness of peoples, cultures and societies through individuals as products, melting-pots and creative manipulators or jugglers of multiple identities. The tendency has been and remains to essentialise, that is 'to impute a fundamental, basic, absolutely necessary constitutive quality to a person, a social category, ethnic group, religious community, or nation'; 'to posit falsely a timeless continuity, a discreteness or boundedness in space, and an organic unity'; or 'to imply an internal sameness and external difference or otherness' (P. Werbner 1997a:228).

As Jean-Pierre Warnier (1999) argues, in the Cameroon grassfields individuals are not entirely under external influences, or at the mercy of forces from within or outside the society to which they belong. Individuals exercise a certain amount of freedom and rationality in their daily actions, and must make decisions and choose between different paths even in the most confining of social worlds. When acting in the society, individuals, in order to achieve their goals, must however take into account and provide for the actions of others. Achievement, in other words, is always within and as part of, or on behalf of a group of people who legitimate and recognise that achievement. In this regard, culture and identification play an important orientational role by providing repertoires and representations for individuals to draw from, in order that they may act in concert with expectations recognised by their groups. By accepting these repertoires, the individuals affirm their belonging while acting on their own behalf, even in conflicts of power and interest that oppose them to other actors. Thus culture could be likened to a compass that facilitates action without necessarily determining it. In this sense, culture is the capacity to bring into play references, frames of action and communication. It is a capital of incorporated habits that structure the activities of those who possess it. Culture is the whole repertoire of action, language and styles which enables a person to recognise their belonging to a given social group and to identify with the group in question, without necessarily being confined by it.

Discussing agency and subjectivity calls for scrutiny of the importance of cultural identity in the lives of individuals and groups. In mainstream anthropology, cultures often appear unique, and geographically or socially localised (for a critique, see Ferguson and Gupta 1997). Culture is seen to be a source of identification for groups and individuals and of differentiation from others. It enables social actors to assert themselves in relation to one another and to their environment. Culture and tradition, however, are not frozen or stagnant; the individuals and groups partaking of any culture or tradition actively shape and reshape it in their daily endeavours. Culture changes because it is enmeshed in the turbulence of history, and because each act, each signification, each decision risks opening new meanings, vistas and possibilities. In order to provide orientation or serve as a compass, culture must integrate change, which by no means entails throwing the baby out with the bath-water. Few changes succeed in the form of a clean sweep, the total replacement of the old by the new. Always something old is in the new, even if the new cannot be reduced to the old. Given accelerated flows and interactions of diverse cultural products as a result of globalisation, does it make sense to talk still of individuals and groups as belonging to given cultures like fettered slaves and zombies, or confined within them like canned sardines? If cultures are subject to influences from without and tinkering from within, and to reformulation in accordance with historical contexts, what does this say of culturally specific conceptualisations of agency and subjectivity? Within the context of globalisation and postcoloniality, it is possible for a single individual to assume multiple identifications that draw from different linguistic, cultural or religious repertoires, depending on the context (cf. Barber 1997; Warnier 1999; R. Werbner 1996). If cultures prescribe behaviour and beliefs, and if an individual or group is exposed to competing cultural codes or styles in this way, should we talk of identity in the singular in relation to that individual or group – especially as every culture takes much time to be transmitted, assimilated or undone? What do we have to say about agency and subjectivity inspired by drawing from multiple cultural repertoires? How do individuals and groups come to terms with the fact that identity in the postcolonial age of globalisation is not determined solely by birth, nor entirely by choices made by individuals or groups?

In Bum as in the other *fondoms*[3] of the Cameroon grassfields, proverbial sayings show an appreciation for the individual as a social being. I focus my discussion of domestication, agency and subjectivity on one of these common sayings: *A child is one person's only in the womb*.[4] But this statement has more than one meaning, and is sometimes richly ambiguous. Its most common usage reinforces the idea of the individual as a child of the community, as someone allowed to pursue the fulfilment of his/her needs, but not his greed. You belong to your mother exclusively only when still in the womb. Once delivered, you are expected to be of service to the wider community, first to incorporate your father, and then to extend your network of mothers and parents to include even the childless, and to bury your greed along with your umbilical cord. Your creativity, abilities and powers have got to be harnessed in order to be acknowledged and provided for. Agency and subjectivity have meaning only as domesticated agency and subjectivity: the freedom to pursue individual or group goals exists within a socially predetermined frame that emphasises conviviality with collective interests at the same time that it allows for individual creativity and self-fulfilment. Social visibility or notability derives from (or is facilitated by) being interconnected with others in a communion of interests. You are not expected to decline rendering service to this or that person because they are not family. Even the passing stranger from a distant land should benefit from your sociality. In other words, this statement is an invitation to parents to endow their children with the necessary community spirit, so that the rest of society can share in the child's successes and good fortune, while relieving the immediate family of the burden of dealing singlehandedly with the child's failures and misfortunes. Because of the vicissitudes of life, it pays to be modest about personal success and measured in one's ambitions, given the tendency towards temporality, transience or impermanence of such individual success.

Through domesticated agency and subjectivity, the collectivity shares the responsibility of success and the consequences of failure with the active and creative individual, thereby easing the pressure on individuals to prove themselves in a world of ever-diminishing opportunities, even for the most talented. Domesticated agency or subjectivity does not deny individuals the freedom to associate or to demonstrate self-reliance, initiative and independence, but simply places a premium on interdependence as insurance against the risk of dependence, where people face the impermanence of independent success. Achievement is devoid of meaning if not pursued within, as part of, and on behalf of a group of people who recognise and endorse that achievement. For only by making their successes collective can individuals make their failures a collective concern as well. Such collectivisation or domestication emphasises negotiation, concession and conviviality over maximisation of pursuits by individuals or by particular groups in contexts of plurality and diversity. Acknowledgement and appreciation should be reserved and room created for excellence, especially for individuals who demonstrate how well they are ready to engage with collective interests. Individuals who refuse to use their endowments towards enhancing their community are most likely to be denied the public space to articulate their personal desires, and, like Cinderella, find themselves dependent on external agents and muses, or confined to singing their little songs in their little corners: 'In my own little corner in my own little chair I can be whatever I want to be.'

In my own case, as a young boy growing up where most settlements still suited the resilient anthropological idea of communities and cultures as geographically homogeneous and bounded units, and at a life stage where I stayed fairly close to home, I found it easy to see, and perhaps become confined, by the first meaning of *a child is one person's only in the womb*. My first six years in life were spent mainly in one village in Bum – Fonfuka, a valley settlement very much isolated from the rest of Bum which was mostly hilly. As a child in Fonfuka, I was hardly aware of the world beyond the hills; and felt that everything actually started and ended with my village. If anything else existed out there, beyond home, it was the other villages of Bum that I sometimes heard mentioned by the odd traveller, visitor, or migrant labourers home on leave (from the plantations of the distant coastal region of Cameroon), or that I glimpsed momentarily in photographs of absent villagers sent home for relatives to use in negotiating a wife for them.

However, that changed as schooling, the search for a better life at the various centres of modernity, and the nation-building efforts of the central government increasingly led me and others to break free of the limitations of distance and isolation. The change also provided for competing institutions of social control. It became increasingly clear that there was or could be another interpretation to *a child is one person's only in the womb*. This second meaning acknowledges that even infants in the grassfields, like the Beng babies in Côte D'Ivoire Alma Gottlieb has studied, are perceived to be highly conscious, and 'accorded a high degree of agency' in both a bio-logical and an intellectual sense (Gottlieb 1998:131). It also points to the fact that a child can outgrow social structures, culture, identity or community of origin to become something more. Or simply that, even as a child, one can stand at the margins of one's own culture and community, playing a delicate balancing act of endorsing and questioning at the same time, and taking advantage of little concessions (openings) here and there to foster one's own ends and ideas of belonging. Just as the fact of having been of the womb can never be refuted, so a child can never completely erase the impact of his or her society, culture or identity of origin, although one is always able to add to it (in an often creative and original manner) influences from elsewhere or from one's very own genius. Indeed, this interpretation had always been there (though not always noticed by the external observer), even before German colonial penetration and transformation of the grassfields from 1890 to 1900, relatively recent though this was in comparison with the coastal and forest regions. In those days exposure to competing ways of seeing and doing came through travel, trade, war, diplomacy, and also by way of the genius or muse of extra-talented individuals (cf. Fowler and Zeitlyn 1996; Nkwi 1987; Nkwi and Warnier 1982; Warnier 1985).

On this point, some beliefs shared by most Bum people indicate that not every individual is endowed with the same talents from birth or creation, hence a certain conviction that the wider society stands to lose much if individuals are empowered to pursue their own ends unharnessed. It could lead to a situation where some found themselves diminished by the achievements of the talented others, especially in a culture where personal success is often thought to be at the expense of others and of the collectivity (cf. Rowlands 1994). In the following section, my remarks on a typology of individuals are not intended to essentialise or to homogenise the people who pass for Bum today, but rather to provide a basic framework for understanding the nature and development of ideas on agency and subjectivity in the grassfields. While such notions are contested and variously applied, underlying them is a fundamental notion of agency as torn between 'with us' or not, even when one is actually 'with others' (e.g. the 'destructive' community of *Msa* or *uwungabe*, below) or alone. Thus, my account of a Bum typology suggests agency or subjectivity has always had a place, but that there is a clear distinction between agency or subjectivity which empowers a community and that which projects individual greed. Individual self-fulfilment cannot be articulated in a social void, for once the child is out of the womb his or her actions necessarily shape and are shaped by the actions of others. As Durham observes in her study of playful interchange in Botswana, 'people are not construed as independent, self-determining actors of full agentive powers prior to any interchange, but … their definition as such must be forged, and perpetually reforged, in each social encounter' (1995:118). An individual 'is not a pre-social being, naturally occurring, set up to be contrasted with more perduring social roles of hierarchy and agentive constraints' (Durham 1995:126). Individual actors need society as a moral regulator for competing agencies, granted that corporate or communal interests are not simply the aggregation of individual aspirations.[5] In other words, paradoxical as it may seem, individuals maximise their interests best when these are pursued in recognition and respect for conviviality and interconnected with others and in communion with collective interests. This is something that does not depend simply on the goodwill of fellow social actors, but on a community or society providing an ordered environment in which all actors can foster various ends, personal and/or otherwise.

Grassfields *fondoms* offer social actors such an ordered environment in which to excel, by treating every individual (male and female) as a potential 'container' or 'vital piggy-bank' capable of mixing and exchanging trans-formable or transformed substances such as breath, saliva, semen and blood (Warnier 1993a:315). Their highly hierarchical and inegalitarian social struc-tures may appear on the surface as a threat to individual self-fulfilment, but a closer look reveals a more complex situation. Their ethos that a person, full as he may be of transmissible life essence (breath, saliva, semen and blood), can only transmit life when coopted as a 'father' or a 'mother' into a descent group, implies that only through marriage or succession can one become a 'container' or a 'vital piggy-bank' for one's family or group. Marriage, how-ever, is not affordable to all (although a father is expected to provide each of his sons with a wife and to marry out his daughters), and some people remain unmarried for long, even for life. Succession to the office of *fon*, notable or compound head, is limited to one son only, chosen by his father in his lifetime. This son takes his late father's name, title, paraphernalia, wives (except his mother) and all his rights in persons and things. As successor, not only does the son take the position of his late father, he becomes 'the father', and must be addressed by his siblings (older or younger) as such (Warnier 1993a:305). Daughters may also succeed their mothers in similar ways, although authority is transmitted mainly through the male line in most *fondoms* of the region.

But such hierarchy and inequality also push the unmarried or unchosen others to migrate to urban areas and various centres of accumulation in quest for alternative channels of legitimation and recognition, in compensation for what they have been denied at home. This would partly explain not only the status of the grassfields as 'a major reservoir of slaves for the Atlantic trade' for over two centuries, but also the fact that 'About one third of the Grassfields population live in diaspora, trading and doing business, and providing cheap labour in urban centres of varying size' (Warnier 1993a: 304). It partly explains, as well, the proliferation of occult metaphors such as *msa*, *famla*, *atchul*, *balok*, *kong*, *kupe* or *nyongo* among grassfielders seeking to come to terms with 'the loss of people through contemporary occult slave trade' in the service of the market economy (Warnier 1993a:310–11).

Given how important being able to pass for an active and effective container of transmissible life essence remains as a measure of success even among diasporic grassfielders, the successful entrepreneurs in the city or diaspora ultimately return to the village to negotiate for recognition and legitimation through redistribution of their personal wealth. This they do by way of marriage, sponsorship of development projects at home, acquisition of land, building of houses, and by purchasing neo-traditional titles of nobility from *fons* and other notables. The cooptation by marriage or succession into a descent line that was denied them from the start is thus acquired via an alternative route (Warnier 1993a and b). Those not successful enough to return to the village from the diaspora in the same way often recreate in the cities or plantation camps and villages the very same hierarchies and inequalities that they purportedly fled from (cf. Tabapssi 1999). In either case, it is evident that it was not so much the principles of hierarchy that these migrants were fleeing from, as the fact that those principles had been used to exclude them. The structures and ethos prove their resilience through negotiations and renegotiations between and amongst the included and the initially excluded.

## Personhood, Agency and Subjectivity in Bum

In Bum, villagers allow for individual creativity and self-fulfilment in general, but frown on the greedy and hurtful pursuit of these. The popular meticulous distinction between good and bad persons of all types speaks eloquently of a conviction that no agency or subjectivity is rewarding for the collectivity, and even for the individual ultimately, if undomesticated. Undomesticated agency or subjectivity is greed, and success that comes from greed can only be achieved through the sacrifice of others, or of their interests, as a full account of the notions of *awung* and *Msa* would demonstrate. *Awung* is believed to be a person endowed with clairvoyance from birth, but who is capable of using his/her supernatural powers in both positive and negative ways. *Msa*, for its part, is believed to be a mysterious world of abundance, infinite possibilities and dangers, which a certain type of clairvoyant individual may visit for constructive or destructive purposes (see Nyamnjoh 1985). Like their fellow grassfielders, Bum people tend to believe that 'personal success is essentially destructive unless seen to be acting for the good of all and this ensures that such achievements should be accompanied by egalitarian redistributory mechanisms' (Rowlands 1994: 17).

In his study of personal success in the Bamenda area of the grassfields, Michael Rowlands points out that in this region it is believed that personal success is always at the expense of others. 'Someone who suddenly acquires wealth or good fortune has done so at the expense of close relatives or friends', who are usually thought to have been 'made into zombies' and 'given to societies of sorcerers to work for them and produce wealth in return for the good fortune given to one of their members' (Rowlands 1994:15). It is believed, he further observes, that

> if someone has success in business or politics, has many wives, many goats, or a bountiful harvest of yams or groundnuts ... that success must necessarily have been at the expense of someone else's career or that he/she will have sucked the fertility out of the families, livestock or fields of someone else. (Rowlands 1994:15–16)

He thus concludes that the Bamenda area

> shares a mercantilist philosophy according to which resources are in a fixed and limited supply and what someone has 'eaten' is appropriated at the expense of the whole society. Life in itself is part of the bargain, and if someone is sick or dies, it must be that someone has sucked away his/her life to feed on it. The wealthy will have to take this into consideration and should people experience misfortune or die among his kin and neighbours, accusations may arise. (Rowlands 1994:17)

Agency or subjectivity as the ability to manipulate oneself into a position of abundance, while everyone else is barely struggling to get by, is perceived as destructive for others and ultimately for the accumulating individual, as a full account of the ambivalence of *Msa* and *awung* would further demonstrate. It is not enough to belong to a group or community; such belonging or community must impact positively on one's kin to be recognised. While it could be argued that, in the popular notions, even those described as villains and sorcerers identify with communities at *Msa,* or constitute themselves into communities of *awung*, the fact that they are seen to be harming their own kin and communities of descent means they are neither recognised nor legitimated.

In this light, we could understand the widespread belief in and postcolonial resilience of sorcery or occult forces in the grassfields not so much in terms of the inability of the people to modernise their beliefs and rituals, but as reflective of collective preoccupation with the conflictual relationship between competing agentive forces in postcolonial societies, where promises of modernity are fast becoming a broken dream for all but an elite few. Sorcery can be as much a source and resource of personal and collective power or powerlessness as a call for domesticated agency and intersubjectivity against various forms of exploitation, marginalisation, inequality and individualism (Ardener 1996:243–60; Fisiy and Geschiere 1996:193–7; Geschiere 1997; Geschiere and Nyamnjoh 1998; Rowlands and Warnier 1988:121–25; Warnier 1993b:139–62). Indeed, the fact that postcolonial accusations of sorcery, like colonial ones, are usually among family members or kin is indicative of how much grassfielders still cherish the solidarity of domesticated agency or intersubjectivity and how ready they are, today as in the past, to protect it from aggression and the hurtful pursuit of personal success (see Fisiy and Geschiere 1996:197; Geschiere 1995:7–35; Geschiere and Nyamnjoh 1998). For what use is a social system which glorifies personal success but in reality has little room for everyone seeking success? Success that is attainable only through sacrificing the humanity of others is considered not worth pursuing.

This ethos is well articulated in ideas of personhood, agency and subjectivity in Bum. It is worth reiterating that these beliefs and categories are not frozen or uncontested. Nonetheless, they are widely shared and invoked, particularly in times of stress, misfortune and uncertainties (cf. Geschiere and Nyamnjoh 1998). It is evident that *Msa* and *awung* are central, in Bum beliefs, to a common understanding of how the world should be organised to maximise the interests of all and sundry. Because not everyone is endowed with the same talents from birth, and because there is not enough of everything for everyone to have more than enough, it is important that the extra-gifted harness their *awung* and knowledge of *Msa* to enable the less endowed or the inept to benefit as well. Using one's talents for personal gratification only is likely to engender more conflict and pain than satisfaction and pleasure, even for the talented individuals.

Most people in Bum believe in a supreme God (*Fyen*) who is responsible for all creation. Some individuals he endows with clairvoyance (*seba* = two eyes), others with innocence (*seimok* = one eye). Those with clairvoyance are clairvoyant: *wutaseba (sg.)/ghetaseba* (pl.) = person(s) of *seba*; also *wuta-fintina* (sg.)/*ghetafintina* (pl.); and those with innocence are the innocent: *ayung/ngwo/mumu* (sg.)//*wuyung/wungwo/wumumu (pl.)* = person(s) of *seimok*. The clairvoyant are said to be endowed with an ability – *fintini* (sg.)/*fintitu* (pl.) – to see and do certain things which their innocent counterparts are incapable of. It is not uncommon to refer to the clairvoyant as clever people: *wutatoffana* (sg.)/*ghetatoffana* (pl.) = person(s) of sense. The innocent are associated with shortsightedness, incapability, and at times foolishness. The verb 'to see' (*yen*) is sometimes used to distinguish between the clairvoyant and the innocent. The former sees (*yenalo*), and the latter sees not (*yenawi*).

To those who share this belief, clairvoyant and innocent are the only two categories of persons in Bum, and a person is either born as one or as the other. However, both categories have two subcategories each. A clairvoyant might be associated either with *uwung* or *Msa*. *Uwung* are further subdivided into two: Wiseperson – *awungadzunga* (sg.)/*uwungudzungu* (pl.) = good *awung/uwung* – and Sorcerer: *awungabe* (sg.)/*uwungube* (pl.) = bad *awung/uwung*. Cunning – *wutamsa* (sg.)/*ghetamsala* (pl.) = person(s) of *Msa* – is the appellation of the second subcategory of clairvoyant, which is also subdivided into two: Sly – *wutamsamdzung* (sg.)/*ghetamsamdzunga* (pl.) = good person(s) of *Msa* – and Villain – *wutamsamba* (sg.)/*ghetamsambe* (pl.) = bad person(s) of *Msa*. The innocent fall into either of two sub-types: Medium – *wut-ni-toffotu* (sg.)/*gheta-ni-toffotu* (pl.) = person(s) with intelligence – or Inept – *ayung/ ngwo/mumu* (sg.)//*wuyung/wungwo/wumumu* (pl.) = person(s) capable of nothing great.

It is hard to resist thinking of *Msa* as analogous to modern capitalism, especially as experienced at the periphery (cf. Ardener 1996:243–60; Warnier 1993b:159–62): its rhetoric of emancipation and empowerment for the individual who sacrifices (breaks free of) family and custom to embrace modernity on the one hand, and, on the other hand, the harsh reality of exploitation, zombification, debasement, depletion and disenchantment it occasions among its converts. Many scholars have explored the relationship between persistent beliefs in *Msa* and other forms of witchcraft and the changing nature of capitalism and its effects on the periphery. Local beliefs in *Msa* predate the transatlantic slave trade, and communication between the grassfields and the coastal regions predates colonialism and plantation agriculture. Yet recent and current discourses or narratives on witchcraft in Bum are heavily coloured by symbols and associations informed by capitalism. Most recent analyses have tended to focus on the globalisation of poverty, uncertainty and anxiety of consumer capitalism to explain the resurgence in witchcraft accusations and beliefs in mysterious centres of accumulation (such as *Msa*, *famla*, *Nyongo*, *Kupeh* or *Kong*) in Cameroon and elsewhere in Africa. While our understanding of witchcraft can certainly not be reduced to the impact of capitalism alone, we cannot afford to ignore its impact either. That is so, at the very least, because the tremendous expansion of the market economy of the past thirty years 'has given a new impetus to the idioms of accumulation and dis-accumulation through various kinds of leakages' (Warnier 1993a:310).

Bum ideas of *Msa* and *awung* are like a statement both against undomesticated agency or subjectivity and the illusion of permanence created by capitalism about personal success. Like capitalism, *Msa* and *awung*, when not harnessed, bring power and opportunities only to a limited minority – those with the clairvoyance and greed to indulge in them. Like global capitalism which caters for the needs of investors, advertisers and the affluent consumers of the world as a whole, the undomesticated pursuit of *Msa* and *awung* enhances self-seeking individuals at the expense of family and the wider community. In other words, it is only by marginalising family and collective interests, by manipulating, exploiting or taking advantage of others, that the selfish pursuit of clairvoyance can afford for its disciples personal success of the type studied by Rowlands (1994; 1995) and Warnier (1993b:163–96) in the grassfields and among diasporic grassfielders. But such success is only an illusion because, again like consumer capitalism, *Msa* and *awung* seem to be an eternal cycle of indebtedness, manipulation, zombification and the craving for elusive satisfaction. The appetites they bring about only grow from strength to strength, and those who yield to their allure become instantly trapped and ultimately consumed themselves, after consuming their sociality to death.

In post-apartheid South Africa, for example, the state, by yielding to the *diktats* of global capitalism, has allowed hurtful agency and subjectivity in the form of individual success to run counter to the liberation dreams of the black majority. Structural inequalities are yet to be resolved in a way that benefits more than just a black elite (Sharp 1998), despite enormous sacrifices by ordinary South Africans during the liberation struggle. The small but bustling black elite who have graduated into the white-dominated middle classes can only afford to wallow in the conspicuous consumption of prized commodities, such as houses, cars, TVs, cellphones and jacuzzis, by breaking the dreams of ordinary South Africans. The price of their rapid and phenomenal personal success is the reality of most ordinary South Africans who are still trapped in shacks, shantytowns, joblessness, poverty and uncertainty, and who can only marvel at the 'indecent speed and ... little visible exertion' with which the black elite have come by their riches and prosperity. These inequities have given rise to the belief 'that it is only by magical means, by consuming others, that people may enrich themselves in these perplexing times', and consequently, to a resurgence in accusations of witchcraft and zombification, and to the scapegoating of immigrants – *makwerekwere*, whose readiness, like zombies, to provide devalued labour is seen as compounding the disenchantment of the autochthonous populations in the face of rapidly diminishing prosperity in South Africa (J. and J. Comaroff 1999a:22–26; 1999b). Global capitalism is thus like *Msa* in posing the greatest threat to domesticated agency and intersubjectivity, or to the philosophy by which personal success has meaning only when inclusive of collective interests as well.

Observations elsewhere seem to buttress further not only our analogy between *Msa* and capitalism but also the fact that under both success seems often at the cost of enormous sacrifices of social relationships and responsibilities. The agency or subjectivity they engender is inherently destructive if left unharnessed. In the Democratic Republic of Congo (former Zaïre), getting involved in the dollarised diamond economy as an alternative to collapsed state structures seems to create more problems than it solves among villagers who have come to believe that 'to be considered in Zaïre, you got to have money!' Some go even further to assert that '"you need money to be considered in the eyes of God, for God only recognizes the rich"' (de Boeck 1998:793). Thus, driven by desperation to capture and tame the wild, unpredictable and ambivalent diamonds and dollars, the young *bana Lunda* men who are at the heart of this economy are ready to sacrifice (by means of sorcery and otherwise) their work power and productivity, their youth, strength and beauty, their fertility and sexual prowess, and their friends or family members. Diamonds and dollars 'totally isolate one and invert the normal ties of solidarity and reciprocity into the destructive internal mechanisms of redistribution by sorcery. The longing or hunger for dollars and diamonds is ... like an incurable festering sore which reopens every time one runs out of money'. This happens pretty often, since diamond dollars tend to 'evaporate', to be drained away on beer, cigarettes and women ('economy of ejaculation') – an 'uncontrolled and wild flow of money and commodities' 'that does not correspond to accepted patterns of self-realisation' (de Boeck 1998:789–99). This impermanence of success even at the personal level reflects the fact that agency or subjectivity as independence only creates dependence, and provides further evidence for interdependence or domesticated agency and intersubjectivity as the only way of curbing the 'radically widening chasm between rich and poor' and the 'uneasy fusion of enfranchisement and exclusion, hope and hopelessness' (J. and J. Comaroff 1999a:19) that *Msa*, global capitalism or modernity seem to bring about in marginal communities.

## Agency and Subjectivity in Contemporary Grassfields

The instances of social control in the past were very much limited to the institutions that *fondoms* like Bum and Mankon had designed for themselves. But in colonial and postcolonial times the individual was exposed not only to new and competing forms of social control, but also to the possibility of taking refuge under these new institutions to pursue particular types of agency or subjectivity that would clearly have been sanctioned by the structures of control traditional to the region. The further away from the *fondom* an individual was (in the colonial army, as migrant labour in distant plantations, or in school in town), the greater the possibility of getting away with undomesticated types of agency or subjectivity (see de Vries 1998, for cases in point from Kom). It must be noted in the case of Bum, however, that the long arm of the *fon* and his secret police (the *Kwefon*) has continued to pursue Bum migrants in distant places who believe their destructive agency and subjectivity out of reach of traditional modes of sanction (cf. Geschiere and Nyamnjoh 1998).

This notwithstanding, it is clear that new or modern instances of power and opportunity have seriously weakened the social institutions of grassfields *fondoms* and their idea of domesticated agency and intersubjectivity (cf. Fisiy 1995; Nkwi 1976). The empowerment and opportunities such instances have occasioned for all individuals, and the dissenting individual in particular, have made the traditional social structures of these chiefdoms more ready to negotiate with and accommodate forms of agency and subjectivity that would certainly have been sanctioned into the margins in the past. On the other hand, successful individuals in the modern and individualistic sense, perhaps because of earlier socialisation into the collectivistic philosophy of their cultural group of origin (for example, the quest for legitimacy and recognition as a 'container'), or perhaps because of awareness of the temporality and impermanence of personal success in the modern world, especially in peripheral states under consumer capitalism, are just as ready to negotiate with and accommodate traditional ideas of domesticated agency and intersubjectivity. The outcome is usually creatively negotiated, the result of concessions by both parties, and serves as the basis of future traditions, to be referred to and negotiated with by others in similar predicaments. Hence traditions are not only being modernised, but modernity is being traditionalised, and the outcome is triumph neither for tradition nor for modernity as such, but rather for the new creation issuing from a marriage of both.

Anthropological accounts of agency and subjectivity in the grassfields point to this quest for accommodation and conviviality between the community and the individual. While cultural meanings of agency and subjectivity have been transformed remarkably by new political and economic developments in the region, nation-wide and beyond, these meanings have themselves continued to influence such developments. Instead of traditional grassfields ideas of domesticated agency and intersubjectivity being pushed aside by the modern power elites, as was widely predicted both by modernisation theorists and their critics, grassfields social structures and institutions have displayed remarkable dynamism, adaptiveness and adaptability to new socio-economic and political developments, without necessarily becoming erased by the latter in the process. *Fons* and *fondoms* have become active agents in the quest by the new elites for traditional cultural symbols as a way of maximising opportunities at the centre of bureaucratic and state power (Fisiy 1995; Fisiy and Goheen 1998; Geschiere 1993; Geschiere and Nyamnjoh 1998; Goheen 1992; Konings 1999; Warnier 1993a).

Certain chiefs such as *fon* Angwafo III of Mankon and *fon* Doh Gah Gwanyin of Balikumbat (currently the only parliamentarian for the ruling Cameroon People's Democratic Movement – CPDM – in the opposition-dominated North West province) have themselves become part of the new elite at the centre of national and regional power. Through their individual capacities or via various associations – such as the North West Fons' Union (NOWEFU) led by *fon* Abumbi II John Ambe of Bafut, and the North West Fons' Conference (NOWEFCO) led by *fon* Doh Gah Gwanyin of Balikumbat – these *fons* stake claims on national power and resources for their region and *fondoms*. *Fon* Angwafo III of Mankon, for example, became the first *fon* to be elected as a member of parliament in 1961 (after resigning from the house of chiefs) in a keenly contested multi-party election in which he ran as an independent. He ignored calls for his resignation as either MP or chief by those who thought it was improper for a chief (whose position is hereditary) to hold an elected office. Upon the reunification of the English and French Cameroons, *fon* Angwafo III became a member of the sole party, which he served as president of the Bamenda section. He stayed on as MP until his retirement from active politics in 1988. However, the launching of the Social Democratic Front (SDF) in Mankon and the dramatic resignation from the ruling CDPM in 1990 of John Ngu Foncha (anglophone architect of reunification and prominent statesman) brought *fon* Angwafo III back to the centre of local and national politics when he was appointed to replace Foncha as the national vice-president of the CDPM. *Fon* Angwafo III has been described as 'a shining example of a pragmatist', and a man of many faces who has skilfully married two different political cultures (Aka 1984:64).

It is in connection with similar quests for state power and resources by the new elites that some anthropologists have understood the growing interest among these elites in investment in neo-traditional titles and in maintaining strong links with their home village through kin and client patronage networks. But such participation and investment have led 'not to the reproduction but rather to the transformation of the structures and relationships of power' (Goheen 1992:406). To maintain themselves as embodiments of community, chiefs constantly renegotiate their positions within the contradictions between state and community, on the one hand, and in relation to competing expectations within the community on the other (cf. Konings 1999). This is as true of Bum and Mankon as it is of the other chiefdoms in the grassfields, and speaks not only of how these chiefdoms continue to explore new ways of domesticating the agency and subjectivity of their sons and daughters at the centre or periphery of modernity (or *Msa*), but also of the mechanisms they have adopted as communities for collective agency and intersubjectivity in changing situations.

Such adaptability or dynamism is displayed both towards macro level changes and towards developments within the family among children. Continuity and change are alike determined by mutuality in concessions. Turning to social structure and agency at the level of the family, I now want to consider how conviviality is negotiated over time; thus providing for both meanings of *a child is one person's only in the womb*. Limiting oneself to one of these meanings denies either the impact of history as a process or the resilience of tradition ('the womb') in the regeneration of social structures or the life of the individual.

At the level of the family, I illustrate with examples of marriages in Mankon that show how people negotiate tradition with modernity through conviviality, and how competing understandings of agency or subjectivity are compromised. To understand my Mankon example better, here is a brief biographical account of my association with *fon* Angwafo III, a further illustration of how ideas of cultures and identities as homogeneous wholes often hide more than they reveal.

I was born in December 1961 in Bum, where I spent the first ten years of my life. My biological father was Ndong, a rich cattle owner of Bafmen origin whom I was to meet for the first time in my third year in college. My mother got married to Nyamnjoh when I was three years old, her father having turned down Ndong's offers to marry her because Ndong was not of Bum. My mother's elder sister was married to *fon* Yai of Bum, and together with his 20 other wives they lived in his LakaBum palace, some 30 kilometres away from Fonfuka where I attended primary school. Without children of her own to send to school, my aunt had persuaded her husband to sponsor me instead. He had accepted but had also insisted that I spend my holidays in LakaBum, and work for him like all the other young men and women he sponsored, including his own biological children. Although not of royal blood as such, I was to spend my childhood and adolescence with two *fons* in two different *fondoms*, *fon* John Yai and *fon* Solomon Angwafo III, of Bum and Mankon respectively. Both *fons* have fathered me socially, and both *fondoms* claim me and my achievements (or the lack thereof) equally. Through me, they have prided themselves on having a son in the corridors of modern opportunities at the national and international levels. And so too I have had to identify with them, for one personal reason or another, in the course of my life.

In both Bum and Mankon, I am a prince in every sense but blood, since neither *fon* is my biological father. When I discovered the latter in my third year in college, he showed more interest in trying to claim me by undoing the impact of all the others on my life and upbringing, than in seeking to catch up with them. But when I refused to change my name from Nyamnjoh to Ndong and to become reinvented by him, he lost interest and I kept some distance. My reaction to similar pressure by the *fon* of Bum to adopt his name, however, was not the same. Instead of giving up the name Nyamnjoh as he repeatedly instructed, claiming it was the name of a commoner, I at one point added Yai to my list of names, and some of my school certificates did actually bear 'Francis Beng Yai Nyamnjoh'. I also remember at one point adopting the nickname 'Frank Human' in exasperation, and asking my classmates and friends to call me that instead of all these names that different claimants were seeking to impose on me for their own strategic reasons. Later on, however, I decided to shade Yai from my list of names, and to stick to the rest. (It was normal for a child to have three names where I grew up – the name at birth, the family name and the christian name upon baptism.) I was conscious I was different from other children whenever people asked me questions to which they were used to receiving simple, straightforward, cliché answers: 'Where do you come from?', 'Who is your father?', 'What is your name?' I found myself having to explain all the time, to prove that I was not lying by claiming this parentage or that identity, when my name or other indicators pointed elsewhere.

If there is any such thing as an identity crisis, mine was not felt from within, but was rather imposed by others. I feel an insider in both communities and, according to many cultural indicators, I may even be more of an insider than most people exclusively assumed to be of either culture, given my connections with the palaces and their institutions as embodiments of culture. But if one were to stick to traditional ideas of belonging, as some have, I would definitely not be classified as Mankon or Bum, but as Bafmen, the home village of Ndong, my biological father.[6] According to the same logic, neither my aunt in the Bum palace nor my social mother in the Mankon palace would qualify to claim me as a son (which they do), their love and commitment notwithstanding. Frozen ideas of identity and culture are like labelling in order to include or to exclude; it is like seeking to confine the child in the womb.

My completion of primary school coincided with the marriage of a princess of Bum to *fon* Angwafo III of Mankon, a childhood friend and schoolmate of *fon* John Yai of Bum. So I was sent to stay with *fon* Angwafo III, who became my guardian during my first two years at Sacred Heart College, Mankon. *Fon* John Yai soon became irregular in the payment of fees for my college education, and I was threatened with dismissal. *Fon* Angwafo III, who cherished education particularly, given his own brilliant achievements in this regard,[7] could not understand why his friend was irregular with the fees. One day I was actually sent away from college, and went to see him in tears. He sat me down and listened. It was only then that he learnt for the first time that I was not a prince of Bum by blood. Faced with the prospect of having me dismissed from school for non-payment of fees, he decided to sponsor me thenceforth. And did so all the way to my MA degree at the University of Yaounde, where I subsequently won a government scholarship to study for a PhD at Leicester University in the UK. Not once did he suggest that I change my name to bear Angwafo, nor did he encourage me when I hinted I was willing to consider doing so. With Ndong at the margins, I was left with three active fathers, two royal and one commoner, and in my own little way have sought to satisfy their competing demands for attention ever since. They have each allocated me a piece of land in their villages on which to build my house, as is traditional in the grassfields. When I married in December 1990, they all were part of the process: all attended the ceremony and each participated in his capacity as a father. Two of my mothers were present as well; only the biological one was absent, having died in 1989.

In 1935, a prince of Mankon (tipped to become the next *fon*) was disowned by his father (*fon* Ndefru III) for daring to marry in church. Incidentally, the woman in question was Bum, sister to a Bum migrant who would be raised to a notable at the 1984 *Nukwi* cultural festival organised by *fon* Angwafo III to commemorate the death of his predecessor (cf. Eballa and Aka 1984). The first migrants to be formally accepted and offered land to settle in Mankon by late *fon* Ndefru III were from Bum. Hence the Bum Quarters of contemporary urban Mankon. In 1985 *fon* Angwafo III consented to attend a church wedding for the first time since succeeding Ndefru III as *fon* of Mankon in 1959. One of his brothers' sons, Ephraim Nde Ngwafo (then law lecturer at the University of Yaounde, where he later became professor and rector), was marrying a woman from Manyu division, a forest area in the South West province of Cameroon. Ephraim was also one of the few among the young generation of princes not only to choose his wife from outside of Mankon, but to venture out of the western grassfields. He had grown up in the South West province where his father had migrated, and knew more of South West and South Westerners than of the grassfields and grassfielders. In addition, he had left Cameroon to study abroad in England and the United States, where he earned his PhD in law. The wedding took place at the Saint Joseph's Metropolitan Cathedral in Mankon. Since his marriage, Ephraim has mobilised the *fon* for other personal projects as well, inviting Angwafo III to co-chair (with the Minister of Higher Education) the launch – in 1993 in Yaounde – of four books he had published. His subsequent appointment as rector of the University of Yaounde II, and cooption into the inner circles of the ruling CPDM party, may not be unconnected with the *fon*'s position and influence.

Shortly after Ephraim's wedding, a prince and biological son of *fon* Angwafo III – a urologist who had lived in the USA for over 20 years – married there, against the *fon*'s will, a woman from the Caribbean. Although ready to allow a marriage to someone from outside of Mankon, the *fon* was not yet ready to concede a marriage with someone as far away as America. He was angry with his son whom he threatened to disown. But as time passed and the son explained his position, the *fon* finally understood him and yielded to the marriage eventually, on condition that his son returned to Mankon with his wife and that he underwent the traditional marriage ceremony as well. This son now lives and works in Yaounde. He is also a key adviser to the *fon*, and two of his children have since returned to the USA for further studies. Following this precedent, another prince who went to the USA for further studies has since married an African-American, and in 1999 came home briefly to present his wife and son to his family in Mankon, and to undergo some traditional rites too.

These rites transformed both marriages from a contract between two individuals (*usa'mangyie*) to marriage by consensus (*ngoo manyie*). The traditional rites entail anointing the groom and bride with powdered camwood and red palm oil, and pouring a drink of raphia wine from the *fon*'s drinking buffalo-horn into their hands scooped around their mouths to avoid spillage. The anointment blesses them with fertility, and the wine transmits to them some of the life essence of the *fon* (as father), thus taking away their symbolic impotence. If the prince was also to become the son chosen to succeed when his father dies, he would inherit the *fon*'s buffalo-horn cup upon his enthronement, and would become 'container' or vital piggy-bank to his brothers and sisters and to the entire *fondom*. He would become *father* to all, and could henceforth pour libation on the graves of dead *fons* and ask for blessings and protection on behalf of everyone in the *fondom*.

While *fon* Angwafo III has had to choose between rigidly defending tradition and losing both sons to the world out there, the sons have also had to choose between rigidly adhering to their individual agency or subjectivity and losing their father and community of origin back home. In both cases, the choice has been for the middle ground, to seek conviviality between modernity and tradition, to settle for interdependence or interconnectedness between the competing world views. In analogous terms, the choice has been to bridge *Msa* and community of origin. On each occasion, the decision taken has served as a reference point for future action.

Thus, having allowed a church wedding in 1985,[8] *fon* Angwafo III needed no further convincing when it came to my turn. In December 1990 I married the daughter of a local notable from the village of Ntambeng in Mankon. It was a more traditional wedding than the others in that once I had made known my intentions to marry Henrietta, the *fon* as wife-taker started negotiations with her family as wife-giver when I was still in the UK. He completed payment of the bridewealth long before I returned home. I had met Henrietta during my days as a student at the University of

Yaounde, and we had fallen in love the year I was elected secretary-general of the Mankon Students' Association (MASA). The marriage started with the traditional rites as described above, which the *fon* performed in person at his palace. Another rite (*miy*) was also performed to prove that I had qualified to wear shoes into the inner courtyard of the palace where the *fon* granted daily audiences, and that I could thenceforth greet or speak directly to the *fon* and could attract his attention by clapping my hands – all things I was not allowed to do until 1990. I had come of age. My family-in-law, satisfied with the bridewealth, officially handed their daughter over to us, and considered her married. As was the custom, Henrietta was led to my house in the palace at night by a singing group of her relatives with bamboo lights (*nka'*).[9] None of her kin were happy to be separating from her, although they all shared her joy at marriage. The idea of night and bamboo light is intended to discourage the bride from rushing back to her parents each time she has a dispute with her husband, something Henrietta has not done since we married, although she pays her parents regular visits (see Monikang 1978 for more on marriage in Mankon).

The *fon* was also actively involved and represented at the next stage – that of the civil marriage, which was performed by the government delegate of the Bamenda Urban Council. It is usually quite a brief ceremony, but the delegate (or mayor) has incorporated some of the rituals of the church, and insists on having the wedding rings slipped over the fingers of the couple by the witnesses. This stage is important, for the mayor issues a marriage certificate which the state recognises, and in which the man has the choice of indicating whether he opts for polygamy or monogamy. The churches insist on this stage and on seeing what option the groom has settled for before deciding whether or not to allow a church wedding as well. Those who opt for polygamy have their applications for a church wedding turned down, since the church, unlike the state, allows only for monogamy. An increasing number of couples settle for this stage only, partly because all they really want is a certificate of marriage to submit to the state bureaucracy for tax purposes, and partly because they are too poor to marry in church. For most, however, the traditional marriage is still important, even if the tendency is to cut down on costs by limiting the process to its most significant or symbolic aspects only – 'knock door' (going to see a woman's parents to ask for her hand in marriage), and payment of the bridewealth.

I opted for monogamy upon persuasion from Henrietta and also because of my status as a Catholic Christian, and therefore qualified for the next stage: the church wedding, which *fon* Angwafo III also attended. Ordinarily, the *fon* does not go to church on Sundays to worship, although he has authorised various churches to operate freely in his *fondom*, and his wives and children are free to belong to any church of their choice. Under 'religion' on his CV is entered: 'Christianity; Non-denominational', and he has the christian name of 'Solomon'. A *fon*'s presence in church at any time is interpreted as a major concession by a traditional authority. The most dramatic concession of them all was made by *fon* John Yai of Bum when he decided upon instant baptism for himself during a Baptist Church field conference in November 1990 in Bum. For over 30 years as *fon*, he had vehemently opposed the setting up of a church in his palace, forcing his wives, children, retainers and others to practise Christianity in secret. I had gone to finalise preparations for my upcoming marriage, and had participated at the baptism and taken some photographs (see Geschiere and Nyamnjoh 1998). On the occasion of my wedding, *fon* Angwafo III was accompanied to church by *fon* John Yai of Bum and his delegation, and also by the *fon* of Babungo, a son-in-law to both of them. Equally attending as one of my fathers was Nyamnjoh. Ndong found an excuse not to attend, even though the wedding invitation card had been designed to accommodate him: 'The families of HRH Angwafo III/HRH John Yai/Thomas Ndong and Ngu Ambrose Ngang cordially invite … to the wedding of their son Francis Beng Nyamnjoh and daughter Henrietta Mambo Ngu.' But two of his sons did attend in their own right, and did bring with them a ram which was used as part of a pool towards the feast.

On 20 June 1998, *fon* Angwafo III's daughter, Doris Manka (professional secretary in a bank in Yaounde), married a magistrate, Joseph Aseh, prince from the *fondom* of Balikumbat. This wedding was attended by eight other *fons*, who were keen to display their solidarity as members of the unions of *fons* mentioned above. Also in attendance was the governor of the North West Province, as a close administrative collaborator of *fon* Angwafo III, and in recognition of the latter's powerful position in the ruling CPDM party. The pattern was the same as for the previous weddings, but since this was a daughter's wedding, the *fon* as wife-giver was expected to personally hand Doris over to the husband in church, in the same way that her brothers and sisters had escorted her to the groom's home a few days back. Having led her up to the altar in church, the *fon* later commented on the wedding: 'It is her choice and I grant her that. If she has saved enough to finance it, I'll encourage her to go ahead.' The venues for her wedding and reception party were the same as for my wedding and Ephraim's. The most recent wedding reviewed here took place on 8 January 2000 at the Ntamulung Presbyterian Church in Mankon; it was between another son of the *fon* (PhD in Engineering) and the daughter of a former vice-minister of agriculture and reverend pastor of the Baptist Church in Cameroon. They were based in the UK and the USA respectively, and had decided to come home for their traditional, civil and church weddings. This accomplished, they flew to the USA where the bride was employed and the groom was hoping to find a job.

In all cases, the wedding rings, bridal dress and groom's suit, shoes and other outfits had been obtained directly from Europe or North America. In Doris's case, for example, the wedding cards were designed and printed in the USA by her sisters of the same mother (of whom, incidentally, I am the adopted son), one of whom also brought along the wedding dress and other exotic modern consumer paraphernalia. In my case, I had toiled as a security guard in Leicester after completion of my doctorate to earn the money I needed, and had bought a seven-year-old Peugeot 305 car from Holland[10] with some of the money in preparation for what was baptised 'the wedding of the year' in 1990 – a landmark soon eclipsed by other families with more wealth to lavish on weddings for public admiration. In all cases, both families involved had each chosen a fabric (Nigerian wax – the preferred Vlisco-made Holland wax being on the expensive side) as the uniform that would identify and distinguish them (cf. 'wealth in people'). These uniforms were stitched differently, depending on whether one's style was local or cosmopolitan, traditional or modern, or a creative mix of all. Some did it the customary way (heavily embroidered gowns or jumpers – grassfields style) while others opted for modern designs inspired by catalogues imported from the West. Video cameras were there to record every moment; so were photographers with all sorts of modern cameras. Some of the guests who were not part of the extended families were clad in the latest Western fashions, while others wore modern African designs influenced by Senegalese, Malian, Nigerian and Beninois styles.

The weddings were massively attended, with guest lists ranging between 1,500 and 2,000. The receptions were rich in champagne, assorted whiskies, wines, beers and soft drinks, and there was also palm wine and locally brewed corn beer. There were cakes and other types of snacks, and there were modern dishes, domesticated and otherwise. There were also *achu*, *fufu* corn, *ndolé*, pepper soup, soya beef, fried fish and other local dishes from the grassfields and from elsewhere in Cameroon. Guests included villagers from Bum who had trekked over 200 km with loads of food, fowls and goats; villagers from Mankon brought into town by specially hired trucks; traditional elites from chiefdoms far and near; local and national politicians from Bamenda, Yaounde and elsewhere; the clergy and modern professionals in Mercedes-Benzes, BMWs, Pajeros and other modern cars, bought directly from the factory or second-hand as reconditioned comfort. Also attending my wedding were two friends I had made as a student in Leicester, an Irish couple-to-be. They flew in to attend, and brought along presents, including champagne glasses that proved handy at the high table during the reception. Other friends in Europe who could not make it to the wedding had sent presents and goodwill messages. My wedding was co-celebrated by 14 priests because of the close association my parents-in-law had with the Catholic Church. Along with traditional and modern music there were Bum and Mankon dances, as well as a choir of Henrietta's friends and mates at the University of Yaounde where she was completing her degree in English and Literatures.

It was an interesting and creative mix, a melting pot of influences and networks of solidarities. Would one call this creative adoption or simply the inability of grassfielders to break with the past in favour of modernity? Is this a conflict between agency or subjectivity and social structures, or is it a case of domesticating agency and intersubjectivity as a way of maximising opportunities? To what extent could either tradition or modernity survive in a context where neither can afford the independence it needs to survive without the other?

Indeed, *fon* Angwafo III has changed remarkably since he came to power in 1959, and tradition has only survived because it has proved itself capable of making concessions to modernity. It is a statement which is equally true of each and every one of us who married in church, in front of the mayor and with the blessings of our father(s) and tradition(s). At first all marriages were celebrated strictly in the traditional way. In 1935 a prince was disowned, and lost the possibility of succeeding his father as *fon*, because he had dared to defy tradition by insisting on a church wedding. Girls who became pregnant before marriage were expelled from the palace and never again was the *fon* to set eyes on them. That used to be the case until the early 1990s. Today princesses have left school pregnant, had their babies and brought them back to present to the *fon*. It was forbidden for women to present themselves before the *fon* when having their period. Today, with modern facilities, it is difficult to distinguish between a woman in her period and one who is not. The *fon* has given up on that ban, preferring to leave it to the conscience of each and every woman. He used to be against his children studying abroad; today, even 10-year-olds are known to leave for the USA. Two of his 50 wives, who are both illiterate (one of them my social mother in Mankon), have been to the USA unaccompanied to assist their daughters in childbirth. My mother returned from the USA in October 1999 after staying there for a year, with a driving licence to her credit, and with new styles of dressing (jeans, shorts, trainers, African-American hair styles), an affected way of speaking with insistence on grammar and disregard for pidgin, a craving to read and write, and tastes that would certainly have sent shock waves through the *fondom* some ten years back. This is a laboratory *par excellence* for the study of negotiated agency and intersubjectivity, collective or personal. We cannot afford not to create theoretical space for such negotiations, interdependence and intersubjectivities, of which Bum, Mankon, the grassfields and indeed Cameroon are only indicative of ongoing creative processes much more widely in postcolonial Africa.

## Conclusion

This chapter challenges frequent impressions in literature that agency or subjectivity is an undifferentiated phenomenon in any society, open to some and not to others, and that those who have it must prove their independence through conflictual and antagonistic relationships with others and with society. The chapter also challenges the parallel impression that imputes agency to the West and celebrates the Westerner and his/her impact on the rest of the world where tradition and custom are portrayed as obstacles to individual progress and achievement. It argues against such reductionist views of agency, acknowledging the fact that agency may take different forms and, most particularly, that it is construed and constructed differently in different societies, informed by history, culture and economic factors. Agency in the Cameroonian grassfields is both individual and collective, and involves a great deal of negotiation and concession by individuals and the communities to which they belong both at the micro and macro levels. It is important to understand how agency is recognised, fostered and contained in various localities, in order best to comprehend the interaction between globalisation and local communities, on the one hand, and, on the other, the creative processes of negotiation and straddling, of the making of interconnectedness, hybridity, intersubjectivities and multiple identities of peripheral societies (or their elements in the diaspora) in the postcolonial era. In the light of the foregoing, we need to theorise afresh agency in African studies as informed by real situations of real people in all their complexities. The way forward lies in recognising the creative and intersubjective ways in which Africans merge their traditions with exogenous influences to create modernities that are not reducible to either but superior to both.

## Notes

1 I would like to thank the Wenner Grenn Foundation for a grant that permitted me to collect much of the data used here. I am also grateful to Milton Krieger, Deborah Durham, Forcheh Ntongah, Henrietta Nyamnjoh, Richard Werbner, Mike Rowlands, Dwayne Wilson and participants at the Leiden University PhD and Post-Doctorate Seminar on 'Personhood and Agency in African Studies' (27–29 September 2000), for useful comments on earlier drafts of this paper.

2 In this regard, we are all familiar with the question: 'Where do you come from, originally?', which seems ready for no answer short of the land of your birth or of the birth of your father. Here is an exchange which reportedly took place between an English woman and a black British girl:

> English woman: 'Where were you born?'
> Black girl: 'Manchester.'
> English woman: 'I mean before that.'

3 In the western grassfields of Cameroon, Kings or Chiefs are known as *fon*, so by *fondoms* here I mean kingdom or chiefdom.

4 In Bum: 'wa wuta mogk mo ke wulah'; in Mankon: 'mu a ni wu ma tehh mutoh'; in Kom: 'wayn wul mo' nin go'ilva'.

5 This does not necessarily imply arguing along with Durkheim (cf. Lukes, 1882; Frisby and Sayer, 1986) that society has a life of its own nor that it is external to us in the same way as the physical world is. For 'While society is external to each individual taken singly, by definition it cannot be external to *all* individuals taken together' (Giddens, 1993:720).

6 Incidentally, Bafmen was also home to my mother's father, whose own father is said to have been brought to Bum as a war captive. But because the practice in Bum was to treat war prisoners and slaves well, he was given a piece of land to settle and to start a family. Bah, my mother's father, gained respect and recognition from the *fon* of Bum, and eventually became a notable and adviser, as well as provided the *fon* with a wife – my aunt.

7 He obtained a Diploma in Agriculture in 1953 from the School of Agriculture, Ibadan, Nigeria and started working for the Southern Cameroons Agricultural Service; and had recently been promoted to Assistant Agricultural Officer Grade I when he resigned to become Fon of Mankon in April 1959.

8 See de Vries (1998) for an example of how grassfields *fons* used to be vehemently opposed to christianity, which they perceived as a threat to their authority.

9 See Funjong (1994) for examples of nuptial songs and their significance in Mankon.

10 A car which *fon* Angwafo III blessed by pouring raphia wine from his buffalo-horn over it, and which has amazed me and others with its resilience. More than 10 years later, the car is still on the road, and the engine is as good as new.

## References

Aka, E. A. (1984), 'Some Vital Information About Fo Angwafo III'. In Y. Eballa and E. A. Aka (eds.) *Focus on Nükwi Nü Fo Ndefru III: Mankon Cultural Festival 23rd–31st December, 1984.* Yaounde: Sopecam, pp. 63–8.

Ardener, E. (1996), 'Witchcraft, Economics and the Continuity of Belief'. In Shirley Ardener (ed.) *Kingdom on Mount Cameroon: Studies in the History of the Cameroon Coast, 1500–1970*, Oxford: Berghahn Books, pp. 243–60.

Barber, K. (ed.) (1997), *Readings in African Popular Culture*. Oxford: James Currey.

Cohen, I. J. (1987), 'Structuration Theory and Social *Praxis*'. In Anthony Giddens and Jonathan Turner (eds.) *Social Theory Today*. Cambridge: Polity Press.

Comaroff, J. and J. (1999a), 'Alien-Nation: Zombies, Immigrants, and Millennial Capitalism'. *Codesria Bulletin* 3–4:17–28.

— (1999b), 'Occult Economies and the Violence of Abstraction: Notes from the South African Postcolony'. *American Ethnologist* 26(2):279–303.

Davies, B. (1991), 'The Concept of Agency: A Feminist Poststructuralist Analysis'. *Social Analysis* 30: 42–53.

de Boeck, F. (1998), 'Domesticating Diamonds and Dollars: Identity, Expenditure and Sharing in Southwestern Zaire (1984–1997)'. *Development and Change*, special issue on 'Globalization and Identity: Dialectics of Flows and Closures', 29(4):751–76.

de Vries, J. (1998), *Catholic Mission, Colonial Government and Indigenous Response in Kom (Cameroon)*. Leiden: African Studies Centre Research Report 56/1998.

Durham, D. (1995), 'Soliciting Gifts and Negotiating Agency: The Spirit of Asking in Botswana'. *Journal of the Royal Anthropological Institute* (NS) 1(1): 111–28.

Eballa, Y. and E. A. Aka (eds.) (1984), *Focus on Nükwi Nü Fo Ndefru III: Mankon Cultural Festival 23rd – 31st December, 1984*. Yaounde: Sopecam.

Ferguson, J. (1999), *Expectations of Modernity: Myths and Meanings of Urban Life on the Zambian Copperbelt*. Berkeley: University of California Press.

Ferguson, J. and A. Gupta (1997), *Anthropological Locations: Boundaries and Grounds of a Field Science*. Berkeley: University of California Press.

Fisiy, C. (1995), 'Chieftaincy in the Modern State: An Institution at the Crossroads of Democratic Change'. *Paideuma*. 41:49–62.

Fisiy, C. and Geschiere, P. (1996), 'Witchcraft, Violence and Identity: Different Trajectories in Postcolonial Cameroon', in Richard Werbner and Terence Ranger (eds), *Postcolonial Identities in Africa*. London: Zed Books, pp. 193–221.

Fisiy, C. and M. Goheen (1998), 'Power and the Quest for Recognition: Neo-traditional Titles among the New Elite in Nso', Cameroon'. *Africa* 68(3):383–402.

Fowler, I. and D. Zeitlyn (eds.) (1996), *African Crossroads: Intersections between History and Anthropology in Cameroon*. Oxford: Berghahn Books.

Geschiere, P. (1993), 'Chiefs and Colonial Rule in Cameroon: Inventing Chieftaincy, French and British Style'. *Africa* 63(2):151–75.

— (1995), *Sorcellerie et Politique en Afrique. La Viandre des Autres*. Paris: Karthala.

— (1997), *The Modernity of Witchcraft: Politics and the Occult in Postcolonial Africa*. Charlottesville: University of Virginia Press.

Geschiere, P. and J. Gugler (eds.) (1998), 'The Politics of Primary Patriotism'. *Africa* 68 (3) (special issue).

Geschiere, P. and F. Nyamnjoh (1998), 'Witchcraft as an Issue in the "Politics of Belonging": Democratization and Urban Migrants' Involvement with the Home Village'. *African Studies Review* 41(3): 69–92.

Giddens, A. (1993), *Sociology*. Cambridge: Polity Press.

Goheen, M. (1992), 'Chiefs, Sub-chiefs and Local Control: Negotiations over Land, Struggles over Meaning'. *Africa* 62(3):389–412.

Gottlieb, A. (1998), 'Do Infants Have Religion?: The Spiritual Lives of Beng Babies'. *American Anthropologist*.100(1):122–35.

Konings, P. (1999), 'The "Anglophone Problem" and Chieftaincy in Anglophone Cameroon'. In E. A. B. van Rouveroy and R. van Dijk (eds.) *African Chieftaincy in a New Socio-Political Landscape*. Hamburg: Lit Verlag.

Mamdani, M. (1996), *Citizen and Subject: Contemporary Africa and the Legacy of Late Colonialism*. London: James Currey.

— (1998), 'When Does a Settler Become a Native? Reflections of the Colonial Roots of Citizenship in Equatorial and South Africa'. Inaugural Lecture as A. C. Jordan Professor of African Studies, University of Cape Town, 13 May 1998.

Mbock, C. G. (ed.) (1996), *Cameroun: pluralisme culturel et convivialité*. Paris: Edition Nouvelle du Sud.

Monikang, A. N. (1978), 'Youth, Marriage and Kinship among the Mankon'. Dissertation for Diploma in Youth Counselling and Animation, National Institute of Youth and Sports, Yaounde (unpublished).

Nkwi, P. N. (1976), *Traditional Government and Social Change: A Study of the Political Institutions Among the Kom of the Cameroon Grassfields*. Fribourg: University Press Fribourg.

— (1987), *Traditional Diplomacy: A Study of Inter-Chiefdom Relations in the Western Grassfields, North West Province of Cameroon*. Yaounde: University of Yaounde.

Nkwi, P. N. and F. B. Nyamnjoh (1997), *Regional Balance and National Integration in Cameroon: Lessons Learned and the Uncertain Future*. Yaounde: ASC/ICASSRT.

Nkwi, P. N. and J.-P. Warnier (1982), *Elements for a History of the Western Grassfields*. Yaounde: University of Yaounde.

Nyamnjoh, F. B. (1985), 'Change in the Concept of Power amongst the Bum'. Unpublished Maîtrise dissertation, FHSS, University of Yaounde.

— (1999), 'Cameroon: A Country United by Ethnic Ambition and Difference', in *African Affairs* 98(390):101–18.

Rowlands, M. (1994), 'Predicting Personal Success in Bamenda', unpublished, pp. 1–20.

— (1995), 'The Material Culture of Success: Ideals and Life Cycles in Cameroon'. In J. Friedman (ed.) *Consumption and Identity*. London: Harwood Press, pp. 116–135.

Rowlands, M. and J.-P. Warnier (1988), 'Sorcery, Power and the Modern State in Cameroon'. *Man* 23(1): 118–32.

Sharp, J. (1998), '"Non-racialism" and Its Discontents: A Post-Apartheid Paradox'. *International Social Science Journal* 156: 243–52.

Tabapssi, F. T. (1999), *Le Modèle migratoire Bamiléké (Cameroun) et sa crise actuelle: perspectives économique et culturelle*. Leiden: University of Leiden.

von Lieres, A. (1999), 'Review Article: New Perspectives on Citizenship in Africa'. *Journal of Southern African Studies* 25(1):139–48.

Warnier, J.-P. (1985), *Échanges, développement et hiérarchies dans le Bamenda pré-colonial (Cameroun)*. Stuttgart: Franz Steiner Verlag.

— (1993a), 'The King as a Container in the Cameroon Grassfields'. *Paideuma* 39:303–19.

— (1993b), *L'Esprit d'entreprise au Cameroun*, Paris: Karthala.

— (1999), *La Mondialisation de la culture*. Paris: Editions la Découverte.

Werbner, P. (1997a), 'Essentialising Essentialism, Essentialising Silence: Ambivalence and Multiplicity in the Constructions of Racism and Ethnicity'. In Pnina Werbner and Tariq Modood (eds.) *Debating Cultural Hybridity: Multi-Cultural Identities and the Politics of Anti-Racism*. London: Zed Books, pp. 226–54.

— (1997b), 'Introduction: The Dialectics of Cultural Hybridity'. In Pnina Werbner and Tariq Modood (eds.) *Debating Cultural Hybridity: Multi-Cultural Identities and the Politics of Anti-Racism*. London: Zed Books, pp. 1–26.

Werbner, R. (1996), 'Introduction: Multiple Identities, Plural Arenas'. In Richard Werbner and Terence Ranger (eds.) *Postcolonial Identities in Africa*. London: Zed Books, pp. 245–70.

# 6 ◎ Uncertain Citizens

## Herero and the New Intercalary Subject in Postcolonial Botswana

Deborah Durham

The most profound, lasting, and pervasive reality of postcolonial subjectivity in Africa is surely the sense of uncertainty. Ironically enough, this sense of uncertainty may be particularly strong in states where democracy and economic promise have been relatively successful (see R. Werbner 1977, 1982 for early postcolonial indications in Botswana). In other postcolonial venues, the broken promises of modernity have circumscribed possibilities for hope and aspiration, the predatory state has established limited modes for action, and disenchantment seems to lead to an ironic embrace of logics of subordination and parodic mimicries of impotent excess, as described by Achille Mbembe (1992). But where the promise of democracy, of civic virtue and 'empowered' citizenship[1] have not been entirely abnegated by the state or by the citizenry, and diverse opportunities for self- and community realisation are sustained, people seem less assured of exactly who has power and what its exercise might look like. Ironically, then, perplexity may be a more serious matter for the optimistic than the levelling parodies, ludic appropriations and self-mocking excesses described for Cameroon. For many in Africa are less zombified by the certainties of the abuse of power on the grand scale, than puzzled by the moral grounds on which they themselves can take effective action.

This uncertainty manifests itself in the small corners of people's everyday lives – in dress and small rituals of deference in greetings (see Durham 1999a) – and in the larger issues of social change that are sweeping the continent, such as who are 'youth' in shifting political and economic relationships (Durham 1998, 2000). Perhaps nowhere are the uncertainties of modernity so pronounced as in citizenship, in the contradictions of the moral nature of civic action. Citizenship is one of the most vexing problems in Africa, and indeed around the world, today. On the one hand, it is

139

connected with modernity, and the deep contradictions that lie between the imaginaries of the 'nation' and 'state', and on the other its modernist dilemma is dialogical with local histories of membership and moral political action (P. Werbner and Yuval-Davis 1999:2,3). Studies of refugees, the homeless and disenfranchised minorities around the world reveal this problematic. Too often, however, the problem of citizenship is reduced to an analysis of normative identity and its consequences: the necessity to conform to specific nation-ised identities, the difficulties of failure to conform. But the difficulties of citizenship are far more complex than simply the ability to claim an identity and the rights that adhere to it. Contrary to the apparent opposition set up by Mahmood Mamdani's title (1996), citizens *are* subjects, and as Mamdani's text makes clear, the subjective nature of citizenship is fraught with uncertainty: it is unequally experienced through the various distributions of power, and it is caught up in diverse and sometimes cross-cutting means of evaluating agency, opportunity and the moral grounds of civic participation. Mamdani is, of course, distinguishing between ethnicised subjects of chieftaincies reified by colonial policies and citizens whose political rights are modernist in their egalitarian universalism under laws. As Nyamnjoh points out, however, Africans 'are both citizens and subjects ... sometimes they are more citizen than subject and sometimes more subject than citizen ... they appropriate both in most creative and fascinating ways' (nd; see also Geschiere and Nyamnjoh 1998). And also uncertain for postcolonial citizens/subjects is the nature of either ethnic or civic action and participation.

Citizens are, of course, subjects, in the sense that political presence in all ways involves complex subjectivity. People in all places and times must evaluate on what moral framework their ambitions, actions and the outcomes of their actions are based, however puzzling this evaluative process may be. This subjectivity is formed out of the intricacies of precolonial, colonial and postcolonial politics and society: it is the distinctively postcolonial nature of citizenship in Africa today to contend with this web of past and present moral frameworks (see R. Werbner 1998, R. Werbner and Ranger 1996), whether through 'connivance' (Mbembe 1992), creativity (Nyamnjoh nd), or in a more perplexed attempt to make sense of one's successes and failures.

James Ferguson starts his recent analysis of urban (or rural–urban) lives in 'modern' Zambia with his realisation that Zambians themselves lack 'a good understanding of what is going on around them' (1999:19) and attributes this to the apparent dissolution of a 'modernist narrative' for Zambians. To the south, in Botswana, the narrative of development, of the spread of the benefits of 'civilisation' and of the possibilities of 'advancement' remains strong, if only too frequently elusive for a large portion of the population.

But the narrative, and its promise, nonetheless still pose puzzles of selfhood, of how, where and why success may be attained, and of how to evaluate failures. Instead of thinking of these puzzles, and the contradictory models from which they seem to emerge, as evidence of fragmentation, however, I will argue that they signal particular political and subjective space which has its own coherence for action and promises for success, as well as for failure and ultimate frustration.

To do so, in my argument, is to enter a difficult academic space. There is, on the one hand, the older idea sometimes traced to Benedict (1934) and Geertz (1973a). It is the idea of cultural meaning as systematic, coherent and holistic, as allowing people confidently to sustain orientations to the world and relationships with others in the face of an underlying pre-conceptual chaos. This cultural coherence, or integration, was often linked (theoretically) to homogeneity and boundedness or isolation (cf. Gupta and Ferguson 1997), or to the strength of its integrative paradigm (Sapir 1949). It is against these assumptions about 'traditional' life, as well as the failures of modernity's promise, that Ferguson (1999) posits an increased fragmentation. He depicts culture as primarily signifying style in a stylistically complex world, where the actor is left alone negotiating possibilities. Ferguson's depiction is to some extent derived from the assumptions of an earlier anthropology, looking at social conditions of the past century as having disrupted any possibilities of wholeness. More radically postmodernist approaches find the actor himself deconstructed in his disparate engagements into fleeting or fragmentary self-consciousness, and so unable to sustain stable forms of meaning (cf. Strauss 1997). Between these, Fernandez for one argues that people seek a 'return to the whole'; that they accomplish this quest through the juxtaposition of contrary and contradictory signs of their lives in poetic forms (1986) which create a semblance of harmony between the diverse elements, albeit unstably. We see this process at work in religious performances, for example, and most vividly in revitalisation ceremonies, including those performed by Herero people of Botswana who will be the subject of this chapter.[2]

I want to argue that the uncertain puzzlement itself forms a resolution, if one of a paradoxical kind. In the sections that follow, I will examine the response in the Herero community in the urban village of Mahalapye to the failure of the Herero candidate, then ranked in the civil service as a *kgosana* (literally 'small chief') or village headman, to be appointed chief of Mahalapye, in spite of his having won a village election. The responses are wide-ranging, and evaluate the failure in terms of suspected tribalist sentiment, party politics, the rhetoric of liberal individualism and achievement, civic nationalism and the power of a bureaucratic imaginary. Running throughout the evaluations are different and complementary discourses on 'representation' and electoral politics that give form to Botswana's 'paternalistic democracy' (Holm 1988) at the end of the twentieth century.

Long ago, members of the Manchester School used the term 'intercalary' to describe the village headman, as he stood between and linked different levels and forms of political integration – domestic and tribal, customary and bureaucratic (Gluckman 1949, Mitchell 1956, Turner 1957; cf. Kuper 1970, R. Werbner 1984). The village chief, or subordinate tribal authority, in postcolonial Botswana today, as across Africa (see Rouveroy van Niewu-waal and van Dijk 1999), is 'intercalary' in the widest sense of the term. Intercalated problematically between uncertain modes of political agency and participation, he is poised between, on the one hand, the electoral politics of the democratic parties, premised on choice, open and fluid memberships, public campaigning and open partisanship, and, on the other hand, the so-called tribal politics of hereditary ascription and status rankings, of exclusions and the subjection of minorities, of gerontocracy and tribal prejudices, and the forging of an overt near-universal consensus masking covert divisions. On this position that straddles community, village and state converge a plethora of very disparate postcolonial realities: the place of non-Tswana 'minorities' in a liberal populace and issues of communal representation, electoral politics in a paternalist and bureaucratic state, the concerns with corruption in the form of private preferences obscuring much-valued open competition for government positions, and the dangerous economic chances taken in a village rapt in a moral panic over theft and violence. In brief, the new village headman or village sub-chief captures all the contradictions that today make Botswana such an interesting place.

A further point must be highlighted to bring out the comparative and theoretical interest of revisiting the village headman in the context of an analysis of postcolonial subjectivity in Botswana. The Manchester idea of an 'intercalary' position interpolates it between spheres that are quite distinct. Against that, postcolonial analysis reveals that the multiple models of civic participation and political subjectivity are not held distinct, but present themselves concurrently in many different contexts. Herero, both headmen and others, live in the midst of multiple models of citizenship, of multiple possibilities for political participation (participation which can be both active or inactive, voluntary or constrained). These models are far more diverse than the now-outdated, Weberian dichotomy of 'traditional' vs 'modern' political forms, of 'customary' vs 'rational-bureaucratic' models of authority – but using these one can look at recent studies of how the customary chiefs' courts and the magistrates' courts of Botswana, ostensibly founded on Roman-Dutch law, overlap and make use of each others' rulings and procedures (see Griffiths 1997). Similarly, as we will see below, the modalities of political participation interpenetrate; elections pervade the arenas of inherited and appointed chiefship, bureaucratic appointments disrupt electoral processes, and inherited privilege is validated by individualist achievement. In the collapse of such dichotomies is the very force of post-colonial analysis.

Another danger of drawing too heavily upon the Manchester approach, or indeed the idea of recently fragmented selfhood, is that both these approaches atomise individual consciousness. Caught betwixt and between different forms of social interaction, the intercalary Manchester man stood as an autonomous agentive individual negotiating the demands put upon him by others (much, indeed, as does Ferguson's cultural stylist). His community being was only a matter of claiming rights and demands; in the midst of these he stood as a choosing, maximising and negotiating individual. To talk of puzzlement, and of confronting diverse opportunities for action, also seems to imply that the 'individual' is isolated in postcolonial Africa and is the ultimate moral unit. But instead, it is the very possibility of such a position that forms part of the puzzlement: is it the Mahalapye headman's status as an individual, his unique qualities and history, and his ability to make independent choices/decisions, or is it his embeddedness in communal actions and communal sympathies, and his nature as representative of group orientations and interests, that explains his fate and is the ground from which he himself acts? The conundrum of being an individual or communal agent is both key, and yet does not align neatly with distinct 'democratic/modern' vs 'traditional/ascriptive' institutions.

At the same time that the discussions by Herero, and others, of their candidate's failure do not produce a sense of returned wholeness, they do achieve some resolution of the multiple moral frameworks within which they evaluate political subjectivity. In these discussions, Herero confronted the various possibilities for political action in the complex political environment within which they live. What is notable is that both individuals and the community as a consensual whole firmly rejected any single account, and any single framework, as sufficient in explaining events. Various suggestions would be made, but the speaker, group of speakers or the person relaying community sentiments always indicated dissatisfaction, or lack of conviction, that one reason was correct. This is particularly significant, I think, when we consider rejection of the 'tribalist' explanation as satisfactory up until the year 2000. I have written elsewhere about the multiple sensibilities of being a minority in a liberal democracy as they are embodied in the wearing of the distinctive Herero dress (Durham 1999a), and how these repeat a profound sense of uncertainty about what it means to be

Herero in Botswana's liberal democracy. The sense of indeterminacy allows for creative response to varied situations; it allows people to avoid some of the pitfalls of direct resistance discussed by Abu-Lughod (1990), whereby acts of resistance are likely to catch up the actor in new subordinations. As such, it allows Herero to escape the most dominant political force in Botswana: bureaucratisation, the subordination and control of ethnicity through centralisation and codification (see also Durham, forthcoming). At the same time, of course, the willingness of village Herero to admit uncertainty forestalled powerful and easily recognised challenge to what were, undoubtedly in my view, patent inequities and failures of promise.

## 'It Is Just Politics'

By 1994, at least, members of the Herero community in Mahalapye were wondering whether or not the hereditary Herero chief, who sat as a junior chief in the main chief's court, would succeed the senior chief of the village after *Kgosi* Ratebelo's anticipated retirement.[3] When I had first arrived in the 'urban village' of some 30,000 residents in late 1988 to do research among the small Herero community there, three chiefs sat in the central village *kgotla*, or chief's court. While the village was divided into numerous wards, each with a headman or *kgosana*, many of these ward *kgotlas* were relatively inactive, and the three officiants were kept busy by their disputes, along with disputes unresolved by *dikgosana* (pl.) at the ward level, the many minor criminal cases brought by the police, and routine registering of cattle and other property. There was a Senior Subordinate Tribal Authority, assisted by a junior one, and finally the Herero chief, whose rank in the main *kgotla* was headman, or *kgosana*, although everyone addressed him as chief, or *kgosi*.

Mahalapye is sometimes said to be an unusual village in Botswana, but this claim must be evaluated in terms of the powerful hegemonic idealisation of a Tswana political system, in which each political level is represented as homogeneous politically and headed by an ideally patriarchal figure assisted by his older male relatives, and the levels are organised into a neat pyramidal structure (Schapera 1991; cf. Durham 1999b). The Tswana 'tribes', actually multi-ethnic polities (Schapera 1952), are generally imagined among Tswana themselves as predominantly Tswana and as organised around a chief descended from the tribe's founder. Wards are idealised as 'typically' overseen either by members of the chief's descent group, or at a lower level by the head of the family group of which the subward unit is entirely composed. But in fact many villages are formed, like Mahalapye, by a diverse group of residents; Mahalapye includes Xhosa, Lozwi, Talaote and

Ngwato as well as Herero (see Kebonang 1988), much as family groups have diverse, non-kin, attached members.

The Herero ward in Mahalapye has, since the arrival of Herero there in the early 1920s, been under a Herero headman; today the ward is very heterogeneous in population, but retains a Herero as headman who hears cases for his own ward and sometimes for residents of neighbouring wards. The current Herero chief is not serving as ward headman, nor did he ever do so, although Herero and some Tswana and others still bring problems and complaints to him in his ward home. Soon after JJ was made Herero chief in 1983, he was 'brought' to the main *kgotla* to assist there. Unlike the ward headman, who was 'on call' for *kgotla* business, JJ worked a 7:30–4:30 day out of an office with a substantial staff, hearing both civil and criminal cases for a salary that was small by professional standards but high for non-professionals. At the same time, JJ often officiated at Herero Ward meetings, especially those directed at Herero community issues, as chief of Herero; he also appeared occasionally in Herero *kgotla* meetings as representative of the main village court. Many Mahalapye residents assume that he was brought to the main *kgotla* to give advice on Herero custom and practice for cases involving Herero – though in the 1980s, to question the logic of this, they frequently pointed to his youth and his upbringing at cattleposts and in South African mines, far from the Herero *kgotla* where Herero custom would be heard. Many Tswana greeted JJ as 'Moherero' – literally, Herero person, but also recognisably an honorific to the Herero chief.[4] In 1990, the junior chief departed the Mahalapye *kgotla* for a village chiefship in another, smaller, village, leaving only Ratebelo and JJ in the main court, and his post remained vacant in mid-1991, when I concluded that period of field research.

This was still the case during my 1994 and 1995 visits: the junior position was empty, and JJ was still technically a headman by civil service classifications. Herero speculated on his promotion. His unmarried status, some thought, might deny him recognition as 'old enough' to be chief; Herero women often complained to me that he 'chased after the girls' and wondered about his aborted marriage and unwise selection of girlfriends. In 1995, a Herero man confided in me the rumour that Sediegeng Kgamane, the Ngwato regent, had talked with JJ about the chiefship, saying that he would not be appointed if he were not married. Others worried about his lack of formal educational credentials – and both these issues would enter into his evaluation as a leader able to judge both household and criminal cases (see Durham 1999b), although when he was not appointed people did not refer again to the marriage issue in conversations with me. In 1996, a fuller tale unfolded, and the speculation widened to encompass and question a much wider range of political subjective possibilities. My version of the story is built up from talks with Mahalapye Herero, and from a newspaper account in *Mmegi/The Reporter* (Letsididi 1997), an independent weekly newspaper in Botswana. The two sets of information were rather similar, and *Mmegi* included a lot of the Herero speculative points, possibly because JJ or one of his close associates seems to have been the reporter's main source of information.

In 1995, *Kgosi* Ratebelo finally started procedures to appoint a sub-chief for the junior position, preparing for his own retirement. According to some Herero men, Ratebelo and 'the old men' (the circle of advisers a chief relies upon, including in Mahalapye the former village chief) chose a headman from one of the other wards in the village, a Tswana and, like JJ, a fairly young man,[5] to be the next sub-chief. JJ heard about the choice and wrote a letter of complaint about the process which he sent to the senior tribal authority in Serowe[6] and to the Minister of Local Government,[7] which ministry administers the 'traditional' courts and their personnel. As a consequence of this complaint, said the Mahalapye Herero I was talking to in 1996, an open village-wide election was held for the position.

The chiefship chapters of the Botswana constitution specify that headmen and tribal authorities be appointed by the tribal chief after 'consultation with the *kgotla* in the customary manner' (Cap.41:01:20), and the ambiguity of this phrasing allows for various procedures of consultation. 'Consultation' is the term used, for example, for the meetings in which representatives of the national government present a policy or act that they plan to implement to the people in *kgotla* gatherings. At these gatherings, people have an opportunity to criticise and disapprove, or to suggest modifications, but the actual power of passing the act or implementing the policy is retained by parliament and the government agencies. Herero in Mahalapye today understand, however, that the 'consultative process' involved in choosing their village chief is an election. When they describe the process, they use either the English word 'election', or the Herero term *okutoorora*, the same term they use for democratic elections for parliament and various councils. In 1989, JJ had described to me how Ratebelo himself had been chosen for his post by village election many years before – letting me know that Ratebelo had been elected probably because previously he had been chair of the village BDP (Botswana Democratic Party, the ruling party in Botswana) committee. It was clear from the discussions I had with Herero that they expected the election of the village chief to proceed much like the elections held periodically for the District Council. In other villages that were also disputing headmen's appointments at the same time, Mosetse and Dukwi, the headmen were also subjected to village elections (see below). I will discuss in later sections, however, some of the ambiguities surrounding elections, appointments and concepts of representation in both party politics and in village Botswana.

According to the Herero versions of the story that I heard in 1996, while the appointment was still being appealed and disputed, an election was held, but only Tswana – and not Herero – were notified of the date and urged to come. Even so, JJ won the election, garnering 300 votes over 223 for Ratebelo's candidate (Letsididi 1997). Nonetheless, the Ngwato regent and the Ministry of Local Government appointed Ratebelo's candidate. JJ appealed this appointment, but eventually lost. Although the appointed sub-chief died soon afterwards, JJ by my visit to the community in 2000 was no longer pursuing the post (indeed, he was talking about retiring from the position he held within five years to pursue private business interests).

In 1996, when I talked most intensively to a number of Herero about the dispute, the Herero community of Mahalapye was experiencing the death of one of its most popular young women, a much-liked former girlfriend of the chief's (and mother of his acknowledged daughter), who had married a Tswana man and had, in Herero eyes, been much abused by her in-laws. Boitumelo's death, and tensions surrounding her burial, had reawakened old complaints that the Tswana 'were killing us all', as one woman had muttered after a string of Herero deaths in 1990, and that the Herero were 'coming to an end'. It was not surprising in this atmosphere of charged ethnic sentiment that people often assessed JJ's failure as evidence of 'tribalism', by which they meant Tswana antagonism to non-Tswana.

At the same time, however, and much more vocally, people also suspected that party politics might be behind JJ's difficulties. Both as a civil servant and as a chief, JJ was not permitted to participate actively in the party politics of Botswana's multi-party democracy, and indeed I never became aware of any open profession of political allegiance or interest by him, or even received any indication of his sympathies, either in the *kgotla* or at home. While Mahalapye Herero, and particularly older ones, were generally thought to be steadfastly loyal to the BDP, a number of younger Herero were known to support the Botswana National Front (BNF), as did many young and urban-oriented people in Botswana. JJ's 'sister' (MZD) was an active campaigner for the BNF, the main opposition party, and had held 'freedom square' political rallies in Herero Ward, laying special emphasis on the BNF's promises to guarantee minority rights and to improve job production, wages and security, and loudly castigating the BDP and its policies through a megaphone. Mahalapye is, however, a BDP stronghold. As noted, *Kgosi* Ratebelo had been chairman of the local BDP committee before his election/appointment as village chief many years before.

JJ himself seems to have worried considerably about the possibility that his appointment was being affected by politics. A Herero man related to me on the telephone in 1999 the rumour that JJ had gone to the Ngwato regent in Serowe and put to rest any impressions that there might have been that he sympathised with the opposition party. The Ngwato royal family has been centrally involved in the BDP; the BDP's founder and Botswana's first president Sir Seretse Khama was the heir to the Ngwato throne, and his son is now Vice-President. The *Mmegi* article also took pains to report that JJ had been a 'card-carrying member' of the BDP prior to his becoming a headman (Letsididi 1997). While it seems unlikely to me that JJ had been an official party member while in his twenties, it is clear that he and other informants for the article believed that party politics was an important aspect of the case.

Two other factors were brought up by various people and the *Mmegi* that are, I think, also important both for the outcome of the case and for JJ's and other Herero understandings of the moral and political nature of his actions, and their evaluation of their consequences. One is the suspicion that JJ's lack of formal educational credentials may have been an issue. Indeed, one Herero told me that a high-level member of the Ministry of Local Government had explained to her that these were the main objections; the appointed candidate had attended secondary school. At the same time, it was widely known in the village that JJ could read and write and was numerate; reservations that he was too young and inexperienced in either Herero or Tswana custom that I heard in 1989 had given way by the mid-1990s to praise for his fairness, lack of bias, and good judgment in the *kgotla*. The *Mmegi* article mentioned one further factor that Herero, in talking to me about this specific dispute, did not: JJ had been involved in the purchase of a cow that turned out to be stolen, and was later accused of bribery in the resolution of the case.

The sense that JJ lacked formal educational credentials and that he may have been involved in shady – not to mention corrupt – business dealings both contrast strongly, in their implications for political and moral subjectivity, with suspicions of tribalism, with the sense that JJ represented Herero custom in the main *kgotla* and with the observations put forth by JJ that he was a chief by royal right and not, like Ratebelo, merely an elected official. Both factors invoke instead the subject of much political rhetoric in Botswana, and the target of many of the state's development initiatives. 'Batswana [citizens of Botswana, alternatively Tswana people] must develop themselves', 'Batswana must work hard to develop themselves' were constant refrains in the speeches of members of parliament and ministerial secretaries touring the country. These phrases recurred almost daily in the government newspaper, which devoted its headlines to official pronouncements. More recently, the recurring term 'empowerment' of citizens invokes the same ideas of productive and self-producing individual. And the idea that it was individuals who were responsible for their own successes and failures, through their own initiatives, decisions and actions, was strong in the Herero community, and in particular underlay JJ 's frequent self-portraiture.

When I talked with JJ about the chiefship in 1996, he dismissively said of the dispute that 'it is just politics'. By this he referred not (directly) to party politics, but to personal chicanery and hostilities animating unreasonable attacks on him. Highly educated Herero from the urban areas often laughed at his use of the term 'politics' to refer to situations where his will was challenged. Cole (1998:116, 123 fn. 10) notes that in Madagascar and across Francophone Africa politics as a term has become synonymous with 'lying'. JJ, calling the dispute a matter of politics, clearly denoted that the accusations and issues were matters of misrepresentation. But in Botswana politics, in the sense of political action, is not so easily pinned down.

While the simple opposition of communal identity and subjectivity with a strong sense of liberal individualism forms a basic contrast, the dichotomy does not easily distinguish the various forums that cross-cut the village headman's political field. The practice of elections, for example, is not a clear example of liberalist political subjectivity in action. In the following sections I want to explore ideas of liberal individualism, representation and morality, and the expectations of elections that I observed in the Herero community and in other reports on Botswana, and to contrast them with chiefship and the *kgotla* as a political and moral forum, with expectations of bureaucratic governance, and with the self-motivated ideals promoted in government rhetoric.

## Liberalism and Group Identities in Democratic States

Representative democratic states, in which citizens' political power is expressed through their representatives in a state apparatus, are fraught with contradictions and difficulties (see Benhabib 1996). One set of contradictions lies in the contrast between, on the one hand, suppositions of the autonomous self-determining individual rationally making political choices based on entirely independent interests and, on the other, of groups of citizens sharing enough interests and orientations to be represented by a designated official. Another difficulty lies in determining the role and character of the elected representatives: are they simply individuals not hierarchically differentiated from those who elect them, who in their very equality or mutuality with their constituency are able to represent them? Or is their representative function hierarchical in one way or another: are they elected because of moral superiority, or because of their distinguished ability to promote the well-being of their constituency through superior knowledge, skill and connections (see Cole 1998, Durham 1999b)?

These contradictions are enhanced by the nature of the state and particularly the postcolonial state. Geertz (1973b) argued long ago, in a much misread article, that the centralisation of power in new states ('independent, domestically anchored, purposeful, unitary', p. 270) underwrote processes of parochialism, communalism, and racialism: 'Though they rest on historically developed distinctions ... they are part and parcel of the very process of the creation of a new polity and a new citizenship' (Geertz 1973b:270), as people explore the grounds on which they can tap into the resources and sources of state power.

This new citizenship in Africa has been particularly fraught. Bayart, surveying state processes in Africa, writes that 'in the context of the contemporary State, ethnicity exists mainly as an agent of accumulation' (1993:55) privileging, from the contradictions described above, the interested individual, and a hierarchy of greed and manipulative skill, as the primary fabric for communal consciousness. Paying more attention to communal sentiments, Nyamnjoh et al. (Nyamnjoh 1999, Nyamnjoh and Rowlands 1998) describe how these contradictions transpire in Cameroon when multi-party representative politics are introduced: a centralised state in which the premise of competition and choice is compromised by hierarchies of access and a dominant political leader who is the persistent source of power, and alienated localities whose commonality is reinforced both through perceived marginalisation and through the means of access they have - their ability to represent themselves in electoral politics and civic associations. Cameroonians, caught between marginalised communalities and frustrated individualist aspirations, manifest their predicament in the uneasy twinship of corruption and witchcraft (Geschiere and Nyamnjoh 1998).

The notion that Botswana is a liberalist democracy, in which citizenship is undifferentiated, is strongly promoted institutionally and rhetorically in the everyday experience of Mahalapye villagers. Government officials in the capital and in sub-district offices readily repeated the line that 'we are all Batswana here' (using the term 'Batswana' to mean citizens of Botswana and not to mean ethnic Tswana – although the irony of the term is inescapable, cf. Durham 1999a, Motzafi-Haller 1998) to all my inquiries on ethnic composition of the population, and none of the censuses conducted since independence in 1966 has asked people to discriminate themselves by ethnicity or race. When, in 1989, government officials attempted to get a count of Herero in anticipation of a mass 'return' to Namibia by the former immigrants, Mahalapye Herero were upset and indignant at being distinguished in terms of their citizenship by the government (although they readily distinguished themselves in everyday village life). The civil bureaucracy is understood by Mahalapye Herero to represent, metonymically, a civil unified state, dispensing centralised power (see Durham, forthcoming) ostensibly undivided by local origins. Civil servants are purposefully stationed around the country without regard for their own origins or current family attachments, and when I visited Herero in their government offices their colleagues often expressed a surprise (undoubtedly ingenuous) that my hostess/host was Herero. Civic buildings – schools, district offices, housing for workers – are relentlessly uniform across the country. Appointment and promotion within the civil service is expected to be through qualifications and accomplishments (see Durham 1999b), and Herero and others referred often in the later 1990s to JJ's qualifications and accomplishments, as well as length of service, as factors that should have contributed to his appointment in his appeal to the Ministry of Local Government.

Herero in Mahalapye embraced enthusiastically the ideals of liberalism and individual accomplishment presented to them in the official rhetoric and programmes. When they talked about the Herero as a communality, their descriptions were either negative, pessimistic or pronouncedly moral in tone. The comment that Herero were dying out, and that they were dying out in the face of Tswana hostility, was one of these forms of communal self-assessment that recurred especially during cold winter months (when deaths increased), and that I still heard in 2000, when HIV had probably increased the death rate. Herero, including JJ, often commented that Herero must be lazy or 'unable' (*kave sora*, they are not able, used intransitively), observing the unkempt compounds and *kgotla* area, or saying that Herero failed to take opportunities while Tswana and others around them were industrious and ambitious for self-improvement. Herero did occasionally comment, while sitting and chatting in the afternoon sun, on how Tswana children had less respect for their elders, how Tswana of all ages had less respect for the *kgotla* (which Tswana will walk across, but which, Herero claimed, Herero respectfully circumscribe), how Tswana women displayed undue deference to men and strangers, and how Tswana behave without proper decorum at funerals.

Indeed, almost all categorisations of ethnic groups offered by Herero were negative, including of themselves.[8] While President Masire and other government speakers in the early and mid-1990s castigated calls for minority recognition by other groups such as Kalanga or Yei, or the opposition party, as 'tribalist' actions disrupting a unitary state, for minority groups like Herero it was Tswana, with a hegemonic grip upon defining the citizenry and excluding cultural recognition of non-Tswana from the public sphere, who compromised valued ideas of equal non-ethnic citizenship. The government and the public sphere in general in Botswana provided few models for discourse about communities as means to success, or more particularly as moral means to success – either as 'tribal' groups, or more recently as villages. Kalanga people are said to be successful, but stories of their success refer to subterfuge (such as the rumour that when they put a 'small mark' on university applications when a Kalanga was Minister of Education, they were guaranteed acceptance; cf. R. Werbner 2000). Early development propaganda praised village projects, such as the building of primary schools by local communities, but village communities today are more likely to be depicted in public pronouncements by ministers and government officials as failing to mobilise work groups for public schemes, or failing to educate their young. Within the Herero community itself, organised groups like the Herero Youth Association and Otjiserandu have indeed had difficulty in mobilising projects, and when they did successfully stage an event or accomplish a project, it was quite notable. National concern with corruption in Botswana in the 1990s looked initially at nepotism, or the favouring of small-group loyalties based on commonalities, as inhibiting individuals' aspirations and rights to non-discriminatory access to national resources. For JJ to be said to be denied the chiefship as a member of a group is very much in line with negative characterisations of group affiliation as people evaluate the means for betterment and development.

The rhetoric of accomplishment in Botswana is the rhetoric of liberal individualism. As noted, government officials repeatedly pronounced that 'Batswana [citizens] must work hard to develop themselves'. Throughout the 1980s and most of the 1990s, individuals were asked to provide development initiative (applying for various schemes the government supported), and to pay themselves for such infrastructural development as electricity in the villages (individuals had to run lines out to their compounds from the nearest – often quite distant – section of the grid at their own expense), or telephone lines. While expecting certain government support for the indigent and food relief during drought, and for education, most Herero accepted that individuals provided the means and labour for development. They accepted, too, the idea of the unmarked, liberalist individual as citizen. Herero repeatedly denied to me, under considerable pressure to identify 'tribalist' bias, that they or other Herero had suffered ethnic discrimination in securing loans from banks, government schemes or lease-purchase agreements.[9] People insisted that when they or others (as individuals) were denied loans, it was because they were unable, under laws governing tribal land, to demonstrate adequate collateral, or that they were unable to fill out the complicated English-language forms properly. Those in school, and their parents, attributed their own and others' failure or success to personal motivations, work effort or individual talents (and occasionally personal hostilities within the community). JJ, for example, was insistent that his nephews remained unemployed and occasionally in jail not because of being Herero, but because they had dropped out of school, because jobs were in the 1990s hard to find for everyone, and because they wasted their time and resources drinking.

JJ himself was, along with many others, the insistent purveyor of tales about making his own success in the world through his efforts and skills. He regaled me with stories of the approbation he had received as a hard-working miner in South African mines (Rustenberg), and of the skills he had acquired as a driver/loader in Gaborone. Like many other Herero men, his life history started with an insistence that he had received nothing from his father in the way of inheritance, and that what I saw around him was all of his own doing. He believed his own success in general to be the result of hard work – and he often wore short pants or other work-associated clothes around his compound, clothes other Herero complained unfitting for a chief – and the result of careful planning, as well as taking all the chances and opportunities he could find. He acquired an old decrepit tractor through a government loan scheme; his compound was usually filled with sand and the products of a cement block business (a popular home enterprise in the village); he built a line of one-room rental housing behind his old house; and rented out to small businesses or for housing the rondavels he had built behind his new house as guest quarters. By 2000, he had acquired a butchery/produce shop in a growing part of the village, and he wheeled and dealed steadily in cattle and other livestock. When JJ was 'brought to the *okuruo* (sacred fire)' by the Herero community to be chief, he was an uneducated and impoverished urban labourer who villagers said 'was raised in the bush'. By the 1990s, his economic ventures brought him the signs of material prosperity (an electrified pink house) and people had begun to treat him as a chief.

In response to comments that Herero were 'unable' (comments he was likely to make himself on occasion), JJ often insisted that the failures and successes of Herero were the failures and successes of individuals. To illustrate this he would then talk about individuals. Among his favourite illustrations was a man who had attained an MA degree in Germany and been married to the daughter of a prominent Herero family, who had herself attained an advanced degree and had a very visible position in government: this man now had nothing – no wife, no job, no cattle, and a notably decayed house on a very undeveloped plot. All of this JJ attributed, first, to the man's personal laziness and lack of ambition; and, second, to irresponsible drinking. Living not far away from the lazy Herero, and often brought up by JJ in tandem with him, was an example of the industrious Herero, a man with little formal education but who, while working as a foreman at the mines, also developed a private chicken/egg business in the mining town, maintained a large herd of cattle with bulls purchased for breeding purposes, financed a general dealership to be run by his wife, purchased a tractor to take advantage of government-paid ploughing schemes and to plough and harvest crops from his own large fields (at a time when many Mahalapye Herero neglected their fields). JJ often also invoked other Herero who had advanced civil service positions, or who had been elected to the District Council, or had had commercial success.

It seems likely to me that in part JJ's self-evaluation as an ambitious, hard-working entrepreneur partly undermined his bid for the chiefship, even though it fulfilled expectations that success was based on individual accomplishment and qualifications. The *Mmegi* article reported that he had 'bought a beast which, as he later discovered, was stolen' and that when an out-of-court settlement was reached between the original owner and the seller, JJ was accused of bribery (Letsididi 1997:10). Although it is, in fact, a chief's role to encourage settlements of disputes out of court, the suggestion of bribery addressed directly the liberalist notion that all citizens should be equally accountable, and have equal access to the means of dealing with the problems of their lives. Bribery is indeed a sign of individual initiative and ambition, both favoured by political rhetoric, yet especially when attached to a chief, it also suggests privileges and resources unequally distributed in the nation. But more ambiguously, the suggestion of bribery by a civil servant also attacked the moral nature of the state – because bureaucracy is structured such that each office partakes of the power of the centralised whole, the moral character of each office is a reflection of the moral character of the whole (see Durham forthcoming). Recent public concern with corruption in Botswana has been fundamentally about the contradictions between the moral leadership expected of the state as a source of power (one that in many ways replaces chiefships) and the self-achieving ethic of an economy that is rapidly expanding and producing novel forms of inequity. Because public morality is associated more often with chiefship in Botswana than the technocratic bureaucracy, whose goal is simply perceived to be development (and whose morality is individualistic), discussions on corruption and bribery open up the intercalary space of leaders and of citizenship in general, a matter we will return to again below.

This is all very subtle, and it is just as likely that JJ's projects for self-advancement had landed him in trouble in more direct and personal ways. JJ had a longer history of acquiring stolen goods than the newspaper was aware of. In 1994, just before the dispute over the appointment, JJ was attempting to work out the loose ends of an incident that might well have prejudiced *Kgosi* Ratebelo in his search for a successor. JJ had bought a pick-up truck, a very new and impressive one, from a private person in the area, using a private bank loan. He had then loaned the truck to Ratebelo when Ratebelo wanted to drive down to South Africa. Almost immediately after crossing the border, people told me, Ratebelo was arrested and jailed: the borrowed truck had been stolen new from the lot in South Africa. The truck, as well as the cow that *Mmegi* reported, were probably not the products of purposeful illegality for JJ, but the outcome of his pursuit of the ideals of a liberal economic agency. He prized his ability to look for and seize the opportunities for wheeling and dealing, for buying, selling and building. When I visited Mahalapye in May 2000, JJ proudly showed me his new butchery/grocery situated near one of the newly paved interior roads in the village, and talked about retiring from the chiefship in order to pursue private business interests. He no longer, it was clear, saw the position of chief, whether salaried bureaucrat or moral arbiter, as consistent with his business aspirations.

## Politics, the Kgotla, and Representation

Village headmen like JJ, convinced of the legitimating power of popular elections and motivated by the moral ideals of individual accomplishments promised by the state, are also caught up uncertainly in the models of chiefship that they inherit and those that apply in the larger chiefdoms of which they are a part. But history and the current chiefships do not offer clear-cut models to which to refer. While some of the ruling chiefs have taken up their positions through simple primogeniture, the model generally thought to predominate since colonialism (see Parson 1990), for many others the process has been more complex.

JJ, when discussing his place in the *kgotla*, was likely to note that while Ratebelo had simply been a member of the BDP – in other words, a politician – he, JJ, was a royal chief. This was a claim to moral superiority, and to certain rights, including representation, that I will discuss below. JJ's own succession, however, was more complicated than simple descent and primogeniture. The last direct patrilineal descendant of Samuel Maharero, the Herero who had led the Mahalapye group to their current settlement and who had also been (prior to leading a rebellion) designated 'paramount chief' of Herero in German South West Africa (Namibia), had died without legitimate offspring. (His never-legitimated son is now ward headman.) The Herero – meaning the older men and males of the core royal group – then 'chose' JJ among the indirect descendant candidates for the chiefship.[10] Certainly part of JJ's expectations of chiefship, however, are based on descent and inherited qualities.

Many histories of Botswana and of Tswana chiefships across southern Africa have noted 'democratic' features of chiefs (Comaroff 1978, Comaroff and Comaroff 1997, Gulbrandsen 1995, Ngcongco 1989). The most prominent of these is that chiefs have been subject to ongoing evaluation by their people: chiefs who lost popular approval thus lost their legitimacy and ability to rule in a variety of ways – people might refuse to acknowledge a chief's legislation, carry out assignments, attend meetings or the cyclical rituals of the polity, or bring disputes for judgment. More dramatically, members of the polity might re-evaluate the complicated genealogies that emerged from pre-Christian Tswana marriage practices to 'discover' that a chief was not, in fact, the proper heir but simply acting on another's behalf (as regent). Analysts often present these processes as continuing today in the form of the elections held every five years for national offices, and for local government positions, which not only recognise the choice of 'the people', but also continue processes of ongoing evaluation and approval of those in power (see Ngcongco 1989, Comaroff and Comaroff 1997); and many Herero have learned of these democratic roots in school. At the same time, however, chiefs were authoritarian, exercising power both in moral and material domains, and imposed many policies to their own benefit or without widespread approval.

Late colonial and postcolonial politics have done much to further blur the 'democratic' nature of chiefship, in such a way as to exacerbate JJ's uncertainty about his claims to the village chiefship. Colonial policies simultaneously reified the principle of primogeniture (see Parson 1990), the power of the state (either colonial or chiefly) to appoint office-holders or to make unilateral decisions, and the idea that chiefs ruled for and by the people's interests. One incident much reproduced in history books, museum displays, and on film, dramatises the obscure nature of *kgotla* politics, at least according to modern political theory. In 1949, when Seretse Khama, heir to the Ngwato chiefship, married an Englishwoman, the regent Tshekedi Khama called a *kgotla* meeting to challenge the marriage and, in effect, Seretse's claims. In the *kgotla*, Seretse dramatically reclaimed his chiefship from Tshekedi by calling for a vote of support (for himself); a vote he overwhelmingly received. As a consequence, the British colonial government removed both Seretse and Tshekedi from office. Seretse became the founding president of Botswana and was committed to democratic principles, an egalitarian citizenry, and development and state policies organised around liberal principles of persons and motivations. Both the idea of chiefs as arbitrary, absolute rulers and the idea of a proto-democratic popular mandate and even election are captured in the scene in the Ngwato *kgotla*.

The idea that chiefs might and should be representatives for the people, and that they also embodied a non-democratic, authoritarian inegalitarianism mingled in the colonial institution of the African Advisory Council (AAC) and the late colonial transitional institution of the LEGCO (Legislative Council). In the AAC, the chiefs were taken as advocates of their people and as representing the will of their people. This was clearer in the LEGCO, where African members were chosen by the African Council, a descendant of the AAC that now included 'new men' as well as chiefs and their colleagues – but European members were directly elected by the European population (see Gabasiane and Molokomme 1987). At the same time, however, the colonial administration and many of the new men distrusted the chiefs as representative of anything other than their own private interests, and sought to circumscribe their powers. The current House of Chiefs can be seen as a further descendant of the AAC: the chiefs, however, represent less the interests of their constituents than their moral nature and orientations, which they may articulate publicly but not legislate on (legislation is the prerogative of the Parliament).

Today, the membership of the House of Chiefs itself is composed of the (so-called) hereditary chiefs of the eight Tswana polities, plus four chiefs from regions outside these polities who are elected from among recognised chiefs every five years in tandem with elections for members of parliament. (A further three members are 'specially elected' by the other twelve.) The elections of 1999 brought an uncharacteristic member to the House of Chiefs – a 32-year-old woman, said to be of Sarwa (Bushman) descent. Rebecca Banika had been elected to the position of chief of the Pandamatenga area recently, and also elected from the various chiefs of Chobe District to the House; she brought to her candidacy five years of experience in government bureaucracy (on the Chobe Land Board). During recent consultations with the population on the matter of chiefs and tribes, it is interesting to note that while Tswana sometimes insist on the royal privileges of the major Tswana chiefships (often, however, grounded in the individual 'heroic' accomplishments of the founders), minority groups such as the Tswapong have indicated that they would like a chief, but would like to elect him (or her?). One speaker at a *kgotla* meeting said that 'it would be possible to elect a chief because merit and competence take precedence over anything else'.[11]

But chiefly elections should not be seen as exclusively the province of rationalist morality. During the time that JJ's dispute was going on, the House of Chiefs complained to the government about politicians meddling in the appointment of a Kwena chief who 'had been elected by the Bakwena in an open *kgotla* meeting'.[12] The House of Chiefs, which has only advisory powers, and chiefs in general, are often seen in Botswana as standing up to bureaucratic impersonality and rationalist technicality. While pronouncements of chiefs are sometimes greeted with scepticism about personal interests, or with disagreement, they do form for many a moral counterpoint to the morality of individualism, trained skill and accomplishment of the state system, within which the uneducated, unskilled and unaccomplished often seem arbitrarily disadvantaged. When in 1999 and 2000 Sir Seretse Khama's son Ian, non-acting chief of the Ngwato, elected MP and Vice-President of the country (as well as former head of the army), began to make overtly moral statements about the self-interested motives of members of his own political party, discussion often turned on behaviour and rhetoric appropriate to chiefs and that appropriate to state and party officials: the two forms were seen as contradictory, and Khama was criticised in many quarters for confounding the two. At the same time that the impersonal individualism of bureaucracy is seen to be countered by a more socially concerned and charismatic morality in the chiefs, fears of Khama's populism, and the rebuke by the House of Chiefs over the Kwena chiefship, converge with ideas of Tswana chiefships as rooted in popular approval against ideas of 'the government', whose monolithic hold on power and resources seems to many to proceed without input from 'the people'. In the midst of these ambiguities about election and representation, it is often implied that chiefs represent the people under them to the government,[13] while elected members of parliament represent government to the people – which they do by travelling around their constituencies to present government policy and proposals for 'consultation' and (ostensibly) feedback, mobilising the classic idea of the *dikgotla* as forums in which chiefs achieved consensus, for government legislations and policies. Ironically, in the dialectic between moral privilege and popular representation, as the government calls hearings on chiefship in 2000, many people have asked that members of the House of Chiefs hold consultations with their constituents, on the model of the *kgotla* meetings, in the manner that elected political representatives and government officials are now expected to do – suggesting quite contrarily that it is the chiefs who are distant from the people and that their pronouncements become the voice of distant, somewhat arbitrary, privilege.

Cross-cutting these uncertain understandings of election, representation, the nature of personal morality, and the source of political agency, is the bureaucratic logic of appointments, which reproduces a centralised source of power in 'the state' or 'the government', a power, and agency, whose morality is very much in doubt. JJ's case was ultimately decided, as we have seen, by the Ministry of Local Government, which justified itself on the liberalist, and opportunistic, grounds of educational qualifications, and in keeping with the technocratic character often attributed to both the state and its bureaucracy. This technocratic logic that both emphasises the needs and power of the centre, and acknowledges individual worth based on specific skills and accomplishments, short-cuts electoral logic outside the *kgotla* as well. Within the political parties, while primary elections may be held to select candidates for parliamentary seats, the outcomes of these elections are sometimes overturned by the central committees of the parties in order to field a different candidate (Mokopakgosi and Molomo 2000). On the surface, then, bureaucratic forms seem to sustain a concept of political participation that is individualist, liberal, and focused on accomplishments rather than such characteristics as inherited status, or inherent or personal connections. Through their reliance upon centralised sources of power, however, bureaucratic forms monopolise a moral space for defining status and making appointments usually associated with the autocratic aspects of chiefship.[14]

The village headmen, or sub-chiefs, participate much more ambiguously in the ambivalent play between the chiefships and state because they are indisputably part of both.[15] Chiefs are not allowed, according to the laws of Botswana, to hold chiefly and political office at the same time. At independence, Bathoen II of Ngwaketse resigned his chiefship and Seretse Khama renounced attempts to regain chiefship of the Ngwato in order to join party politics. JJ's accusations that Ratebelo had been chairman of the BDP committee before becoming sub-chief were an indictment of allowing self-serving and divisive party politics to intrude into a sphere that pronounces morality in the name of consensual unity. Suggestions that JJ may have been denied the chiefship because of political affiliations indicted the BDP, dominant nationally and locally, for intruding its divisiveness into the *kgotla*. When villagers praised a judgment in which JJ had chastised the police for bringing a particular case to court, they were praising his fairness or refusal to take sides (a quality chiefs are supposed to exercise), and his commitment to a popular morality against a state perceived to be pervaded by 'politics', as well as a distant and sometimes arbitrary power as discussed above. When speakers in the *kgotla*, where citizens are invited to voice their opinions on national issues, as well as on specific court cases being tried, began to talk what was recognisably 'party politics' they were roundly shushed by the people around them or, if they persisted, told by the chief to leave the arena. The rhetoric of party politics is very *ad hominem*, attacking directly the personal qualities of individuals, and it is incendiary and pointedly antagonistic and pronounced with the goal of forcing people to take sides (see

Gulbrandsen 1995, Lekorwe 1989). The rhetoric of the *kgotla*, while also directed at evaluating personal moralities, is couched in a language of shared values, and aims at forging consensus (Comaroff 1975): the end of *kgotla* discussions is an impression of shared values and shared decisions (even though many may feel that they do not in fact share the decisions, and that the overt impression of consensus masks exclusions and covert divisions, including the presence of minorities of all sorts).

The claims of chiefs and chiefships to represent consensual and communal moralities – moralities of common sentiment, fear and disposition – oppose, in certain ways, the liberalist notions of representation that often seem to lie behind party representatives. Botswana's citizenry is repeatedly criticised for the irrational, personal attachments voters have for parties (and there is a certain truth to this, as there also is in the United States), and yet stated party platforms and the ways that people in the village often spoke about them were identifiably liberal, individualist, and oriented towards goals of self-improvement. People claimed to support the BDP because its programmes would allow them some access to the means of 'development' (even though these can also be seen as hand-outs in the manner of the old chiefs). They admired one Herero who ran for District Council (for the BDP) and won because of his very visible success as a farmer and businessman, taking opportunity of financial assistance policies, agricultural initiatives and loans. A Herero man from the BNF also ran for the District Council repeatedly; but while he too was an entrepreneur, running a small general dealership in a farming area, he was not visibly successful, and most Herero were indifferent to or opposed his candidacy, even though he was a central figure in organising weddings and funerals, and contributed much to the community. People supported someone whose success lay in self-improvement and who, they thought, would support government policies that would allow them to do the same; they did not support someone whose success lay primarily in facilitating community events. Throughout the mid-1990s, others among Mahalapye Herero supported the BNF because it would provide them, or those they perceived to be like them, other programmes that would allow individual efforts to be successful. (The BNF also garnered some support in the late 1990s in Mahalapye and elsewhere for promising government representation of tribal minorities.)

As Gulbrandsen has argued recently (2000), discourses of power in Botswana continually return to an evaluation of morality, an evaluation that was open and public and ongoing for chiefs in the *kgotla*; as people turn this discourse on the central government, which in its bureaucratic monopolies and centralised power replicates some of the logics of chiefship, they evaluate that power with similar concern for its morality in ways that go beyond recognising individualist aspirations and assumptions about the abilities of individuals to act independently. In so far as the government has maintained its primary goals of development (and its commitment to liberalism), people evaluate both the government as a whole for its ability to provide such, and office holders for their individualist abilities to be 'developed' or financially successful, educated and achieving. It is in this way that office holders, whether elected to councils or parliament or appointed in bureaucratic positions, come to represent citizens as egalitarian individuals whose individual motivations and capabilities are the grounds for action and civil participation.

And it is the communal claims to morality, the implications of speaking a consensus (however contrived silencing may produce it) expressed by chiefs, both the lower-level chiefs/headmen in the village *kgotla* and the major chiefs and elected chiefs in the House of Chiefs, that has made them the focus of debates on the place of ethnic minorities, now also called 'tribes', in Botswana. In 1999, Kamanakao, an association organised to promote Yei recognition and to counter a colonial and precolonial history of oppression under the local Tswana chiefship (the Tswana polity), brought the government to court to demand reconsideration of the clauses of the constitution that recognised only the eight Tswana tribes as official 'tribes', rejecting the idea that Tswana chiefs morally represented them (Nyati-Ramahobo 1999; the case had not yet been heard in courts at the time of my writing). While Charlton (1993) has suggested that the discourse of tribalism and minorities may have been started by Western political scientists bringing their native concerns to studies of Botswana, non-Tswana have long-standing concerns with the nature of their citizenship in both the earlier Tswana polities and in the cultural hegemony of the Tswana state (see, for example, Murray 1990, Ramsay 1987, Solway 1994). In the first decades after independence, Botswana's rapid economic expansion, based on diamond mines, allowed many in the country to dream of advancement either through their own initiatives or the success of their children. But by the early 1990s an economic slump and the recognition that the job market was becoming oversaturated with secondary school graduates, and that even university degrees were not guaranteeing employment and easy opportunity (Good 1992, Hope 1996), caused people to re-evaluate the promise of liberal individualism and the truth of an undifferentiated citizenry (see Solway 1995, 1998). It is surely not an accident that this is the same time at which 'tribalist' and anti-tribalist discourses picked up steam.

The Kamanakao case asks the government to reconsider recognition of so-called minority 'tribes' in the political centre, the House of Chiefs. As part of their preparation for the case, Kamanakao and Yei people chose a chief in a complicated process involving submission of applications for the position, vetting by groups of elders and educated elite, and final approval by the people. In his induction ceremony a member of the association pronounced that 'the role of the chief is to try and capture the remnants', meaning the failing remnants of culture and language – but also implying the people whose unity as Yei was rapidly dispersing.[16] Partly in response to this case and to increasing criticisms from across the minority communities of exclusive permanent recognition of the Tswana chiefs in the Botswana constitution, the government established a commission to study the issue, and in August 2000 began 'consulting' the population in *kgotla* meetings around the country. But programmes asking for representation such as the Yei have accomplished would be impossible for many other groups (unless, like the Yei, they significantly reorganise their cultural and social forms to parallel those of Tswana polities). Herero, for example, lack not only territorial integrity, but also a history of political unification (apart from the much resisted 'paramount chieftaincy' of Samuel Maharero, created by the Germans). JJ would not be acknowledged chief by Herero in other parts of Botswana, nor would Mahalapye Herero recognise as their chief a Herero from Rakops, Maun, Lentswe-le-tau, or any of the other Herero communities scattered across the country.[17]

The ambiguities of a chief as representative of a people based on moral likeness, as appointed functionary, and as leader based on personal skills and invidualist characteristics were revealed in newspaper reports of other villages' headman problems at about the same time as JJ's case. In the villages of Dukwi and Mosetse, also in Central District, the rights of the Ministry of Local Government to approve appointments, the right of the Ngwato Tribal Authority (regent) to appoint a headman, and the rights of villagers to choose their headman ran up against ideas of representation and the moral capacity of the chief/headman to enact the unity of a village. Both villages had significant populations of Kalanga and what people in Botswana refer to collectively as 'Sarwa' (Bushmen, with a wide variety of language and social/cultural practices). When a group of Kalanga in Dukwi protested against the Ngwato regent's appointee, according to some (Sarwa) residents 'chosen by the majority of the people in the village', and nominated a Kalanga for the post, accusations flew. While newspaper accounts reported the case as about Kalanga wanting a Kalanga headman, and Sarwa wanting a Sarwa, or perhaps needing one of each for each subsection, what was particularly significant is the sense of uncertainty in the interviews with villagers and the reporters' accounts. Is choice the choice of a majority of individuals, each exercising autonomous preferences? Or is it a choice by a unified moral community, with the chosen then embodying that community

– and hence a choice that can be made by leading figures of the choosing group, as some residents accused the Kalanga minority of doing. Do the villagers make their decisions and exercise their agency as motivated individuals pursuing self-interest, or do they act as representatives of moral communities? Perhaps this dilemma is clearest in the confused reporting on the Kalanga cabal said to have filed the protest against the appointed headman: on the one hand, reporters and some residents accused them of acting 'tribalistically' and to be defending Kalanga interests as a whole against Ngwato hegemonies (a claim with considerable historical depth; cf. Ramsay 1987). On the other, however, several Kalanga and many Sarwa residents quoted in the articles accused the Kalanga agitators of pursuing private personal interests, motivated by business and other concerns.[18] While the case is still pending, it is unlikely that any court judgments will resolve the uncertainty or basic contradictions, for these contradictions are wound through the fabric of democracy in the postcolonies.

## Conclusion

No one who has read any of the classic literature on chiefships and succession in the Tswana polities will be surprised to hear that a headman or chief's position is in dispute. But the grounds of the disputes have become more complicated than the mustering of factions, the contesting of genealogies in bids for support, the suspicion and reality of backroom and night-time meetings and power blocs, the forging of networks of dependency and alliance. Of course these remain salient and are part of the ongoing contests – as the accusations in the Dukwi case make abundantly clear, and the genealogical searches for chiefs and headmen to represent 'minority tribes' all over the country attest. Many of the tensions I have described here were well established in Botswana villages at the time of independence in 1966, as the close ethnography of an Ngologa village by Adam Kuper (1970) vividly demonstrates: there tensions within the village community between hierarchy and a democratic egalitarianism were met with a skills- and knowledge-based bureaucratic civil service and the new forms of citizen and electorate.

Over the past thirty years and more, what seemed initially to be a tension between two distinct systems – a modern Western bureaucracy premised on liberalist notions of rational individuals and egalitarian citizenship, and an African system premised on communal responsibilities and rights and hier-archical exercise of powers – has been conflated into a more ambiguous field of uncertainty about the premises of political subjectivity and action. Every form of political action is inflected with contradictory expectations and orientations. To some extent similar tensions are inherent to democracy everywhere, and in particular where democracy is fostered in a national setting. This tension is situated in the hyphen in the nation-state, where ideas of common sentiment confront ideas of rationalist individualism; it is situated in the contradictions between egalitarianism and leadership; and in the ways in which representation is a dilemma in all such systems (cf. Scott 1996 on the paradox for women's representation in France). But the contradictions of democracy are revealed in new particularities in post-colonial venues, where they emerge in surprising and uncertain ways in the role of *kgotla* debates, in attempts to understand minority citizenship, in the development of new elites, and across Africa in the institutions of chiefship (cf., for example, Coplan and Quinlan 1997 on Lesotho; Nyamnjoh and Rowlands 1998 on Cameroon).

In Botswana, the insistence on elections for headmen, and a desire for chiefs as representatives by minorities, situate chiefship on this cusp, an intercalary point hovering between two broader and pervasive forms of organisation of actor and society. On the one hand, insistence on election rests on the rights of individuals in the language of liberalism. It brings to bear the sets of associations JJ regularly invokes in his life story: choice, accomplishment, approbation for jobs well done, promotion, the whole sector of jobs and competitive achievement. On the other, though, elections also suggest the politics of representation – and when it is chiefs, the representation of ethnicity. Elections, too, suggest in Botswana the field of party politics: openness in debate, the absence of hidden prejudices or secret conniving, and also the divisive language and open accusations and partisan-ship that are ideally part of 'politics' – as against night-time meetings, prior arrangements, gerontocracy, preference, and hiding of difference under the guise of consensuality that are characterised (or caricatured) as *kgotla* political form.

As JJ and others sought to depict his predicament, and to capture, at least as an idea, the village chiefship, it constantly slipped around between being a government office job to which JJ was entitled by work qualifications and prior service (but also subject to arbitrariness of appointment), an elected position on which the citizenry should vote for individual merit and out of respect for individual not group qualifications, and the sense that chiefship was something different, something in which royal status was associated with the ability to stand above and for group unity. All Herero, and everyone in Botswana, face these conundrums everyday in their lives. Am I acting on my own responsibility, out of universal egalitarian rights? What expectations of myself do I and others bring to my participation here, or in the ward, or at a funeral, or for this job or loan application? Citizens are of course subjects, in the sense that political participation involves complex subjectivity, a complex set of expectations about self, relations to the political field, and the forms of political action one might undertake or be subject to. And the predicament of that subjectivity is not the neat constitution of subjects in too-powerful disciplinary tactics (cf. Foucault 1979), but an uncertainty that lies at the heart of action and evaluating one's successes and failures. Herero hold on to that uncertainty: in discussing JJ's case, or their own projects, Mahalapye Herero consistently refused to attribute matters completely to 'tribalism' - but were often equally uncertain they were individual failures. Theirs is, in a popular language today, a hybrid agency, hybridised between a strongly asseverated liberalism and the renewed relevance of group experiences. But while this uncertain, or hybrid, subjectivity allows them flexibility and the ability to integrate - uneasily - the different expectations they encounter - it also has kept the Mahalapye Herero from directly challenging either or any of the ways in which they, as citizens and subjects, are disadvantaged.

## Acknowledgments

Field research in Mahalapye and Gaborone, Botswana since 1988 has been funded at various times by Fulbright-Hays, NSF, Wenner-Gren Foundation, NEH, the American Philosophical Society, and Sweet Briar College Faculty Grants. The people of Mahalapye have always welcomed me and included me in their conversations, for which a simple thanks or acknowledgment seems inadequate. Jackie Solway has contributed significantly through ongoing conversations on Botswana over the years, and also by bringing me copies of newspaper articles from later 1996. Jackie, Dick Werbner, Francis Nyamnjoh and Keith Adams have made direct comment on the matter of this chapter, not all of which has been particularly well integrated but all of which was valuable.

## Notes

1 Citizen 'empowerment' was a catchword in political and state rhetoric in Botswana at the end of the 1990s and in 2000.

2 For a fuller ethnography of the Mahalapye Herero community, see Durham 1993; chapters 5 and 6 deal with 'revitalisation' movements.

3 I use one of the Herero chief's nicknames, JJ, but use a pseudonym for the Senior Subordinate Tribal Authority of Mahalapye. The case was reported in numerous newspapers, and it would be impossible to disguise entirely the Herero's identity. The Tswana chief, however, was rarely named in the press.

4 The term was more recognisable as an honorific in that Tswana in Mahalapye still generally used the prefix ma- (as in Maherero) for Herero as a group. The prefix pair le-/ma- (singular/plural) is used for several non-human items, and for 'immoral' humans like thieves (magodu) and non-Tswana (e.g., lekgoa, white person).

5 JJ was then around 40, a fairly ambiguous age. Unmarried, he was likely to be considered a 'youth' but as a chief presiding in kgotla, and head of a complex household, he was also easily a mature man. He married in 1999. Cf. Durham 1998.

6 Serowe is the district capital of Central District, and the capital village of the Ngwato

'tribe'. It is worth emphasising that while more and more in Botswana since the 1980s 'tribes' have been represented as ethnic entities, in the past they have been understood more as complex polities generally composed of people of different ethnic origins. The Ngwato tribe is one of eight tribes headed by a Tswana chief that were acknowledged by the British and used for a form of indirect rule; recognition of these eight tribes remains in the postcolonial constitution and the chiefs of them sit permanently in the House of Chiefs (to which other chiefs are also elected for shorter terms). The Ngwato tribe today is headed by a Senior Tribal Authority, Sediegeng Kgamane, who is the regent for Ian Khama, who has been in the army and is now the Vice-President of Botswana, and has never taken up his inherited chiefship officially.

7  Since 1985, the time of my first visit, this Ministry has been part of several reorganisations, and has had a variety of names: the Ministry of Local Government and Lands, the Ministry of Local Government, Lands and Housing, and the Ministry of Local Government and Housing. To avoid confusion, for this paper I refer to the Ministry which has consistently had the portfolio overseeing chiefs as the Ministry of Local Government.

8  Other citizens of Botswana use ethnic categorisations and discuss group success in different ways. People in the urban area often complained that Tswana claimed superiority (although I must note that my knowledge of this comes from others *claiming* that Tswana behaved in this disapproved manner, not from actually observing it). For Herero in Mahalapye, ethnic affiliation is an impediment to success that can best be attained by embracing the ideals of unmarked, liberal citizenship.

9  In 2000, when national debates on tribalism had become much more intense, a member of the BNF, which had for many years included attacks on tribalism in their attacks on the ruling party, told me that she had encountered discrimination in being allotted a plot in a new Mahalapye suburb. Other Herero had received plots there in the early 1990s, and while there were complaints about preferences to the rich and connected, there were no complaints about ethnic discrimination then.

10  JJ's own descent is through Samuel Maharero's third son, and more immediately through JJ's mother. As his mother never married and his biological father never legitimated paternity, JJ may be considered part of the Maharero patriline – although Namibian chiefs sometimes dispute the claim. Herero have historically had a system of double descent, which continues in attenuated and sometimes confused form in the present. Chiefship follows only the patriline, the *oruzo*.

11  *Botswana Daily News*, 'Allow Batswapong to Have Paramount Chief – Residents' 22 August 2000; read at <http:www.gov.bw/cgi-bin/news.cgi>.

12  *Botswana Gazette* 'Hands off Chieftainship and Mind Your Own Business – Chiefs Tell Politicians' 16 October 1996, p. 4.

13  Cf. Durham 1999b on the claims that chiefs represented the voice of the people, coupled, however, with rebuttals that chiefs were authoritarian and given unfair privilege.

14  For more on the contradictions of bureaucracy and its involvement in the creation of specifically *national* communities, see Durham forthcoming, Herzfeld 1992, Anderson 1991.

15  In July 2000, Margaret Nasha, Minister of Local Government, said that about 80 per cent of civil and criminal cases in Botswana were handled in the *dikgotla*. She also said that 'Kgotla is pivotal in Botswana's system of participatory development through consultation' and commented on 'the prominent role played by kgotla in the development process, maintenance and sustenance of Botswana's cultural heritage and upholding of the democratic principles' (*Botswana Daily News* 12 July 2000, 'Kgotla Pivotal in Botswana System'; <http://www.gov.bw/cgi-bin/news.cgi>).

16  The address reminds one of the praise poem addressed to the Kgatla (a Tswana polity) chief Molefi Kgafela in 1931, 'seek for the strays, child of Makuka, bring home the human strays', referring to the migrant labourers who had left for South Africa. See Schapera

1965:117. The address to the Yei chief was reported by Caitlin Davies in *The Mmegi*, which I read on the web 3 May 1999, <http://www.mmegi.bw/main_stry_frnt_pg2.htm>.

17 Indeed, there was a certain amount of hostility and/or competition between these Herero (and Mbanderu, a Herero 'section') communities. In 2000, I heard about recent efforts to establish some cooperation among them regarding the induction of their chiefs, and this cooperation was something people contrasted with past autonomies. It probably was related to the 'tribal' movements of Yei and other minority groups.

18 On the affair, see articles in *The Voice* 5–25 July 1996, p. 3; the *Botswana Daily News* 25 July 1996 (no. 137), p. 4; and the *Midweek Sun*, 24 July 1996, p.1.

# References

Abu-Lughod, Lila (1990), 'The Romance of Resistance: Tracing Transformations of Power through Bedouin Women'. *American Ethnologist* 17(1):41–55.

Anderson, Benedict (1991), *Imagined Communities: Reflections on the Origin and Spread of Nationalism*. Revised edition. London: Verso.

Bayart, Jean-François (1993), *The State in Africa: The Politics of the Belly*. London: Longman.

Benedict, Ruth (1934), *Patterns of Culture*. Boston: Houghton Mifflin Company.

Benhabib, Seyla (ed.) (1996), *Democracy and Difference: Contesting the Boundaries of the Political*. Princeton: Princeton University Press.

*Botswana Gazette* (1996), 'Hands Off Chieftainship and Mind Your Own Business – Chiefs Tell Politicians'. *Botswana Gazette*, 16 October 1996, p. 4.

Charlton, Roger (1993), 'The Politics of Elections in Botswana'. *Africa* 63(3): 330–70.

Cole, Jennifer (1998), 'The Uses of Defeat: Memory and Political Morality in East Madagascar'. In Richard Werbner (ed.), *Memory and the Postcolony: African Anthropology and the Critique of Power*. London: Zed Books.

Comaroff, John L. (1975), 'Talking Politics: Oratory and Authority in a Tswana Chiefdom'. In Maurice Bloch (ed.), *Political Language and Oratory in Traditional Society*. New York: Academic Press.

— (1978), 'Rules and Rulers: Political Processes in a Tswana Chiefdom'. *Man* 13(1):1–20.

Comaroff, John L., and Jean Comaroff (1997), 'Postcolonial Politics and Discourses of Democracy in Southern Africa: An Anthropological Reflection on African Political Modernities'. *Journal of Anthropological Research* 53(2):123–46.

Coplan, David, and Tim Quinlan (1997), 'A Chief by the People: Nation versus State in Lesotho'. *Africa* 67(1):27–60.

Durham, Deborah (1993), *Images of Culture: Being Herero in a Liberal Democracy (Botswana)*. Unpublished doctoral dissertation, Department of Anthropology, University of Chicago.

— (1998), 'Mmankgodi Burns: Missing Youth in Botswana'. Paper presented to the African Studies Workshop, University of Chicago, 3 March.

— (1999a), 'The Predicament of Dress: Polyvalency and the Ironies of a Cultural Identity'. *American Ethnologist* 26(2):389–411.

— (1999b), 'Civil Lives: Leadership and Accomplishment in Botswana'. In John L. Comaroff and Jean Comaroff (eds.), *Civil Society and the Political Imagination in Africa*. Chicago: University of Chicago Press.

— (2000), 'Youth and the Social Imagination in Africa: Introduction'. *Anthropological Quarterly* 73(3):1–8.

— (forthcoming), 'Passports and Persons: The Insurrection of Subjugated Knowledges in Southern Africa'. In Clifton Crais (ed.), *The Culture of Power in Southern Africa: Essays on State Formation and the Political Imagination*. Portsmouth: Heinemann.

Ferguson, James (1999), *Expectations of Modernity: Myths and Meanings of Urban Life on the*

*Zambian Copperbelt.* Berkeley: University of California Press.

Fernandez, James (1986), *Persuasions and Performances: The Play of Tropes in Culture.* Bloomington: Indiana University Press.

Foucault, Michel (1979), *Discipline and Punish: The Birth of the Prison.* New York: Vintage Books.

Gabasiane, O. and A. Molokomme (1987), 'The Legislative Council'. In F. Morton and J. Ramsay (eds.), *The Birth of Botswana: A History of the Bechuanaland Protectorate from 1910 to 1966.* Gaborone: Longman Botswana.

Geertz, Clifford (1973a), 'Religion as a Cultural System'. In *The Interpretation of Cultures.* New York: Basic Books.

— (1973b), 'The Integrative Revolution: Primordial Sentiments and Civil Politics in the New State'. In *The Interpretation of Cultures.* New York: Basic Books.

Geschiere, Peter (1997), *The Modernity of Witchcraft: Politics and the Occult in Postcolonial Africa.* Charlottesville: University Press of Virginia.

Geschiere, Peter and Francis Nyamnjoh (1998), 'Witchcraft as an Issue in the "Politics of Belonging": Democratization and Urban Migrants' Involvement with the Home Village'. *African Studies Review* 41(3):69–91.

Gluckman, Max (1949), 'The Village Headman in British Central Africa'. *Africa* 19:89–101.

Good, Kenneth (1992), 'Interpreting the Exceptionality of Botswana'. *Journal of Modern African Studies* 30(1):69–95.

Griffiths, Anne M. O. (1997), *In the Shadow of Marriage: Gender and Justice in an African Community.* Chicago: University of Chicago Press.

Gulbrandsen, Ornulf (1995), 'The King is King by the Grace of the People: The Exercise and Control of Power in Subject–Ruler Relations'. *Comparative Studies in Society and History* 37(3):415–44.

— (2000), 'Ritual Murder, Subjection and Discourse on Occult Forces: The Case of Botswana'. Paper presented to the 16th Satterthwaite Colloquium on Religion and Ritual in Africa, 16–19 April, Grizedale and Satterthwaite, England.

Gupta, Akhil and James Ferguson (1997), 'Culture, Power, Place: Ethnography at the End of an Era'. In Akhil Gupta and James Ferguson (eds.), *Culture, Power, Place: Explorations in Critical Anthropology.* Durham: Duke University Press.

Herzfeld, Michael (1992), *The Social Production of Indifference: Exploring the Symbolic Roots of Western Bureaucracy.* Chicago: University of Chicago Press.

Holm, John (1988), 'Botswana: A Paternalistic Democracy'. In L. Diamond, J. Linz, and S. Lipset (eds.), *Democracy in Developing Countries, Vol. 2: Africa.* Boulder, CO: Lynne Rienner.

Hope, Kempe Ronald (1996), 'Growth, Unemployment and Poverty in Botswana'. *Journal of Contemporary African Studies* 14:53–67.

Kebonang, Boammaruri Bahumi (1988), 'The Socio-economic and Political History of the Herero of Mahalapye, Central District, 1922–1984'. Unpublished BA thesis, Department of History, University of Botswana.

Kuper, Adam (1970), *Kalahari Village Politics: An African Democracy.* Cambridge: Cambridge University Press.

Lekorwe, Mogopodi (1989), 'The Kgotla and the Freedom Square: One-way or Two-way Communication?'. In John Holm and Patrick Molutsi (eds.), *Democracy in Botswana.* Athens: Ohio University Press.

Letsididi, Bashi (1997), 'Loser Takes All: Mahalapye Chieftainship Crisis in Perspective'. *Mmegi/The Reporter,* 12 December 1997, p. 10.

Mamdani, Mahmood (1996), *Citizen and Subject: Contemporary Africa and the Legacy of Colonialism.* Princeton: Princeton University Press.

Mbembe, Achille (1992), 'Provisional Notes on the Postcolony'. *Africa* 62(1):3–37.

Mitchell, J. Clyde (1956), *The Yao Village: A Study in the Social Structure of a Nyasaland Tribe.* Manchester: Manchester University Press.

Mokopakgosi, Brian, and Mpho Molomo (2000), 'Democracy in the Face of a Weak Opposition in Botswana'. *Pula: Botswana Journal of African Studies* 12(1).

Motzafi-Haller, Pnina (1998), 'Beyond Textual Analysis: Practice, Interacting Discourses, and the Experience of Distinction in Botswana'. *Cultural Anthropology* 13(4):522–47.

Murray, Andrew (1990), *People's Rights: The Case of Bayei Separatism*. Human and Peoples' Rights Project Monograph No. 9. Institute of Southern African Studies, National University of Lesotho.

Ngcongco, L. D. (1989), 'Tswana Political Tradition: How Democratic?'. In John Holm and Patrick Molutsi (eds.), *Democracy in Botswana*. Athens: Ohio University Press.

Nkala, Gideon (2000), 'Hail the Queen of the House'. *Mmegi/The Reporter*, 28 January–3 February 2000. On line version <http://www.mmegi.bw/main_stry_frnt_pg8.htm>.

Nyamnjoh, Francis B. (1999), 'Cameroon: A Country United by Ethnic Ambition and Difference'. *African Affairs* 98:101–118.

— (nd) 'Expectations of Modernity or a Future in a Rearview Mirror? A Review Essay'. Ms.

Nyamnjoh, Francis B. and Michael Rowlands (1998), 'Elite Associations and the Politics of Belonging in Cameroon'. *Africa* 68(3):320–37.

Nyati-Ramahobo, Lydia (1999), 'Oppression in Democracy: The Case of the Wayeyi of Botswana'. Paper presented to the annual meeting of the African Studies Association, 13 November, Philadelphia PA.

Parson, Jack (ed.) 1990, *Succession to High Office in Botswana*. Ohio University Monographs in International Studies, Africa Series No. 54.

Ramsay, Jeff (1987), 'Resistance from Subordinate Groups: BaBirwa, BaKgatla Mmanaana and BaKalanga Nswazwi'. In Fred Morton and Jeff Ramsay (eds.), *The Birth of Botswana: A History of the Bechuanaland Protectorate from 1910 to 1966*. Gaborone: Longman Botswana.

Rouveroy van Nieuwaal, E. Adriaan van, and Rijk van Dijk, (eds.) (1999), *African Chieftaincy in a New Socio-Political Landscape*. Leiden: African Studies Centre; Hamburg: LIT Verlag.

Sapir, Edward (1949), 'Culture, Genuine and Spurious'. In E. Sapir, *Selected Writings in Language, Culture, and Personality*, edited by David G. Mandelbaum. Berkeley: University of California Press.

Schapera, Isaac (1952), *The Ethnic Composition of Tswana Tribes*. Monographs in Social Anthropology No. 11. London: London School of Economics and Political Science.

— (1965), *Praise-Poems of the Tswana Chiefs*. Oxford: Oxford University Press.

— (1991), *The Tswana*. Revised edition, with John L. Comaroff. London: Kegan Paul International, in association with the International African Institute.

Scott, Joan Wallach (1996), *Only Paradoxes to Offer: French Feminists and the Rights of Man*. Cambridge: Harvard University Press.

Solway, Jacqueline (1994), 'From Shame to Pride: Politicized Ethnicity in the Kalahari, Botswana'. *Canadian Journal of African Studies* 28(2):254–74.

— (1998), 'Taking Stock in the Kalahari: Accumulation and Resistance on the Southern African Periphery'. *Journal of Southern African Studies* 24(2):425–41.

Strauss, Claudia (1997), 'Partly Fragmented, Partly Integrated: An Anthropological Examination of "Postmodern Fragmented Subjects"'. *Cultural Anthropology* 12(3):362–404.

Turner, Victor (1957), *Schism and Continuity in an African Society*. Oxford: Berg.

Werbner, Pnina and Nira Yuval-Davis (1999), 'Introduction: Women and the New Discourse of Citizenship'. In Nira Yuval-Davis and Pnina Werbner (eds.), *Women, Citizenship and Difference*. London: Zed Books.

Werbner, Richard (1977), 'Small Man Politics and the Rule of Law: Centre Periphery Relations in East-Central Botswana'. *Journal of African Law* 21:24–39.

— (1982), 'The Quasi-Judicial and the Experience of the Absurd: Remaking Land Law in North-Eastern Botswana'. In Richard P. Werbner (ed.), *Land Reform in the Making: Tradition, Public Policy and Ideology in Botswana*. London: Rex Collings.

— (1984), 'The Manchester School in South-Central Africa'. *Annual Reviews in Anthropology* 13: 157–85.

— (1998), 'Smoke from the Barrel of a Gun: Postwars of the Dead, Memory and Reinscription in Zimbabwe'. In Richard Werbner (ed.), *Memory and the Postcolony*. London: Zed Books.

— (2000), 'The Minorities Debate and Cosmopolitan Ethnicity in Botswana'. Keynote Address to the Conference on Challenging Minorities, Difference, and Tribal Citizenship, University of Botswana, Gaborone, 10 May 2000.

Werbner, Richard, and Terence Ranger (eds.) (1996), *Postcolonial Identities in Africa*. London: Zed Books.

# 7 ◎ Subjectivity and Subjunctivity

## Hoping for Health in Eastern Uganda

Susan Reynolds Whyte

The 11th Conference on AIDS and Sexually Transmitted Diseases held in 1999 was well covered by the BBC. One of the first broadcasts from Lusaka tried to capture some local colour. It opened with drumming and singing; the correspondent had left the conference centre for a compound somewhere in the outskirts of the city, where a traditional healer was performing a ceremony for an AIDS patient. The BBC man explained that most Zambians believed AIDS was caused by witchcraft. Such vast oversimplifications are heard in Uganda too, in various versions: 'You know those people in the village always blame sickness on spirits.' 'The traditional people say AIDS is witchcraft.' 'They think it's caused by a curse.' It is not only Europeans who characterise African views this way. Ugandans make such statements to each other and to people like me, as if to explain, and also distance themselves from, a way of thinking. Recently I talked with the AIDS counsellor at the local hospital in Bunyole, Eastern Uganda.[1] He regretted that very few people were willing to come for an AIDS test: 'Most believe in traditions. We need to make them aware that it's not witchcraft. Instead of wasting money on traditions, they should come for counselling.'

Subjectivities in postcolonial Africa are shaped by global cultural flows (Appadurai 1990) as well as national political economies. The international interest in the AIDS epidemic, the deterioration of African health care systems, and the commercialisation of traditional healing are dimensions that can help us to understand these subjectivities. But I am going to argue for the importance of another approach as well – one that goes beyond describing the characteristics of subjectivities and their historical conjunctures. As ethnographers, an important part of our job must be to inquire about what people as subjects are trying to do – what they are hoping for, how they deal with their life conditions, and how things unfold for them over time.

I want to start with the empirical issue of how people in Eastern Uganda deal with grave problems – like seeking health care and dealing with AIDS – using ideas as plans of action. I will suggest that we can approach the theme of African subjectivity from a position of what we could call *situated concern*. My argument is that through our fieldwork and in our writing we should try to follow people as intentional subjects engaging each other and the contingencies of their lives in a mood that is often more subjunctive than indicative or imperative.

Health problems are a good vantage point from which to explore subjectivities. Illness is a space where the intimacy of bodies is touched by state institutions and global flows, as well as by the dispositions of families and neighbours. It is a space where biography crosses history – that site where anthropologists and sociologists should set their problems, as C. Wright Mills (1959) reminded us. Sickness requires us to acknowledge the double face of subjectivity, for people are subjects in relation to affliction, in that they form ideas about it and act upon it, and they are also subject *to* it as it strikes them down and sometimes resists their attempts to manage it. They undergo and undertake. What is at stake, as Michael Jackson puts it, is the attempt to exert some degree of control in the sense of steering 'a balance between what is given and what is chosen such that a person comes to experience the world as a subject and not solely as a contingent predicate' (Jackson 1998:21).

For students of subjectivity, health poses the problem of uncertainty. Whether we talk of risk and outcome, experiences of suffering and struggle, doubt about the meaning of pain and loss, or the insufficiencies of health care systems in postcolonial African states, illness and treatment are dubious affairs. They allow us to explore the elements of contingency, indeterminancy and ambiguity in subjectivity.

But let me start where I promised, with empirical problems as people are facing them in Bunyole in Eastern Uganda.

## Although They Tried...

Two of our neighbours, Hasahya and his teenage son Mahanga, had come to ask for help with the boy's school fees. Most families in Bunyole have difficulties with school fees, but Hasahya's problems were worse. Had I not noticed the mourners gathered at their home when we passed there? Would I come with my camera and take a picture of the widow and her children? Hasahya's wife, the mother of Mahanga, had not yet been dead a year. She had left seven children, and now her firstborn son had died too, leaving a widow and three children. It was the boy Mahanga who told the story about his mother and brother, while his father patiently helped to answer my questions.

> My mother had divorced and gone to Buganda. After two years she came back sick – with many sores on her body – and thin. She had a sister, whom she loved very much and she told her secretly that she had tested positive. That sister told us. My mother was staying with her brother near here, but my father was helping her, injecting her with penicillin and giving her drips. He's a sweeper at the hospital. Though they were divorced, she was the mother of his children so he still helped her. She was here sick for five months.

> As you know, the traditional people can't believe someone is dying of AIDS or another disease. They think something is on the person. They went to the diviner and found that her dead father wanted a gift of food (*ehing'ulo*) – a goat and a hen. [Did you give it?] We tried – plus some millet beer. But though they tried, there was no way of changing – the disease continued. They took her to the hospital. She was admitted and died from there.

> Then it was my brother Patrick. He started to be sick in January. They tried a divination – some things came. It was the spirit Omuhyeno – of someone who died badly, who was pushed in the lake and drowned. It caught Patrick when he crossed the lake at Jinja. The spirit wanted a cock and a she-goat to be slaughtered by day, and a sheep by night. They did the ceremony at the end of January and he was possessed [by the spirit]. After that he was okay, walking around. But then the sickness came again. We took him to the hospital in March and he was admitted. They gave him a drip – two bottles – and tablets. He stayed there a week, and came home, finished two weeks, and died. He was 30 years old.

I asked what it was that killed Patrick. His brother said: 'That Omuhyeno.' But then he added doubtfully: 'We looked for the cause, but it refused to appear.' 'Could it be the same disease his mother had?' I asked. 'No,' replied the boy. 'Yes,' said his father, 'Because the body became thin and he was about to become mad. That disease affects the brain.'

Mahanga's story was familiar enough. It is not simply that many people are dying of AIDS these days. Even before AIDS, sickness and death, especially of children, were all too common experiences in Eastern Uganda. What is familiar is the process of trying out (*ohugeraga*) ideas – about the spirits of ancestors or the vengeful dead. People make a plan and they try rituals, even knowing they might fail, as did the family of Mahanga.

Mahanga's mother, unlike many others, went for an AIDS test – that fearsome digital mechanism that answers positive or negative. But the problem with an AIDS test is that it does not show any way forward – at least not for most people in rural areas far from AIDS support programmes. Divination did suggest a plan of action for both mother and son. Though as the sickness unfolded, Mahanga came to doubt that the divination had shown the truth. Time will tell, we say, and time told that the cause had refused to appear. And now that they both had died, Mahanga's father could assert, with the authority of a hospital employee, that the symptoms had been like AIDS.

We could say that people in Eastern Uganda believe that AIDS has supernatural causes, or that some do and some do not. But such an indicative statement misses the element of situated concern and ignores the process of trying out. It neglects that unfolding of social experience in which people are intentional subjects. And it overlooks the uncertainties that so often attend undertakings.

## Uncertainty in Stories and Life

As Richard Bernstein reminds us, one of the primary themes of 'the pragmatic ethos', which in many ways anticipated the concerns of what is loosely called postmodernism, is the recognition of contingency or chance (Bernstein 1997:388–9). John Dewey developed this discussion most systematically in his Gifford Lectures, published in 1929 as *The Quest for Certainty*. He spoke of the precarious nature of existence, and of chance as a fundamental property of experience with the world. His view was that certainty is an illusion – but we try for some measure of security. That is, we try to secure that which we value by confronting problems, recognising the uncertainty of outcomes, reflecting on possible ways forward, and interacting to realise intentions.

There is an intriguing parallel between the classical pragmatist view of subjective experience in an indeterminate world and current theorising about narrative. Stories have a structure in which intentional agents struggle towards an ending that is not yet certain. In narrative time, one thing leads to another; there is an unfolding of intention and consequence and a sense of moving towards outcomes which are imagined on the basis of what has happened so far. For the pragmatists, this was the character of life, not only stories. Transitivity is the quality that William James emphasised – the directionality rather than the conclusion: 'reality is movement from terminus to terminus, a pursuing of goals, and arriving at conclusions. It is on its way to something' (Perry 1996:371–2).

And just as Dewey saw problems as that which calls forth intelligent action, so Trouble is the 'engine of narrative' (Bruner 1996:142). Conflict, difficulty and suffering lend suspense and provide the counterpoint to human agency. 'Nothing is guaranteed in the realm of human action. We do what we can but – in the realm of narrative at least – there are always impediments' (Mattingly 1998:95).

There is one more commonality that follows from the others: the mood in which intentional subjects address possible outcomes. Jerome Bruner drew attention to the subjunctivising language of narrative[2] that 'highlights subjective states, attenuating circumstances, alternative possibilities.... To make a *story* good, it would seem, you must make it somewhat uncertain, somehow open to variant readings, rather subject to the vagaries of intentional states, undetermined' (Bruner 1990:53–4).

Subjunctivity, according to Webster's dictionary, is: 'that mood of a verb used to express supposition, desire, hypothesis, possibility, etc. rather than to state an actual fact: distinguished from *indicative, imperative*'. The indicative is the voice of certainty, the imperative the voice of command, but the subjunctive is the mood of doubt, hope, will and potential. Whether or not we accept the view that life itself has narrative structure (Mattingly 1998), it seems to me that we can think of subjunctivity as a quality not just of narratives,[3] but of at least some aspects of life. Where people are negotiating uncertainty and possibility, subjunctivity is an aspect of subjectivity.

I understand subjunctivity in terms of *situated* concern; it is the mood of people who care about something in particular. Subjunctivity does not characterise systems of thought. It is not like Mary Douglas's danger and potential in the liminality between categories.[4] Nor is it like the ambiguity and uncertainty of postcolonial subjectivity – what Mbembe and Roitman in their article on 'Figures of the Subject in Times of Crisis' call the 'profoundly provisional and revisable character of things' (Mbembe and Roitman 1995:342). When they talk about insecurity, and the uncertainty that flows from a confusing multiplicity of meanings, they describe a kind of generic subjectivity that informs everyone, a collective consciousness that is full of ambiguity, a shared cultural pattern abstracted from action. But making people cases of postcolonial subjectivity gives very little sense of what particular individuals are actually trying to do in the postcolony. Subjunctivity is not a characteristic of the times. It is about the specific uncertainty that particular actors experience as they try something that matters to them – as they undertake to deal with a problem. That is to say, it is a mood of the verb, it is about action, and especially interaction.

## The Iffiness of Afflicting Agents

One more thing we need to bear in mind. Intentional, hopeful, doubting subjects are subjects in relation to others. Subjectivity is always intersubjectivity. Michael Jackson proposes that intersubjectivity is about relations not only with persons, but also with other forces of our lived worlds. Here subject takes its other meaning, as topic of attention, and we acknowledge the way that we attribute significance to the phenomena with which we interact (Jackson 1998:6–7). The sickness that came back, the disease that Mahanga's family could not change, was a subject with which they engaged, as was the spirit Omuhyeno that came in the divination and to which they offered a goat by day and a sheep by night. They attended to those subjects, and experienced the reciprocal acting upon each other, being implicated with each other, that is what intersubjectivity can mean.

Being implicated with a subject that acts upon you as you act upon it is an indeterminate business when you do not fully know that subject or what it is going to do. In that situation subjunctivity keeps possibilities open. At least, that is how I understand the way people in Bunyole deal with the subjects that they suspect may be agents of misfortune. Those who bring affliction can be other living people, who invoke the ancestors in a curse or who use powerful substances to bring all kinds of ills. Cursers and sorcerers are almost always people with whom you are closely involved: senior relatives, co-wives, rivals, neighbours. You know them, but you do not know their hearts. Other sources of affliction are the shades of the dead or spirits of various kinds. Of those, people say: 'what you do not see though it looks askance at you – don't quarrel with it'.

This being implicated with what you do not really know helps explain why the language of ritual so often reveals doubt, conditionality and possibility.[5] In divination the project is to identify and communicate with the agents of misfortune who come and speak when the diviner is possessed. Diviners can even seem to be talking to the spirits of living persons, who reveal why they cursed, for example, and what offerings and ceremonies are needed. But the diviners say that the agents sometimes lie. In one session that I tape-recorded, the mother's brother (a person often suspected of cursing) appeared first. The diviner said to his clients: 'This one has begun by giving us lies'; and he later remarked that some agents have quick heads – they rush into the divination for no reason, or quarrel without any grounds (Whyte 1997:70–71). They are just deceiving.

In speaking to agents of misfortune, whether in divination or in a ritual of offering, the language expresses a lack of certainty about the agent. Prayers begin with *if*: 'Eeee Nalulima, if it is you, if you are in the house here of this little child…'(*ibid*.:144). Doubt is there. Even a curser, removing a curse, speaks to the ancestors and the cursed person with the words: 'If I am the one' (*ibid*.:158–9). But, more than that, the mood is subjunctive because it is full of conditionality and possibility, hope and desire. It acknowledges contingency but evokes possible futures. Speaking to a curser who was thought to have made a wife barren, the diviner said:

> If you are the one, I would like all of you to have a good heart ... ah, you remove the curse from this person, that she may go and become a woman where she is [married], so that she may be respected in that home. And when you call to visit there, a little child will go to fetch her from the garden saying, 'Ah, grandma has come.' (Ibid.:78)

If that curser is the one, we *wish* she would have a good heart, and then things *could be* different. The barren bride, the Dry Tree as they called her, could have a child and be respected as a woman. *Imagine* going to visit her in the future – there *would be* a child in the home to go and call its mother.

Entreaties suggest visions about what the implicated parties could hope for. A spirit could get another bigger ceremony with a better offering if only the sick mother and child recovered. Listen to the words spoken to the little spirit Mukama, the invisible twin, suspected of sickening a mother and baby:

> Perhaps it's you who has been kicking that child of yours and your mother – you've been sitting in her chest, you prevent her from cultivating. Ah, we have wanted you to leave your mother, that one. A person digs before she gets the means of [helping her relative]. And if she does not dig, [what about] the goat you are demanding?... You leave that child, that child of yours. When tomorrow comes, it will be bouncing on its mother's breast. Let people say, 'So that's how it was, Mukama was the one who was beating this little child.'... You may be declaring and yet you are not Mukama. But if it is you Mukama, soon we will return here, and we'll eat those things. (Ibid.:142)

They beg Mukama to relent – if it is Mukama. They hope to see the baby lively and happy in the morning so that people will know by the consequences of the ceremony that it *was* Mukama. They want the mother to be well so that she can take her hoe to dig millet. Only then could she get the goat needed for the bigger ceremony for Mukama. So it is not just doubt, but hope for a better future that hangs on the ifs and maybes.

Time will tell. The prayer is spoken in the spirit of pragmatism which William James described as 'an attitude of looking away from first principles ... supposed necessities and of looking towards ... fruits, consequences' (James 1974:47). For James it followed that: 'The truth of an idea is not a stagnant property inherent in it. Truth *happens* to an idea. It *becomes* true, is *made* true by events' (ibid.:133). The diviner suggests that truth might happen to the idea of Mukama. If the child recovers, then people will say, 'So that's how it was, it was Mukama.'

## Presumptive Treatment with Biomedicine

There is plenty of evidence about subjunctivity in the explanatory idiom that is used for dealing with the agents thought to bring misfortune. But what about ill-health that is treated in the genre of biomedicine? After all, biomedicine has been government medicine in Uganda for a century now (Foster 1970; Iliffe 1998) and has pervaded every part of the country. Pharmaceuticals are widely available in shops and small private clinics, as well as in non-profit health facilities. For the most common ailments, they are far more frequently used than herbal medicines (Adome *et al.* 1996).

Treatment by pharmaceuticals is symptomatic treatment in a double sense. It addresses immediate manifestations of illness rather than the human and spirit agents that might be behind the problem. And, from a medical point of view, it addresses patients' complaints more than signs of under-lying disease entities and processes. The patient tells the symptoms to a health worker or drug shop attendant, and gets the appropriate drug for each. For fever, you get chloroquine; for cough it is Septrin (co-trimoxazole, an antibiotic recommended for pneumonia); for diarrhoea, you get Flagyl (metronidazole). Public health professionals point out that this 'pill for every ill' approach encourages polypharmacy – the unnecessary use of too many medicines at once (Kafuko *et al.* 1994). More sympathetically but still in a medical discourse, one could call this 'presumptive treatment'. Not knowing for sure what caused the symptom, you treat for likely common and danger-ous diseases.

From the patients' point of view, biomedical treatment, and especially pharmaceuticals, offer a way forward. Concrete tokens of care are exchanged and valued as a way of dealing with problems. Although people are aware that different drugs have different indications, most are not so concerned with the correctness of choice according to some abstract system of treatment guidelines. Rather they are interested in relief of symptoms. This encourages a rather open and experimental attitude toward medicines, limited mainly by lack of money. I believe that this pragmatic attitude encourages and is encouraged by the increasing commercialisation of biomedicine; at storefront private clinics and small medicine shops, people are able quickly to acquire those tokens of power and hope that they can try out on their symptoms.

Thoughtful health workers are aware that, without systematic examina-tion, treatment is less certain. When people come to buy medicines, often for a patient at home, they get medicine for symptoms. A government health worker with a private business remarked about a customer who had bought drugs for his wife that he wanted to show her that he cared. But instead of bringing her for a proper examination, he just bought different drugs without ever trying to get to the root of the problem (Whyte 1991:139). Still the health worker sold the drugs, without examining the patient.

There seems to me to be a parallel between the ways people use medicines and how they deal with possible agents of misfortune. It is not so much a matter of knowing the truth about a problem in the sense of assimilating it to some absolute categories. Rather you want to alleviate it and that means that you get to know it by trying to act upon it. It is the prospect of what can be done that is important.

## Exams and Tests

Now this does not mean that people are uninterested in investigations that might provide guidelines for action. In fact many people value medical examinations, as we learned in a study on quality of care in six health facilities in the district (Nshakira *et al.* 1996). They noted how health workers touched them, looked at them, and whether they used any instruments like thermometers or stethoscopes. Laboratory examinations of blood, urine, stools or sputum are appreciated by many – except for the fact that they cost extra. But I am not sure that examinations are valued because they identify a disease. Rather they suggest that care was taken and that the most modern technology was offered. Thus they support decisions about treatment. They point towards possibilities and prospects.

In Uganda, laboratory tests do not have the kind of scientific truth status that they have in Denmark. Many health units do not have functioning labs, reagents are in short supply, technicians may not be well trained, they may be absent from their posts, and microscopes tend to go missing. I have often heard doubts expressed about lab results, both by medical professionals and by educated lay people. People without schooling may not doubt the accuracy of lab work in the same way, but for them the measuring of body products by machine is more of a step on the way to treatment than a necessary basis for selecting correct treatment. So even though parasite counts or bacteria identification should be indicative, the way they are discussed and used is often subjunctive.

All of this has become increasingly poignant in the era of AIDS. The efforts put into informing the Ugandan public about HIV/AIDS, and the prevalence of the disease, ensure that most people are aware of it (Seidel 1990, Schopper *et al.* 1995). The education campaign stresses that it is impossible to know by someone's appearance whether he or she is infected. But once the disease is well developed, many are aware of the symptoms: herpes zoster (*kissippi*, the belt) and other skin disorders, weight loss (slimming) and diarrhoea. That the condition is contracted through sexual contact is also well known, and when someone dies of suspected AIDS, it is a cause of great worry for his or her sexual partners. 'They have been screened', is the ironic comment.[6] Most of all, AIDS is associated with suffering and death. Being a victim is stigmatised, not so much because of how you contracted it, but because of the prognosis.

In Bunyole, when people say that someone has AIDS, they imply that the person is mortally ill and unlikely to be cured. But to say that someone is affected by spirits or sorcery is to suggest that something can be done to help. Depending on how concern is situated, one idea or the other might be propounded. It is often seen as an unfriendly or hostile move to say that someone has AIDS, and health workers generally do not force people to confront that diagnosis if they do not want to know. Usually those closest to a sick person talk carefully about the illness, not naming the death sentence. As I have described elsewhere (Whyte 1997:213–19), they sometimes declare their uncertainty ('It's in God's hands, we don't know what will happen'). But I think such assertions of possibility are understood as preparations for the worst. More distant acquaintances talk more directly – although even here the word AIDS, or Slim, is not necessarily pronounced. There are ways of saying things that make it clear enough.

But the situated concern with AIDS is not simply a matter of how close the speaker is to the sick person. It is also a question of timing. After someone has died, when there is no more trying, then it might be said that she died of AIDS. Hasahya and his son Mahanga were reaching that conclusion as they told about the recent death of Mahanga's brother. Retrospectively, AIDS explains why someone died; prospectively, it is difficult as a vision of how to live. The great accomplishment of The AIDS Support Organisation (TASO) and some Christian communities is that they have offered support for living positively towards a future, no matter how long or short it might be.

Against this background, it is easier to understand the way AIDS tests are used. In Uganda, AIDS tests are mostly available in towns. Counselling is offered before and after the test, which makes it very different from other medical tests, where patients may not even be told their results. NGOs like TASO provide some social and limited material support to people who are found HIV positive and who are willing to accept their HIV status and join the organisation. But many people do not take the step of openly identifying themselves as persons with AIDS. By not telling anyone the results of the test, you can keep possibilities open. If your health is good, you may recast the future hopefully. 'After all, it was only a lab test...' (Clarke 1993:268).

In late 1997, AIDS testing was finally made available at Busolwe Hospital in the middle of rural Tororo District. Although many people welcomed the idea, few actually took the test. Only 83 people were tested in all of 1998, and most of those were referred by TASO which had opened a branch about 15 km from the hospital. The counsellor, Henry Mpambiro, explained that people saw no point in being tested:

Now there is no drug, so why should I test? What help would I get?' they ask. We tell them the benefits – that it helps you to make plans, if you have children.... With proper counselling, fears and suicide and depression decline.... But there's a problem about telling spouses: a few agree, but many fear because the spouse will leave. For us here, it's still difficult, but in Kampala they have coped with it. You are living with it. The period of dying is not known. You think you will die tomorrow – but you may live with it for ten years.

So much has been said about the way African people think about the causes of misfortune (the BBC correspondent was in good company). Listening carefully to people in Eastern Uganda suggests that they are situating themselves more in relation to prospective than to retrospective concerns. Henry Mpambiro and his colleagues offer plans, and anticipate problems. At the same time, he mitigates the dreaded certainty with a note of subjunctivity: you may live with it for ten years.

## Subjunctive Civility

So far I have been talking about the subjunctive mood in which people deal with misfortune and its agents, the subjects that might have acted upon them. Now I want to turn to another side of the matter: the way that people who are working together to deal with misfortune relate to each other. Here too, the spirit of subjunctivity is at work. It is revealed in some of the exchanges I have heard between diviners and their clients. When many different possible agents had appeared in a divination, the clients were confused: 'Among all those cases, ah, we do not know where the truth is and where there is no truth.' And the diviner replied: 'You go and do [the curse removal ceremony]. There is where God can give you luck. You, when you divine through so many spirits, don't you go on touching this, touching that, touching another.' That is, you try one diviner and you try another. As he said, 'If she does not get any benefit, let them go and divine elsewhere. A single divination does not heal a person.' A famous practitioner once said something that captured it all: 'Let us struggle and we'll see where things end, when I've done for you that which doesn't prevent people from dying.' (Whyte 1997:22, 72–4). Diviners advise on what rituals should be done, but families decide whether to do them, and which should be done first. Since families are large, there may be different views on these matters. You may think one thing, but be deeply implicated with people who think something else.

Recently I was talking with a man who is a sincere Christian, the son of one of the most influential clergymen in Eastern Uganda, now dead. John is the appointed heir of his father. And he is a respected person in his own right, educated in the US, a former lecturer at the university, now holding an important position in the local area. He asked me about the book I wrote and when I told him a little about it, he wanted me to know about his daughter – a girl of 20 years.

> First she got malaria and then it affected her brain. She began to act so strangely. The family says it's a spirit – that my dead father wants something. My way is healing through prayer. But I will do the ceremony. I will pray – if they want to slaughter a goat, it's okay. Here if you refuse to do a ritual, the family says you are not trying to help. I hope to take her to Kampala for medical treatment too.

What John's remarks bring home is the attentiveness to other people's ideas and sensitivity to their opinions of him. The contrast to his attitude would be the stories told of the early days of Christianity and Islam in Bunyole when religious leaders were said to have campaigned against traditional beliefs. The act of burning down spirit shrines epitomised their convictions. Even today, it is said that the small group of Islamists in Busolwe, the Tabliqs, set the little thatched houses for spirits alight. But John's stance ('if they want to do it, it's okay') is by far the most common. I want to suggest a term for it.

To the two -ities on offer here – subjectivity and subjunctivity – one more can be added and that is civility. Civility can mean courtesy, but in its etymology it implies politics or politic behaviour, that is, having practical wisdom. And civil has to do with the interrelations of a community of citizens. Tolerance is not quite the same thing. It means to endure or forbear; to allow, permit, to not interfere with others' views and practices; to recognise and respect others' beliefs without necessarily agreeing or sympathising. Tolerance means freedom from bigotry or prejudice. But I would use civility to emphasise intersubjectivity – the way that people are interdependent in trying to pursue goals. To be so assertive in one's religious certainty as to deny others their ideas would be to lose community support. 'They'll say you aren't trying to help.'

This too involves subjunctivity – the conditionality of being implicated with other people. The parallel in narrative analysis is the recognition of multiple perspectives and diverse readings (Good 1994:153–6). As Bruner points out, the appreciation that a story is somebody's story means that narratives are viable instruments for social negotiation (Bruner 1990:54–5). I want to take that idea further in underlining the intersubjective interests that frame the acknowledgment of other positions. It is a matter of being careful about what others will think and what consequences that might have. Others concern you.

When Mahanga told about dealing with the terrible sicknesses of his mother and brother, he moved back and forth between saying *we* and saying *they*. 'As you know, the traditional people can't believe that someone is dying of AIDS. *They* went to the diviner. *We* tried the ceremony. But though they tried....' When he says 'the traditional people believe', or when John says that families here want to offer goats to their dead, they are speaking with understanding and involvement as well as a touch of distance. They are concerned.

Civility is a recognition of your involvement with other social actors, also into the future. It does not imply equality or similarity between people, but rather 'practical wisdom' about the intertwining of concerns. It is predicated on continuity in personal relationships and strengthens the possibility of mutuality to come. The subjunctivity of civility has to do with the unknowability of both the future and other actors. Civility involves a degree of respect and reservation about final truths.

## Technical Know-How and Technical Know-Who

When you are desperately in need of help, it is not only a question of accepting the ideas of various relatives about what should be done. It is also a matter of dealing with the providers of care. For our purposes here, use of biomedicine provides an excellent example because of its historic connection with the colonial and postcolonial state. What kinds of intersubjectivity are in play here?

Much has been written about the deterioration of the Ugandan health care system (Dodge and Wiebe 1985, Macrae *et al.* 1996, Asiimwe *et al.* 1997, Okello *et al.* 1998). Despite a massive input of foreign aid, policy changes, and restructuring in the public sector, utilisation remains low and complaints high. The litany of problems includes: the demoralisation of health workers due to poor and irregular salaries; misuse of resources at all levels; shortages of medicines and supplies; fees and other demands for services that used to be free; ineffective management and supervision; poor quality of care. Alongside the public sector, a thriving private for-profit sector provides biomedical treatment and pharmaceuticals for self-medication. Much of this is 'informal' in the sense that it is not recognised by state authorities – though much of what goes on in the public facilities is informal in that sense too.

The complexities and frustrations of trying to use or work in this (non)system can be extreme. Sometimes there is nothing for it but the derisive, ironic and complicit laughter to which Mbembe (1992) has drawn attention. 'In Uganda, drugs have legs – they can walk out the back door of the clinic all by themselves,' commented someone about the disappearance of medicines from public facilities. 'We Ugandans are too clever,' one health worker told me, in describing the variety of tricks for smuggling medicines out of the health unit, cooking the patient registers, etc. 'It's not just a matter of medical know-how,' I have heard people say, 'but also of know-who.' Connections are important when you need the knowledge, drugs and procedures that are widely available if not widely accessible.

Yet it is important to note that these ironic comments are not just aspects of a free-floating subjectivity. They have their particular place in social exchange – in moments of companionable reflection, friendly chat with a familiar researcher, justification for or criticism of something that has happened. By drawing attention to moral ambiguities and criteria for efficacious action, people create a form of intersubjectivity in certain contexts – whether sympathy, solidarity, distance, or knowing insinuation. In other situations, as subjects trying to solve problems or achieve something, they put irony aside or subsume it in a larger design. A parent whose child is acutely ill is positioned and oriented. Derisive laughter belongs to other contexts.

Working with colleagues in 1996 to assess the quality of care in district health units, we interviewed exiting patients and also held focus group discussions in the catchment areas of the facilities. The focus groups expressed criticism of the health services – the fees, the shortages of drugs, the indifference of the health workers. But there was almost no disapproval in the exit interviews; standing so close to the unit, with a sick child, having finally been seen by a health worker, people were grateful for whatever they had received.

Not so the father of 4-year-old Suzan Maguleti Nawile, whom I spoke with in 1997 shortly after she died of what may have been pneumonia. We sat under the temporary shelter built to receive mourners, deciphering the words written in Luganda on a page torn from a school exercise book.[7] It was a brief *elepoti* for a brief life, but like all the 'reports' read at the open grave, it placed the person in terms of kinship and religion, numbered her years, and acknowledged the support of those who came to bury her.

The young father spoke quietly about his firstborn child:

> She wasn't a baby, she was already big enough to go to the borehole for water. She fell sick with fever and trembling. We took her to the hospital and they examined her and said her lungs were swollen so she couldn't breathe well. Her breathing was fast and her heart pumped hard. The body was hot. They told me that since I was alone and did not have the things necessary for admission, I should go home and come next day with someone to care for her and she would be admitted. They gave her an injection and I got some tablets, but she

kept on vomiting all the medicine. In the evening we never thought she would die – she even ate something. But the sickness got worse, she had convulsions, and passed away. No one expected it.... The problem at the hospital – they want money. After examining, they send you to buy medicines at their clinics. If you are given a bed, you have to pay every day. It's money that makes people die here.

Suzan Maguleti's father could be openly critical; he and the other mourners were explaining to themselves what had happened, rather than hoping and acting in the mood of subjunctivity. From his account, it seems that he was weak on technical know-who; he did not have any advocate at the hospital. He also went to the hospital unprepared. In the 'do-it-yourself bureaucracy' (Mbembe and Roitman 1995:343) of contemporary government health care, admission to hospital requires a caretaker, food, supplies and money.

How different was the situation of Hasahya's family. As a cleaner in the hospital, he could facilitate the admission of his ex-wife and his son, and he could ensure a good standard of home treatment as well. Knowing someone who works or has worked in a medical facility is a great advantage to the family seeking health care. You gain access to their knowledge and skills, to the channels through which resources, especially medicines flow, and you may also be able to avoid having to pay for services. You will be treated with more consideration, because you are not just an anonymous patient, but a relative, friend, colleague or neighbour.

The importance of technical know-who means that criticism of health workers is almost never made to their faces. Confrontations are practically non-existent. Who would dare to alienate a person on whom they may be dependent sometime in the future? Some critical health workers themselves recognise that civility can have a negative side. There was recently an instance of drunken negligence on the part of a health worker that led to the death of a patient. Another health worker spoke of the need for public support in disciplining alcoholics:

The public needs to help. You should go and round up all the drunkards and make them walk around the roundabout with their pots on their heads. But people say they can't do that to health workers, because next time they may need them.

Practical wisdom says that you should not burn bridges you may need to use. In a larger sense, too, ridiculing health workers as drunks – without dignity and respect (*ehitiwa*) – would make the health system itself less worthy of hope and trust.

Earlier I referred to the idea that subjects are trying to exert some degree of control, not necessarily as masters, but rather as helmsmen steering a course. For people trying to steer through health problems, this kind of control involves interrelationships with institutions and practitioners. Drawing on pre-existing links and exercising civility towards people in key positions are ways of navigating. But there are other ways as well. Going to a little private clinic or a drug shop gives more leeway than going to an outpatient department that is more formalistic and impersonal. Being a customer rather than a patient gives steerage; you can decide what medicine you want, how much you can afford to pay; you can ask questions and expect to be treated with civility – since the provider is concerned with you in his business endeavour. The problem of technical know-who is one of leverage – the increased means of accomplishing some purpose. Being a customer, for some people at least, is also a form of leverage.

## Directions

The chanciness of health in conditions of poverty, insufficient medical services, and heavy loads of infectious diseases reminds us that uncertainty is an aspect of subjectivity. As researchers we can choose to emphasise the historical conditions to which the health of citizens is subject. War, budget priorities, corruption, poor management, user fees and donor policies have affected the health system that Ugandans have developed since independence. They are sources of uncertainty, as are the diseases against which people are struggling, most dramatically epitomised by AIDS. As a field-worker, however, I wanted to bring out another dimension: the perspectives of people trying to manage under these conditions.

The concept of subjunctivity was a way of focusing on the intentions, hopes and doubts of people looking toward an immediate future whose contours were not certain. I pointed to the situated concern of subjects facing problems and to the directionality of their efforts. Subjunctivity is not just about uncertainty; it helps us attend to purposes and consequences. It asks us to take seriously the question of what people are trying to do – not that that is ever a simple question. People reflect and doubt and hope because they have situated concerns – usually in the plural.

The notion of civility is related to subjunctivity, in that people are implicated with other subjects they do not fully know or control. Civility is recognised as a virtue in Eastern Uganda. It is good to attend to others, to recognise their moral privilege to an account of how things are (Rorty 1982:202). Showing respect to others brings respect, whereas confrontation and anger are usually thought to make people look foolish. But, analytically, civility may also help us to focus on the interdependence of subjects. How are they interdependent? With respect to what purposes? In what time frame? To what extent do people recognise that interdependence?

The wry term 'technical know-who' has the distancing quality of irony, and it is used in situations where people are reflecting, not when they are in the midst of dealing with a problem. It is related to the notion of civility, in that it recognises the importance of interrelationship. But it has about it an air of calculation, scheming and cold rationality. While those are relevant sometimes, they are misleading as primary characteristics of civility or inter-subjectivity.

Neither subjunctivity nor the uncertainties about other persons inherent in civility are peculiar to the postcolonial period. Scepticism, doubt and hope are not prerogatives of postcolonial or postmodern times. The extreme emphasis that some scholars place on the uncertainties of the present era imply that life was more certain in colonial or precolonial times. In contrast, the classical pragmatists like John Dewey recognised that existential problems always present uncertainties to social actors. But uncertainties themselves change, as do the means available for dealing with them.

What then is particular to this postcolonial moment in Uganda? The immediate answer might seem to be the ravages of AIDS and the fears and hopes surrounding life with the epidemic. But, in a broader sense, we must attend to the way consciousness of AIDS and other health problems has been shaped, and the health care options available for dealing with them. The combination of increasing commercialisation of medical care and donor/government efforts to sensitise citizens about health and implement new programmes has had the effect of making people more demanding and more critical concerning biomedical care. I see this as a matter of degree; there is a well-established pattern of critical evaluation concerning specialists in African healing too. The difference is that nowadays there are more options for biomedical care than there were in colonial times, and there is greater awareness of the failings of the government health care system.

The nature of civility in these postcolonial years is a fundamental question for social scientists. At the microlevel of fieldwork in one locality, civility emerges as a sense of interdependence concerning common goals in a shared future. It entails a recognition of others with their interests, and of your implication with them. Whether civility borders on complicity is a matter for careful consideration. The term complicity implies a negative evaluation by an outsider, while for the actors involved what is important is often the maintenance of relationships and possibilities for the future.

The failure of civility can take the form of assertions of absolute right and wrong or the denial of relationship with certain kinds of others. In talking of civility and incivility, we must specify the level of sociality with which we are concerned. But whether we speak of neighbourhoods or nations, incivility is about power and/or indifference, situations where social actors pursue futures to which certain others are irrelevant. Subjective assessment of these matters is a continuing process. When people in Bunyole criticise health workers for self-interest and lack of commitment to their jobs and patients, they blame them for incivility. When they refuse to accuse them publicly, they act with civility and consider possible futures.

The approach taken here has so emphasised the practices and uncertainties of actors that it may seem to neglect the forces of subjection that oppress them. In one sense there is always a danger in more phenomenological approaches that broad historical processes and forces are left aside since they are beyond the compass of the immediate lifeworld. Studies of subjectivity need the historical dimension of political and cultural economy; the concept of postcolonial subjectivity makes no sense without it, since the very term postcolonial denotes a historical period. What I have tried to show is the importance of *also* understanding forces of subjection from the point of view of those who experience them and deal with them, who undergo and undertake. Only in this way can we avoid generalisations about subjectivity that risk becoming stereotypes if not caricatures.

The notions of subjunctivity and civility suggest that subjectivity is situated and directed, hopeful but aware of fallibility. It is deeply social, not just in the sense of being informed by abstract historical processes, but also in the day-to-day interactions between subjects that insure that subjectivity is always intersubjectivity.

## Notes

1 This chapter is based on fieldwork with people in Bunyole County, Tororo District, in 1969–71, and at intervals since 1989. Since 1992, I have been working with researchers at Child Health and Development Centre and Makerere Institute of Social Research on two long-term projects in Tororo District: Tororo Community Health (TORCH) and Community Drug Use. Many thanks to colleagues in Uganda and to the Danish International Development Agency for continuing support.

2 A more technical discussion of how language subjunctivises reality within narratives may be found in Bruner 1986:25–37.

3 Byron Good (1994) and Frode Jacobsen (1998) have followed Bruner in using the notion of subjunctivity to analyse narratives of illness. As ethnographers, however, both go beyond a narrow focus on stories to suggest the situational implications of subjunctivity for persons, families and groups.

4 Good (1994:205 n.20) refers to Victor Turner's use of the distinction between 'the indicative quotidian social structure' and the 'subjunctive antistructure of the liminal process'. This structural distinction differs from the positionality and directionality that I am emphasising.

5 Heald (1991) makes a similar argument based on fieldwork among the Gisu of Eastern Uganda. She suggests that scepticism and doubt are inherent in the institution and process

of divination. The stereotypes of 'gullible savages' and sophisticated Westerners are totally misleading. In fact, Westerners may be more willing to accept the authority of their medical specialists than rural Ugandans who are accustomed to playing an important part in constructing knowledge about their own conditions.

6  The uncertainties and struggles for help associated with HIV/AIDS have been well described in Asera *et al.* 1996 and 1997.

7  This is the report of the late Suzan Maguleti Nawile. She was a daughter of Mr Esau Hisa and Mrs Grace Nahire. By clan she was Muhibiga, a niece of the Benge clan, a grandchild of the Bahambe on the side of her father and of the Bajanja on the side of her mother. She was born on 12 December 1993 and reached the age of 4 years. She was baptised on 27 February 1994. She died when she had finished three years in religion. The one who baptised her at Hahoola church was Namukuba. We thank all the people who have come to dig the grave and construct the shelter and those who gave money. As for the 'dismantling death' ceremony, we will inform you later.

# References

Adome, Richard Odoi, Susan Reynolds Whyte and Anita Hardon (1996), *Popular Pills: Community Drug Use in Uganda.* Amsterdam: Het Spinhuis.

Appadurai, Arjun (1990), 'Disjuncture and Difference in the Global Cultural Economy'. *Public Culture* 2(2):1–24.

Asera, Rose, Henry Bagarukayo, Dean Shuey and Thomas Barton (1996), 'Searching for Solutions: Health Concerns Expressed in Letters to an East African Newspaper Column'. *Health Transition Review* 6(2):169–78.

— (1997), 'An Epidemic of Apprehension: Questions about HIV/AIDS to an East African Newspaper Health Advice Column'. *AIDS Care* 9(1):5–12.

Asiimwe, Delius, Barbara McPake, Frances Mwesigye, Matthias Ofumbi, Lisbeth Ørtenblad, Pieter Streefland and Asaph Turinde (1997), 'The Private-Sector Activities of Public-Sector Health Workers in Uganda'. In Sara Bennett, Barbara McPake and Anne Mills (eds.) *Private Health Providers in Developing Countries: Serving the Public Interest?* London: Zed Books.

Bernstein, Richard J. (1997), 'Pragmatism, Pluralism and the Healing of Wounds'. In Louis Menand (ed.) *Pragmatism: A Reader.* New York: Random House.

Bruner, Jerome (1986), *Actual Minds, Possible Worlds.* Cambridge, MA: Harvard University Press.

— (1990), *Acts of Meaning.* Cambridge, MA: Harvard University Press.

— (1996), *The Culture of Education.* Cambridge, MA: Harvard University Press.

Clarke, Ian (1993). *The Man With the Key Has Gone!* Chichester: New Wine Press.

Comaroff, Jean and John Comaroff (eds.) (1993), *Modernity and its Malcontents: Ritual and Power in Postcolonial Africa.* Chicago: University of Chicago Press.

Dewey, John (1929), *The Quest for Certainty: A Study of the Relation of Knowledge and Action.* New York: Minton, Balch and Company.

Dodge, Cole P. and Paul D. Wiebe (eds.) (1985), *Crisis in Uganda: The Breakdown of Health Services.* Oxford: Pergaman Press.

Foster, W. D. (1970), *The Early History of Scientific Medicine in Uganda.* Nairobi: East African Literature Bureau.

Good, Byron J. (1994), *Medicine, Rationality, and Experience: An Anthropological Perspective.* Cambridge: Cambridge University Press.

Heald, Suzette (1991), 'Divinatory Failure: the Religious and Social Role of Gisu Diviners'. *Africa* 61(3):299–317.

Iliffe, John (1998), *East African Doctors*. Cambridge: Cambridge University Press.

Jackson, Michael (1998), *Minima Ethnographica: Intersubjectivity and the Anthropological Project*. Chicago: University of Chicago Press.

Jacobsen, Frode F. (1998), *Theories of Sickness and Misfortune amongst the Handandowa Beja of the Sudan: Narratives as Points of Entry into Beja Cultural Knowledge*. London: Kegan Paul International.

James, William (1907, reprinted 1947), *Pragmatism and Four Essays from the Meaning of Truth*. New York: New American Library.

Kafuko, Jessica, Christine Zirabamuzaale and Dan Bagenda (1994), *Rational Drug Use in the Rural Health Units of Uganda: Effect of National Standard Treatment Guidelines on Rational Drug Use*. Entebbe: Uganda Essential Drugs Management Programme, Ministry of Health.

Macrae, Joanna, Anthony B. Zwi and Lucy Gilson (1996), 'A Triple Burden for Health Sector Reform: 'Post'-Conflict Rehabilitation in Uganda'. *Social Science and Medicine* 42(87): 1095–108.

Mattingly, Cheryl (1998), *Healing Dramas and Clinical Plots: The Narrative Structure of Experience*. Cambridge: Cambridge University Press.

Mbembe, Achille (1992), 'Provisional Notes on the Postcolony'. *Africa* 62(1):3–37.

Mbembe, Achille and Janet Roitman (1995), 'Figures of the Subject in Times of Crisis'. *Public Culture* 7:323–52.

McPake, Delius Asiimwe, Francis Mwesigye, Mathias Ofumbi, Lisbeth Ortenblad, Pieter Streefland and Asaph Turinde (1999), 'Informal Economic Activities of Public Health Workers in Uganda: Implications for Quality and Accessibility of Care'. *Social Science and Medicine* 49(7):849–65.

Mills, C. Wright (1959, reprinted 1961), *The Sociological Imagination*. New York: Grove Press.

Nshakira, Nathan, Susan Whyte, Jessica Jitta and Gonzaga Busuulwa (1996), *An Assessment of Quality of Out-Patient Clinical Care in District Health Facilities, Tororo District*. Kampala: Child Health and Development Centre Document.

Okello, D. O., R. Lubanga, D. Guwatudde and A. Sebina-Zziwa (1998), 'The Challenge to Restoring Basic Health Care in Uganda'. *Social Science and Medicine* 46(1):13–21.

Perry, Ralph Barton (1948, reprinted 1996), *The Thought and Character of William James*. Nashville: Vanderbilt University Press.

Rorty, Richard (1982), *Consequences of Pragmatism (Essays 1972–1980)*. New York: Harvester Wheatsheaf.

Schopper, Serge Doussantousse, Natal Ayiga, Georges Ezatirale, William Jean Ido and Jacques Homsy (1995), 'Village-Based AIDS Prevention in a Rural District in Uganda'. *Health Policy and Planning* 10(2):171–80.

Seidel, Gill (1990), '"Thank God I Said No to AIDS": On the Changing Discourse of AIDS in Uganda'. *Discourse and Society* 1(1):61–84.

Whyte, Susan Reynolds (1991), 'Medicines and Self-Help: The Privatization of Health Care in Eastern Uganda'. In H. B. Hansen and M. Twaddle (eds.) *Changing Uganda: Dilemmas of Structural Adjustment and Revolutionary Change*. London: James Currey.

— (1997), *Questioning Misfortune: The Pragmatics of Uncertainty in Eastern Uganda*. Cambridge: Cambridge University Press.

# 8 ◎ Ancestral Incests and Postcolonial Subjectivities in the Karembola (Madagascar)

Karen Middleton

## Why Do Karembola 'Love to Practise Incest'?

Maraze and I were walking home from Betsikoboke in the late afternoon sun when we passed a hamlet where around thirty people had gathered to perform a sacrifice. A fine red ox lay upon the red earth, its feet bound together, its head turned to the east. 'They're performing a sacrifice to atone for incest', Maraze explained after chatting to kin. 'The young man and woman have slept together; but it's forbidden because she is his "mother" and he is her "child". The sacrifice will make their union possible by lifting the taboo.' 'We Karembola love to practise incest' (*tea'ay ty manambaly faly*), Maraze added mischievously. 'We have a liking for forbidden unions' (*tea'ay ty fanambaliañe an-paly*).

Writing about the Bara people of the southern highlands of Madagascar in the immediate postcolonial period, prior to the fall of the First Malagasy Republic in 1972, Huntington (1978) recounts a rather similar incident. A young Bara man arrives at the ethnographer's hut in a state of great excitement, declaring that he is about to commit incest. Several days later, Huntington is invited to witness an atonement sacrifice. From an early twenty-first-century perspective, Huntington's analysis of this episode belongs squarely in what Gupta and Ferguson (1997:1–2) dub the 'peoples and cultures' approach in anthropology. In structuralist mode, Huntington explores how Bara incest prohibitions disclose a local cultural logic of power and regeneration. In functionalist mode, he demonstrates how Bara incest practices and discourses reaffirm categorical distinctions between kin and non-kin. It is typical of the anthropological tradition of conceptualising the 'problem' of incest in ahistorical terms (for a notable exception see Hutchinson 1985) that there is little evidence here either of incest as changing cultural practice or that the local logic of power and regeneration, and the concern with inner and outer boundaries, might have anything to do with a world beyond Bara lineages and clans.

In this chapter, I set myself a puzzle. During the 1980s and 1990s, Karembola villagers of southern Madagascar were deeply preoccupied with incest. Wherever I went, people told me of the 'ancestral taboos' that regulate sexual relations, often tapping them out one by one upon my legs. They then proceeded to recount how 'people today break them all'. This perception seemed to be vindicated by the many cases of alleged incest that filled my notebooks. Karembola showed none of the unwillingness to discuss the subject which, as Beidelman (1971:181) once remarked, often makes incest difficult to investigate in the field, and which has meant that, despite its centrality to conventional anthropological understandings of African societies, there is relatively little solid ethnographic material on the ideology or the practice of incest. This chapter explores the significance of contemporary incest discourses and practices for Karembola subjectivity. It asks why incest figured so prominently on local political and cultural agendas, and how this intense, often explosively emotional, concern with the nature of moral and personal connectedness related, if at all, to broader political and economic forces that were shaping Karembola lives.

Incest discourses are discourses on personhood, power and social identity that are carried out in the language of kinship. Yet over the past twenty years or so the study of kinship, once the focus of anthropological theory, has come to be seen by many anthropologists as belonging to our discipline's past. While recent work on gender (e.g., Collier and Yanagisako 1987, Strathern 1988) and reproductive technologies (e.g., Edwards *et al.* 1993, Franklin and Ragoné 1998) has rekindled interest in the subject, it has not been particularly concerned to explore the pertinence of kinship discourses and practices to postcolonial subjectivity. The unease with which many students of contemporary African social life approach the subject of kinship is evident in a recent essay on 'witchcraft' by Geschiere (1999) in which the author half apologises to the reader for focusing on the family and 'house' that plainly figure prominently in his field data.

As Geschiere notes, however, Africanists for a long while neglected the modern dynamics of witchcraft discourses and practices because witchcraft had been a staple in 'Anthropology-land' (Geschiere 1999). This changed, we are told, when theoretical interest in witchcraft discourse was redirected 'from *ahistorical* questions of social control, responsibility or micropolitics in interpersonal relations to *historical* questions of moral and political economy within the state under changing conditions of capitalism' (Werbner 1996:1, emphasis added). Is it possible that the same is true for incest? Might we be able to talk of the 'modernity' of incest in the way that Africanists talk of the 'modernity' of witchcraft (Geschiere 1997; see also Apter 1993, Auslander 1993, Bastian 1993, Matory 1994, Rowlands and Warner 1988, Shaw 1997)? Do contemporary Karembola incest discourses and practices, like new forms of witchcraft in Africa, 'crystallize perceptions of the alienation of labour under (post)colonial capitalism, of the social consequences of a cash economy, of the contradictions of urban and international migration, of disparities generated by cash-cropping, and of the dislocations of boom-and-bust cycles to which communities and regions are subject through integration into global markets' (Shaw 1997)? Do they, like spirit possession, reveal 'an intense awareness of the effects of outside forces on the local political economy' (Sharp 1995:76)? Has ritual around incest proliferated in the Karembola as a concomitant of 'modernity' because it provides 'ironic commentary' upon 'problematic forms of wealth, power and technology', a discourse about 'a totalizing moral economy in which the acquisition of money and power links parochial means for producing and destroying human value to potent foreign sources of wealth' (Comaroff and Comaroff 1993: xxv)? Or are the data I shall record in this chapter more meaningfully grasped as part of a longer cultural tradition that has relatively little to do with 'postcolonial subjectivity' *per se*? What kind of reading should I offer of Karembola sacrificing cattle in the setting sun to enable a 'son' to sleep with a 'mother', and of Maraze laughing as she told me that Karembola love to practise incest?

The answer I give to this question is equivocal. On the one hand, I shall explore contemporary Karembola incest discourses and practices for cryptic allusions to broader historical forces of social and economic transformation, including postcolonial state and political domination, and new forms of capitalist enterprise and economic decline. Yet I also stop short of explaining them in these terms. While Karembola incest discourses and practices can be 'opened up' to reveal commentary on 'the contradictions and opacities of (often oppressive) expanding national and world systems' (Comaroff and Comaroff 1993: xxx), for the most part the never-ending incest histories that filled my notebooks had meaning and significance for Karembola because they wove densely textured, inward-looking subjectivities. Rather than foreground regional and global forms of connectedness, this is a subjectivity that focuses closely on the micropolitics of interpersonal relationships. To be sure, there are historical reasons why Karembola have chosen and indeed been able to cultivate interiority and intimacy, and one of the aims of this chapter will be to explore what these reasons are. As a result, however, this is yet another instance where the world system perspective 'frame becomes too big for the picture' (Gable 1995).

## Karembola Today

One of the difficulties in writing Karembola ethnography is that Karembola specialise in producing symbolic discourses and practices that appear to conceptualise the self and collectivity in remarkably unfashionable ways. Thus, Karembola imagine that they live in a world where power is essentially based on the gift of a woman and the life she makes possible; where this gift creates a spiritual debt that grooms can never redeem; where cattle follow paths that are determined by their origins, and taboos and sacred powers prevent their value-conversion into commodities; where people have primordial identities based on ancestry and (imagined) rank. While the *fin de siècle* ethnographer is under peer pressure to write of modernity and globalisation (see Englund and Leach 2000), Karembola do their best to live in what after Geschiere (1999) we might term 'Anthropology-land'.

Karembola are not, of course, a people without history. Local narratives single out two key experiences as having shaped their contemporary selves. Both are curiously distant in time, however. The first was conquest by French colonial troops in the early years of the twentieth century. The second was the eradication in the 1920s of a prickly pear upon which Karembola and their cattle had come to depend. It is not difficult to understand why Karembola remember this event so powerfully. First, it transformed their relationship to the colonial economy when, following a famine that drove thousands to migrate, the Deep South became a reservoir of 'unskilled' wage labour for other parts of Madagascar (Middleton 1997, 1999). At the same time, it also transformed their relationship to the past. For Karembola, time thereafter became scythed in two: 'the time of the ancestors when "Malagasy cactus" [the prickly pear] was still living' and 'the time of foreigners when "Malagasy cactus" had died'. Even so, the primacy Karembola narratives give to this event has the effect of making their twentieth-century history appear otherwise curiously static. Nothing of parallel significance appears to have happened since, or rather nothing – droughts, famines, cattle anthrax, elections, even independence in 1960[1] – which cannot be subsumed under this metonym for conquest by foreign power. Indeed, while the term *vazaha* ('foreigner', 'stranger') has a wide range of referents (including European or white people, Malagasy government officials, and Malagasy who act like Europeans), French colonisers remain for Karembola the archetypal *vazaha*, and successive postcolonial regimes are seen for the most part as a continuation of colonial rule (see Cole and Middleton 2001). In this respect, Karembola would probably agree that to speak of the 'postcolonial' for Africa is to mark the end of an epoch falsely by placing a break where none exists (Werbner 1996:5; cf.

Chabal 1996, Ranger 1996 on the pitfalls of the 'postcolonial' as a theoretical subject).

I have described elsewhere how Karembola dramatically enact their sense of impotency, and distance from the past, in contemporary rituals around sacrifice and death (Middleton 1997). Themes of defeat and decline feature strongly in Karembola cultural productions. Drawing on symbols of *longue durée* – ancestry and its negation, slavery – Karembola present themselves as a conquered people living in a ruined land. And yet I have also shown how in many respects it would be more accurate to say that carefully elaborated imagery of powerlessness and peripherality masks the experience of centredness and considerable autonomy.

It is worth exploring some of the political and socio-economic factors that have engendered this paradox. To begin with, the Karembola region is an extremely arid region of Madagascar. While this has meant that Karembola have had to contend with poverty, drought and famine, it has also meant their homeland has never attracted European concessions or settlers from other parts of Madagascar. Consequently, while the demise of 'Malagasy cactus' had a profound and lasting impact, Karembola were never dispossessed of their land. Subsistence farmers continue to herd cattle, sheep, and goats, and to work the land with hoes to produce 'ancestral foods' (*hanen-drazañe*): manioc, maize, sweet potatoes, pumpkins, melons and legumes. In many ways, local production systems were more poorly integrated into regional and national markets in the 1980s and 1990s than they had been in the colonial and immediate postcolonial periods. In the socialist 1970s, for instance, Karembola supplied goats' wool in considerable quantities to a carpet-weaving state collective in Ampanihy; they stopped when they were not paid. This is part of a wider isolation. For instance, while many households possess a radio, for twenty years radios have been seldom heard in Karembola villages – for want of batteries during the socialist era, and for want of money to buy them since 'structural adjustment' has made them freely available.

The aridity of the Karembola region, together with its location at the very tip of Madagascar, with nothing but the Southern Ocean between it and Antartica, has also meant that the postcolonial state simply has not bothered to struggle for control of social space. Far from any turbulent inter-state border, vital port or mine, this rural people has been more or less left to its own devices. The infrastructure of a centralised, modern state – schools and medical services – was never really developed during the colonial period. Consequently, the 'waning' or 'withered' state of the late twentieth century has had comparatively little impact upon local communities accustomed to relying upon their own efforts. The state has also had limited powers in matters of cultural identity. For their part, Karembola have been largely apolitical. They have not engaged actively in either the production or the contestation of imagery of the Malagasy nation-state and its leadership. The profound cynicism they express as self-designated 'authentic *gasy*' [Malagasy] about the symbols and rhetoric of nation building is voiced entirely amongst themselves. They did not participate on any scale in the disturbances that rocked the south in 1971, heralding the fall of the First Malagasy Republic (Althabe 1972; Covell 1987:44–5), nor in the violence that erupted during the 1980s against Indo-Pakistanis (*karany*) who control regional trade networks. The violence of 1947 (Cole 1998, Tronchon 1986) also passed them by. While elections I witnessed generated intense battles for control of local councils (*fokontany*), participants appeared largely indifferent to or cynical about the broader national implications. In encounters with government officials, Karembola always stress their passivity before state power: 'don't we simply nod our heads when *vazaha* speak?' Yet behind the metaphors of conquest, marginalisation and powerlessness, state intervention in this region has often been ineffective, and Karembola have continued to regulate their own affairs.

The impact of out-migration from the Karembola over the decades since the demise of 'Malagasy cactus' has been substantial. As Karembola emphasise, 'to the north the many, here but the few'. Patterns of migration have changed in recent decades, however, because wherever possible Karembola nowadays prefer to migrate as families (cf. Feniès 1957). As a result, there appears to be little of the demographic imbalance that characterises many African rural communities with histories of dependency on migrant labour, namely, the preponderance of the old and the very young, or of women over men. At the same time, my sense is that during the 1980s and 1990s migrants were returning to the Karembola in far fewer numbers than before. The practice of bringing home for burial the corpses of those who have died in other parts of Madagascar had certainly become less common. Despite extended periods of fieldwork in the Karembola, I have never witnessed this quintessential Malagasy act of reaffirming the link between people and their ancestral land. This is partly because the cost of hiring bush taxis to transport 'wet corpses' over long distances is now prohibitive. (Karembola taboo the practice of temporary burial and subsequent exhumation that enables many Malagasy peoples to return more cheaply the shrivelled remains of dead relatives years later as bundles rolled up in mats.) But it is also the case that, as Karembola communities in exile have grown in number, they have often established tombs, and new identities, in the places where they have settled (see e.g., Astuti 1995; Sharp 1993:71). While those who remain behind in the Karembola rue the severance of kin connections, it has spared them the challenge of contending with the competing political and cultural agendas of those who, after many years away, might in one way or another seek to recast their natal villages as a 'virtual reality' (van Binsbergen 1999; see, e.g., Piot 1999). The 'bovine mystique' (Ferguson 1985) still prevails in the Karembola, and those migrants who do return mostly convert the money they have earned into cattle with legs (cf. Comaroff and Comaroff 1992). This is the paradox in Karembola historiography: namely, that a region of Madagascar known for its high rates of outward labour migration is also known for its cultural insularity (cf. Althabe 1972).

Although Karembola insist that their bodies and minds have been completely colonised by foreigners (Middleton 1997), there is in fact little of the cultural pluralism that characterises, for example, the multi-ethnic migrant towns of north-west Madagascar (Sharp 1993, Lambek 1998). While officials and gendarmes from other parts of Madagascar reside in the local market and administrative town of Beloha, the Karembola villages to the south are still inhabited by *tompotane* ('masters of the land') and their uxorilocal dependents. To a striking degree, 'alterity' is an experience produced and enacted by Karembola themselves. This takes the shape of *doany* cults during which Karembola become possessed by the dead spirits of Sakalava monarchs who once ruled in north-west Madagascar where Karembola migrate to work on plantations. It also emerges in the form of angry spirits of dead Karembola who impose *vazaha* ('foreign', 'colonial') patterns of work upon mourners (Cole and Middleton 2001). One might say that, in the absence of significant others, Karembola take it upon themselves to make visible the alleged dominance of foreigners, just as they take turns to play the role of 'stranger' (*rahambañe*) in each others' rituals, despite being for the most part kin.

*Doany* cults are one context in which Karembola register their experience of strangers, migration, and unfamiliar values. At the same time, increased proselytisation by the Roman Catholic Church, following the transfer of responsibility for the Androy from French authorities to the Spanish Lazarists and the Spanish branch of the Filles de la Charité, has resulted in a growing incidence of possession by 'priests' (*mompera*) and 'nuns' (*masera*). These 'newly arrived' (*vao niavy*) cults constitute important dimensions of Karembola contemporary existence, and, as elsewhere in Madagascar (Sharp 1995, Lambek 1998; cf. Stoller 1995), are richly evocative of modernity, historicity, and alterity. If I had wished to produce imagery of Karembola postcolonial subjectivity – cosmopolitan, divided, shifting, alienated – that would be easily recognisable to Africanists, then I would have elected to focus on these cults. However, I believe that such a focus would give a partial and misleading view of Karembola subjectivities in so far as the majority of late-twentieth-century Karembola discourses and practices around the person were far more muted plays upon what Karembola themselves define as 'traditional Karembola customs' around kinship, marriage, ancestry, and death.

I am suggesting that over the last two decades the Karembola political and moral imagination has been remarkably inward-looking. It has focused on the vagaries of microclimates that determine the outcome of subsistence production; on struggles for control of wealth and labour with greedy affines and the spirits of the recent dead; and on the fertility of women's bodies, and of cattle bearing the marks of ancestries, that weave an intricate, tangled web of moral obligations between Karembola as they move between hamlets (Middleton 2000, nd). To a great extent, Karembola have invested their sense of social value in highly particularised local landscapes of fields, cattle pens, villages, and megalithic tombs. This is a landscape where historical subjectivity is not primarily present in dramatically new religious cults or bodily disciplines, such as Zionism or Pentecostalism, that offer radically different understandings of fertility and power (see, e.g., Comaroff 1985, Meyer 1999). On the contrary, for the most part Karembola work their experience of coloniality/postcoloniality – what they term the reality of 'living in a foreign land' – into 'Karembola traditions' through finely nuanced symbolic shifts and reversals. History here is internalised within seemingly unchanging mental, social, physical, and symbolic landscapes, where the difference between past and present is continuously translated into subtle contrasts between keeping and breaking ancestral taboos (cf. Middleton 1997). Karembola typically define themselves as people who 'continue to follow ancestral custom but constantly make mistakes' (*be mañarake fombandrazañe feie maro diso zahay*).

Corporeal experiences and bodily disciplines change dramatically when Karembola venture beyond the Karembola. In cities like Tuléar and Antananarivo, men find themselves between the shafts of rickshaws, pulling *vazaha* and their wealth, 'like oxen put to the yoke'. Back home Karembola work some of these experiences into mortuary ritual (Cole and Middleton 2001). For the most part, however, unmechanised subsistence activities, coupled with ritual idioms that celebrate the productivity of kin-based relations, define persons and their relations to land and labour. Thus, while this chapter focuses on the subjectivities of a rural people at the periphery, it is important to recognise, when placing Karembola ethnography in the broader context of African 'postcoloniality', that this is no more a disorientated peasantry overwhelmed by changes beyond its control than it is a literate, Westernised urban world.

It might be thought that I am building an argument for a 'moral economy' in which the effort Karembola invest in 'Anthropology-land' symbols of kinship and marriage imaginarily or effectively opposes or negates the pull of the market economy and the state (cf. Gudeman and Rivera 1990; Hyden 1980, 1983; Taussig 1980). In an essay on a social milieu that is strikingly *dissimilar* to that of the Karembola – diamond-smuggling on the borders of south-western Zaire – de Boeck has criticised such theories for their over-simplistic binary oppositions between the 'rationality' of the capitalist market and an irrational 'economy of affection' (de Boeck 1999:179). My data also point to the need to move beyond simple binary oppositions, though for somewhat different reasons. Rather than read the prominence of incest discourses and practices among Karembola as evidence of the enduring salience of social ties based on kinship, locality, and 'affection', or, alternatively, of their 'breakdown' before global forces of social and economic transformation, I shall argue that they constitute highly imaginative play on contemporary predicaments.

## Contemporary Incest Practices and Discourses

At the time of my fieldwork, Karembola were keenly interested in the question of 'what makes the self live'. In many ways, they were surprisingly optimistic about the possibility of realising a state of bodily and material well-being today. The prayers they addressed to God and the ancestors stated their desires very plainly: 'Give us sons, give us daughters, give us rain, so that our cattle may multiply, our crops flourish, and our wives give birth.' The classic simplicity of the invocation, however, masks a sophisticated and subtle understanding of the processes and powers that 'make the self live' (*mahaveloñe teña*). This understanding turns upon the concept of *asy*, a complex, highly ambivalent notion of sacred efficacy or spiritual essence, with the power for both good and evil, to give life and to kill.[2] This places indeterminacy and precariousness at the very heart of social reproduction. Contemporary incest discourses and practices play to these understandings in many ways.

Karembola have several expressions that can be glossed in English as 'incest'. *Mandika faly* ('to overstep taboos') denotes all kinds of taboo-breaking; one can generally infer from context that the speaker has the transgression of sexual prohibition in mind. Another term, *mila faly teña*, has the more precise meaning: 'to have sexual intercourse with a taboo partner'. The third expression, *manambaly faly,* has an interesting ambiguity since in the Karembola dialect, as in many Malagasy dialects, the term *manambaly* (literally, 'to have a pair' or 'partner') covers both sexual congress and marriage. Thus, the statement 'We Karembola love to practice incest' (*tea'ay ty manambaly faly*, literally, 'to have taboo partners') can also mean 'We love to marry incestuously' (*tea'ay ty manambaly faly*, literally, 'to marry taboo'). This mutability between marriage and incest is indicative of the highly ambiguous ways in which incest practices are seen by Karembola to relate to the project of making the self live.

*The primary value of closure*
Although I translate the above expressions into English as 'incest', Karembola incest prohibitions are not identical to American-English taboos, nor are their understandings of the powers released by taboo-breaking the same.[3] For example, neither sexual liaisons nor marriages between the children of brothers are considered to be incestuous.[4] On the contrary, Karembola praise such unions for their ability to create and conserve *asy*, spiritual force, political power and material wealth. 'Those who marry in one house are blessed', they say repeatedly, 'because there is nothing different, all are of one kind' (*masiñe ty manambaly añate traño raike fa tsy misy raha hafa, karazañe raike avao*). This is a model of the social order in which key reproductive relationships ideally involve identity (Middleton 2000). It is a world from which exchange is abolished, so that 'wealth [in people and cattle] never leaves to go to strangers' (*tsy miakatse mandeha an'ondate*) and 'the polluting substances of outsiders gain no entry to the house' (*tsy militse an traño ty raha tiva boak'an ondate hafa*). In Lévi-Strauss's words, this is 'a world in which one might *keep to oneself*' (Lévi-Strauss 1969 [1949]:497). The perceived dangers of cultural plurality are precluded because 'people of one house are like-minded' (*ondate traño raike miray hevitse*). Moreover, to marry in the house is to inhabit a world where 'nothing changes' (*tsy miova*), where what people are, and what they do, is fixed *ab origio* rather than created by historical events. Instead of engaging with the world beyond the hamlet, agnates 'return again and again to their primordial root' (*mihere an-pototse, hatrahatra*) (Middleton 2000).

The elaboration of such imagery by a late-twentieth-century people who have experienced both the very dramatic intrusion of colonial power and the constant seepage out of human resources in labour migration inevitably puts one in mind of Bayart's observation that globalisation is accompanied everywhere by *clôture culturelle* (Bayart 1996). To hear Karembola extol the virtues of marrying in the house is a salutory experience since on standard socio-economic measures theirs is probably the most 'deprived' and marginal-ised region of one of the poorest countries in the world. While we imagine Karembola as peripheral to progress, development and modernity, they portray those who marry among brothers as being at the centre of a veritable *asy* powerhouse generating purity, fertility and wealth. It is as if all that were needed to maintain their world in perpetual regenerative cycles was contained within one tiny timber house.

It is very important to appreciate that this seeming fantasy of a world without difference does not exist only as an ideal which at best is created only temporarily in the context of ritual. Examples of unions between patrilateral parallel cousins were to be found in almost every hamlet. Everywhere I went in the Karembola, people pointed to 'brother–sister' couples by way of introducing themselves. In effect, Karembola seek actively to constitute the primary value of closure as an embodied subjectivity. The emphasis is on demonstrating and experiencing consubstantiality – 'brotherhood' (*firahalahiae*) – through bodily practices in the here-and-now. 'Brothers' and 'sisters' are said to acknowledge the ancestors they share in common, and their mutual rights and obligations, by 'eating one another' in the act of sexual intercourse as well as by 'sharing water and food'. This is an intensely emotional subjectivity, in which people feel keenly whether they are recognised, esteemed and cared for by others through everyday practices around sex and food. 'We belong to one another', Karembola say of close agnates. 'We are members of one another; we participate in each other's moral and bodily being.' In fact, the more Karembola talked about 'brother–sister' marriages, the more I was put in mind of the relational self that has been typically attributed to the ontologies, cosmologies and psychologies of African peoples – that is to say, a self 'infused with the presence of others, both human and nonhuman' (Piot 1999:19), where bodily being is the existential ground of a self enmeshed in a web of multiple influences (see Jean Comaroff 1980:644; Jackson 1982:22–3; Jackson and Karp 1990; Riesman 1986). The relational self, and its place in the processes by which Karembola 'make themselves live', figure centrally in Karembola incest discourses and practices.

### Can we ever know?

Soarano was no more than twenty years old, and in the final days of her second full-term pregnancy, when she haemorrhaged to death. Over the hours as she lay dying, the baby dead in her womb, her husband's people consulted several diviners in quick succession as to the cause. The first, a man possessed by *doany* (the spirit of dead Sakalava kings), said that Soarano had committed incest but did not reveal her tabooed partner's name. Soarano's affines had therefore pressed her to disclose the man's identity so that the requisite sacrifice could be performed. 'Speak out! Speak out!', they cried. 'It's a taboo that has already been removed, back home among us,' the dying woman had protested. 'It probably was a very big taboo,' an elderly woman commented, 'considering that the diviner still sees it. They undoubtedly did try to lift it back in her village but it has proved too strong.' Another diviner, calling upon *kokolampo*, nature spirits local to the Karembola region, confirmed that 'a very difficult taboo had been broken' but again did not specify.

It should be noted that, despite the allegedly high incidence of culturally defined incestuous activity, Karembola are unequivocal about forbidden categories of kin. While 'brothers' and 'sisters' are ideal sexual and marriage partners, intergenerational unions – between 'children' (*anake*) and 'mothers' (*rene*) or 'fathers' (*rae*), and between 'grandparents' (*raza*) and 'grandchildren' (*zafe*) – are taboo (*faly*). Thus, when Karembola said that 'a very difficult taboo had been broken', this implied that Soarano had slept with a 'father' or a 'son' (perhaps a father's brother or a brother's son). Informants were also agreed that taboo breaking has harmful, even fatal, consequences. 'Those who commit incest see no children, no cattle, no harvests. They fall sick and even die. Everything comes to nought.' For Karembola, the consequences of incest are broader and more generalised than among the Bara, where incest causes infertility in the couple or in their offspring (Huntington 1978). As Karembola see it, incest creates a form of 'pollution' (*handra*) or 'moral blame' (*hakeo be*) that attacks every form of fertility, bringing misfortune (*haoreañe*) to people, crops and herds. Again, the self 'infused with the presence of others, both human and nonhuman' (Piot 1999:19) is evident, a self upon which other people, spirits and natural phenomena continuously impinge. Thus, the consequences of breaking incest prohibitions do not afflict only the couple responsible. Stressing the mutual entanglement of people, Karembola insist that the 'more serious transgressions annihilate ancestries' (*faly loza mandany raza*).[5] Indeed, I have often heard Karembola blame their collective passion for incest for the hardship and poverty they suffer as a people, and particularly the droughts that have afflicted their land over recent decades. 'We suffer because this land is filthy with fathers and mothers seeking children' (*mijaly zahay fa maloto tane toy ama ty rae, ty rene mila ty ana'e*).

Yet Maraze had indicated that, despite the dangers, Karembola love to practise incest. Marrying incestuously, one man explained, was safer than marrying strangers since 'by marrying in the hamlet one can be certain of taking from a good land' (*militse an-tanañe, mangalake amy ty tane soa*). 'One knows that there is no blemish, and that the union will turn out well' (*tsy misy handra'e; ho vaño avao*). 'By marrying kin, even if [they are] forbidden', explained another, 'descendants are not lost' (*manambalia an-dongo, kanefa faly, tsy motso teranake*). In effect, all the reasons Karembola give for 'marrying in the house' become reasons for incestuously endogamous unions.

Nor, according to Karembola, is this a particularly modern phenomenon, since the very same motives also drew the ancestors to break their own taboos. Fortunately, the ancestors also instituted sacrifices that (in theory) made it possible to have safe sex with forbidden categories of kin and to marry incestuously. 'Ndriañanahare [God] regrets it when taboos are broken; but once there is blood it no longer matters; there is no moral blame, no harm, because the cattle make it good.'[6]

For Karembola, then, the morality of incest is highly ambiguous. It is not, as among the Merina of the Highlands of Madagascar, the 'conceptual antithesis to kinship', 'the ultimate wrong' while kinship is the ultimate right (Bloch 1971:67). Rather, like other forms of taboo breaking, incestuous activity releases a fearsome power (*asy*) that can be turned by sacrifice to good or bad. Incest can easily render cattle sterile, cause women to bear 'creatures' (*biby*), harvests to fail, and people to die; but, if handled well, it can make people *masiñe* ('blessed', 'efficacious', 'fertile'). Its power lies in its essential indeterminacy.[7] Taboos make things *masiñe* but so too can breaking them. The very boundary between morality and immorality is permeable in this cosmology, as when ancestors turn incest into marriage, and moral blame into blessing. Consequently, Karembola are never certain of how incestuous practices relate to their primary project of sustaining the self in life. They cannot predict whether such practice will conserve *asy* or disperse it, enhance vitality or make people more vulnerable. Soarano's incestuous coupling with a 'son' or a 'father' had proved disastrous, but, if the sacrifice had been effective, their union might have been holy instead. The essence of incest, as Karembola perceive it, is that it involves incalculable risks.

In so far as taboo breaking is conceptualised as intrinsic to 'Karembola custom' (*fomba Karembola*) because the ancestors also broke taboos, the problem, as Karembola see it, is less that people today commit incest. It is more that they are unable to handle the power that taboo breaking releases. The ancestors knew how to master these powers to their advantage. Today, however, 'the great men are either dead or gone abroad, and only children remain'. 'Children', by definition, lack the moral power, the wisdom and the ritual knowledge to be able to transform moral blame into blessing. 'They commit incest indiscriminately, and then hope to make amends by sacrificing a goat! This saddens Ndriañanahare and the ancestors, and causes drought.'[8] 'People nowadays are unable to follow ancestral customs because they live in a foreign land.' For instance, breaking the 'great taboos' (*faly be*) is said to require the sacrifice of one or more cattle at the clan altar (*hazomanga lava*); but this is no longer possible because the altars have fallen, and Karembola today 'just sacrifice at the house' (Middleton 1997).

It is clear that ritual divinations play a key role in mapping incest, and the particular readings of social experience incest entails, onto the (often dramatic) immediacies of bodily experience (cf. Csordas 1990). The blood ebbing from Soarano's body, when it ought to have created life, had put the diviners in mind of deadly, incestuous couplings. It made known both her singular, personal history and her relations with multiple others, living and ancestors alike. Yet people did not agree as to the meaning of this particular observable bodily experience. Its moral and social significance was open to provisional and contestable readings. Keen to refute the charge of incest, Soarano's kin suggested that murder (sorcery) by her affines was to blame for her death. With the spirits' reluctance to name names, compounded by Soarano's refusal to confess her taboo partner's identity before she died,[9] rumours and suspicions were rife.

From this perspective, the self 'infused with the presence of others' is a source of great uncertainty. As Whyte argues for Bunyole, Uganda (1997: 32, 33, 230), it is an explanatory idiom which problematises social relations. Uncertainties as to bodies are also uncertainties about the interconnectedness of people and their agencies. While I do not think that Karembola incest discourses paint as dark a picture of personhood (malicious, treacherous, evil) and of community life as do witchcraft discourses in some African societies, they do convey a sense of the essential opacity of the causes of suffering, misfortune and affliction. Behind the very simple 'rules' of sexual prohibition Karembola drummed upon my legs, their imagination was taken with the essential 'open-endedness' of social knowledge and human existence past, present and future (cf. Lambek 1993:385), and with their own vulnerability and inability to master the powers at play. Undoubtedly the most common response to the various explanations offered for Soarano's death among Karembola not directly involved was 'Perhaps. Who's to know?' (*Asa. Fanta teña vao?*). The understandings of intersubjective experience that are constructed in incest discourses and practices are always ambiguous and incomplete.

*The ambiguity of closure*
An alleged case of incest between an actual brother and sister a few months later revealed just how uncertain the articulation of incestuous or legitimate, fruitful or deadly unions is. I do not know whether the pair had actually slept together, nor am I clear how often diviners explain affliction in this way. I should also like to underscore how very shocked people were. 'Death is the only outcome of such a serious delict,' I was told repeatedly, 'cattle can never make it good.'[10] Already experience had confirmed their accursed condition: one sibling had died, and other family members were sick.

Another informant used no uncertain language to describe his sense of horror at what had happened: 'cattle had suckled swine'. And yet it could be argued that the diviner had done no more than draw upon everyday bodily experiences of sickness and mortality to conjure up the reality of a world based on absolute intimacy and total closure, a social order in which all actors 'stem from one house' (*hirik-an traño raike*).

The ease with which the fertile proximity of brother–sister unions slips into the mega-infertility of actual brother–sister couplings – the epitome of closure – underscores the essential mutability of *asy*, the concept that informs Karembola understandings of the person and his/her agency in the world. It also reveals closure, solidarity and self-generation to be ambiguous ideals. In fact, despite their avowed fear of incorporating 'things from the exterior, the substance of others' (*raha hirik'ambalike, raha tsy an-teña*), and their reluctance to share with outsiders (*tsy mizarazara am'ondate hafa*), Karembola know that fusions with 'strangers' beyond the hamlet can prove highly fertile, generating wealth and 'many kin', thereby creating 'persons of worth'. Indeed, the local ritual economy is organised around encounters of *mpirahambañe* (strangers) linked by 'gifts' of women, and therefore depends upon people marrying out. It would not exist if people truly 'stayed in the house' (Middleton nd). The unknown element makes *rahambañe* marriages difficult, even dangerous, but Karembola constantly contract such unions knowing that stranger allies can be a source of fertility and potency. A desire for 'closure' and 'stasis' coexists with a desire for movement and communication through the creation and renewal of exterior links.

I am suggesting that Karembola incest discourses and practices play in a profoundly ambiguous way on the articulation of 'open' and 'closed' societies, of people 'owned' and 'rooted' in ancestries and people who move and change, and of fertile and infertile fusions of the other and the self. The interplay of competing models of social resources and of strategies for their deployment is open-ended because Karembola can never be certain how best to go about securing life. Are talents (cattle, people) best hidden 'within houses' and kept from 'strangers', or are Karembola more likely to 'prosper' (*manjary*) if their bodies and minds are turned outwards and put to work in exchanges with 'the world beyond'? Each option carries both difficulties and attractions, and the outcome is impossible to predict.

For the most part, this uncertain play on fertile and infertile fusions of the self and other is carried out by Karembola among and for themselves. As I noted, 'strangers' (*rahambañe*) in Karembola rituals are more often than not distant kin. However, it also lends itself to the expression of broader experience. For instance, fears of sharing vital substance (*asy*) with strangers resonate powerfully with the sense Karembola feel of having lost so many kin to other parts of Madagascar as migrant labour. Marrying in the house, by contrast, reasserts the rootedness of people and their labour in primordial identities. Yet the values ascribed to contrasting modes of reproduction are constantly inverted. For if incest practices and discourses metaphorically express the generative possibilities of remaining in familiar landscapes known intimately, they also emphasise the dangers of a world seemingly turned in on itself. In this case, Karembola may better flourish by engaging with strangers in unfamiliar modes of production and reproduction far away in Tuléar or Mahajanga, just as they do in exchange relationships closer at hand. Incest discourses and practices disclose a multi-faceted vulnerability, in which human vitality can be either threatened or enhanced from both within and without.

These ambiguities make it difficult to see the effort Karembola invest in 'Anthropology-land' symbols of kinship simply as restating the enduring value of social solidarities based on kinship and 'affection' in the face of global and national forces of transformation. To a certain extent, incest discourses and practices are a 'relocalising' strategy, one of many in Madagascar that draw moral persons and wealth back into local networks, reanchoring them in local landscapes, often through rituals around ancestors focused commonly, though not only, on the symbolic and actual construction of tombs and ancestral lands (see, e.g., Bloch 1971, Cole 1998, Feeley-Harnik 1991, Middleton 1999, Raison-Jourde 1983). Far from being the 'negation' of kinship, Karembola incest discourses and practices emphasise the indebtedness between people. They speak of a surfeit of kinship rather than its decline.

On the other hand, it could also be argued that these discourses are relatively insignificant in revaluing local social relations and commitments because Karembola are in any case both deeply dependent upon one another and peripheral to state power and market economy. Moreover, analysis needs to consider the significance of social and moral subjectivities felt not simply as kinship but more specifically as incest. While the incessant cases of incest point up the continued salience of relatedness based upon ancestors, they do not ascribe to this kind of relatedness a wholly positive value in socially reproductive processes today. On the contrary, Karembola incest discourses articulate highly ambivalent and unstable cultural understandings of the relative value of local and external sources of fertility, power and social worth. The 'love agnates bear for one another' may create unparalleled *asy*, 'bringing pleasure to God's eyes' as they accomplish the seemingly impossible feat of 'chewing the food in the other's mouth'. But this intimacy of 'same substance' and 'like mindedness' can just as easily annihilate. 'Holding to the self in perpetuity', 'seeking nothing different', may prove empowering, a trick learned from the ancestors that Karembola manage to pull off against all odds in modern times, enabling Maraze to declare with pride, amusement and satisfaction that 'we Karembola love to practise incest'. Staying in the house can make Karembola *masiñe* ('efficacious', 'powerful'), as indeed they are in their own domain, given the virtually absent state. But primordial attachments often end in moral blame and pollution, becoming yet another factor Karembola invoke to explain their poverty and impotency, the high rates of bovine and human mortality, both cause and consequence of the demise of great men, yet another metaphor for 'living in foreign land'.[11]

## Moral Communities

One day seven men appeared in our village with a plaint against Iavimasy. They accused him of 'stepping across incest prohibitions' (*mandika faly*) by having sex with two of their kinswomen. At first I was puzzled by the reference to 'incest' because, as far as I knew, Iavimasy was related to neither woman. It was explained that the women were taboo to one another (*mpifaly*) because they belong to different generations, and that by sleeping first with one and then with the other, Iavimasy had made 'mother' and 'child' commit incest. This, I learn, is not uncommon. Third parties 'regularly step across taboos' (*mandika faly sanandro*, literally, each day), connecting 'fathers', 'mothers' and 'children' incestuously. A few months previously, a woman had made Iavimasy and his mother's brother commit incest by having sex with them both (at different times). A diviner had discovered the *faly* (the broken taboo) when the mother's brother fell sick.

It will be clear that, on account of the multiple ways incest can happen, as well as the comprehensive degree to which Karembola calculate taboos, incest, rather like witchcraft in many African societies (Geschiere 1999; Parkin 1986:216; Shaw 1997), is omnipresent in social relations, waiting to be made known. The endless movement of women between hamlets over two centuries has created a milieu in which all Karembola 'share and share ancestors' (*mizarazara razañe*). This thick web of connectedness, which Karembola portray by placing both hands together, all ten fingers interlaced, makes the likelihood of committing incest ineradicable from the condition of being Karembola. Even when a Karembola man goes to Beloha market, and spends five minutes having sex with a seeming stranger behind a bush, he cannot shed the sedimented weight of Karembola history. He may be unaware of the taboos that are broken in that fleeting moment or he may know but seek to hide them; but diviners – practising geomancy (*sikily*), or consulting local *kokolampo* or the *doany* spirits of Sakalava monarchs, who show remarkable familiarity with Karembola taboos and genealogies[12] – 'always see'.

As I noted, divinatory practices play a key role in making incest a pervasive feature of everyday personal and social experience in the Karembola on account of the regularity with which they interpret instances of bodily affliction and general misfortune in terms of incest.[13] What is particularly striking is the way ritual divinations create incest as a recurring feature of social relationships between 'strangers' as much as between close kin. The result is to author an extreme type of relational personhood in which being Karembola means being enmeshed in commitments, constraints and influences that extend far beyond known relatives, those upon whom one depends closely and with whom one is directly involved. Local incest discourses and practices produce and reproduce a subjectivity in which the boundaries between the self and the other are so permeable that incest in some form or another becomes a possibility between just about everyone who might belong to this imagined Karembola community.

Viewed as historical practice, these endless divinations of incest express a curious relation to the past. On the one hand, they enact the impossibility of ever reckoning, let alone dismantling or disempowering, the multiple relatedness between Karembola that stems from the past.[14] Indeed, these latent presences – the 'unknown taboos' continuously surfacing in multiple incidents of incest – inscribe the past on people who have not experienced it. Focused on ancestors, this appears to be an inward- and backward-looking account of contemporary Karembola personhood. But discourse on incest suddenly shifts, attributing its *ever-increasing* incidence to modernity or what Karembola define as 'living in a foreign land'. Thus, Soarano's body not only embodied her singular, personal history as well as her relations with multiple others. It also stood for the social body in which Karembola saw enacted a broader malaise. Each particular case of incest triggers a more general narrative of moral decline and cultural impoverishment, in which Karembola describe how difficult it is for them to respect taboos because 'foreigners own the land today' or 'because we've been seized by foreigners', or even 'become foreigners ourselves'.

These discourses also ascribe a double value to kinship (*filongoa*). On the one hand, even strangers come through incest divination to be participants in a single moral community. Yet these practices also elaborate the dangers inherent in a surfeit of intimate, potentially incestuous, connections. A 'love for incest' epitomises the mutual entanglement that makes Karembola one people but also drains their wealth. Local identities and practices based on ancestral connections may contest legal-bureaucratic inscription and political-economic valuation (Feeley-Harnik 1991); but this world saturated with kinship also puts Karembola at risk. Not only can the living never *know* all the taboos the past has created between people. There is always the possibility that a sacrifice may fail to atone for a breach, perhaps because the animal was the wrong sex, size or colour, or because too few were killed; or because the sacrifice was made at the house; or because the couple had broken other as yet 'unseen' taboos. The dying woman had insisted that 'the taboo had been dealt with' (*fa efa*, literally 'completed') but, as one informant commented sardonically, 'clearly, one never can be sure'. In this way, incest discourses and practices simultaneously enact and challenge the appropriateness of kinship and local forms of community as the basis for generative power in Karembola life cycles today.

## The Micropolitics of Incest

At first sight, Karembola incest discourses and practices appear defiantly 'traditional' in that they are discourses on identities inscribed in people from the past. Rather than invoking a personhood which is created in ongoing practice (cf. Astuti 1995), they are about people who are forbidden to one another because of ancestors. Yet the pre-eminence of primordial identities in Karembola self-depiction is also deceptive. For as Karembola are shuffled between generations in the course of incestuous unions, drawing on ancestral power through sacrifice to turn classificatory 'mothers', 'fathers', and 'children' into 'brother–sister' pairs, they also have the capacity to 'become' (*manjary*) other than what they were by birth.

Even so, it is curious that these incest discourses and practices make no explicit reference to the profound transformations of social identity which have been experienced by the 'many [Karembola] gone to the north'. Instead they focus obsessively on the possibilities of detachability and negotiability among those who remain behind. The ceaseless incestuous activity that permeates everyday existence in the Karembola has an intense dynamic; but its 'territorial' range is extremely limited, and the endlessly shifting identities it deals in are visible only to those close by. This is truly running on the spot.

Owing to the link Karembola draw between authority and generation, however, these transformations, seemingly minuscule from a global perspective, have very important status implications for individuals in local contexts. In lifting a taboo in order to marry a 'daughter', for instance, a man is said to 'decline in rank' (*mifotsake ambane*, literally 'fall below') *vis-à-vis* the woman's agnates. This is because men, who would be his 'sons' and 'brothers', become his 'brothers' and 'fathers' respectively. Conversely, a man who marries a 'mother' is said to climb in status.[15] Karembola use terms like 'status climbing' and 'status loss' to describe these realignments because idioms drawn from kinship and marriage to a large extent define identities and constitute local forms of power relations in the Karembola today. Being a 'father' rather than a 'son' or 'brother' matters greatly to individual Karembola men because it can mean the difference between speaking first in oratory or having to listen, or between commanding another's labour or being commanded by them. Ahistorical from the world system perspective, these minutiae of interpersonal relationships are experienced as deeply historical from the perspective of individual biographies.

For Karembola, then, managing incest is a highly political activity, which is central to the processes that create and undo big men (*ondate be*). To 'own a kin group free of incest pollution' (*manam-poko tsy misy handra*) is to show oneself wise and upstanding, with the spiritual power to create and maintain fertility in people, cattle pens and fields. This is a milieu where people gamble their claims to authority upon the highly precarious margin between incestuous, deadly unions and blessed, fertile ones. Moreover, the management of incest practices and discourses is closely linked to the politics of marriage alliances: men and women gain strategic advantages by making otherwise taboo unions possible or by thwarting another's ambition by insisting that a sacrifice has failed to removed the taboo.

For this reason Karembola compete to control the techniques that produce and reproduce knowledge of bodily and moral conditions, and explain sickness, abnormality, and mortality in people and their herds. In addition to the divinatory practices already mentioned, individuals employ an extensive repertoire of ordeals, oaths and oracles to coerce other Karembola into revealing incestuous activity or to refute accusations of incest which have been levelled at themselves. Karembola explained how they found the possibility that people might be concealing broken taboos frightening because, if unremedied, this can cause them, too, to fall sick or die. However, they also took pleasure in describing the cunning and acumen that managing incest involves. It is about knowing when to allege incest and to demand an atonement sacrifice, and when to remain silent. It is about knowing how to tell the oral histories (*lily*), or perhaps the 'lies' (*vande*), that 'remember' the multiple connections between people and define particular relationships as incestuous or not. It means judging when to accept blame and acknowledge ancestral commitments by providing cattle for a sacrifice, and when to be selfish and risk a serious rift with kin by refusing to 'cough up'. Incest, Karembola say, calls for Karembola to *mahay politike* ('to know how to be political'), an expression that is used throughout Madagascar to refer to the wily ways of city politicians.[16]

This politics of incest has a rather contradictory dynamic. In contrast to many African societies (see, for example, Cruise O'Brien 1996), the older generation of Karembola men retains considerable authority over women and younger men. Their ability to manipulate incest discourses and practices in particular is enhanced by their claims to superior command of genealogy, the knowledge that is precious in this political economy.[17] However, while sacrifice is supposed to transform incestuous 'parent–child' unions into proper, blessed unions, Karembola also worry at the breakdown in authority and respect between generations such negotiability implies. And indeed the politics of incest is centrifugal to the extent that never-ending accusations and counter-accusations fuel indeterminate contests for power between intensely competitive but essentially equal groups. In bemoaning their inability as 'children' to manage incest – tame its destructive aspects and harness its rewards – Karembola reveal their inability as a relatively devolved people to manage social power to cumulative effect.

Karembola incest discourses and practices also appear to relate contrarily to broader trends in local political and kinship organisation over the last half century. Incestuous activity seems to be associated partly with the contraction of personal horizons: agnates 'seek one another' to ever closer degrees until, in case of actual sibling incest, intimacy finally collapses on itself. But incest is also expansive, bridging ever increasing social distance by drawing 'strangers' into incestuous intimacy. Socially expansive and implosively intimate, these discourses and practices register contradictory notions of the self. Thus, incestuously endogamous unions can be seen as reaffirming enduring ties between close agnates in the face of the decline of cult practices that once sustained agnatic identities. But equally, as smaller, more autonomous communities have become more viable, incest discourses and practices can be seen as counteracting the declining importance of extended political ties by creating social bonds of *filongoa* (relatedness, cognatic kinship) to span an 'imagined Karembola community'.

I cannot in this chapter explore in greater detail how the politics of incest relate to power struggles between affines, to the ongoing construction of deeply parochial landscapes of small hamlets and monumental tombs, or to the local cultural rhetoric of ancestry and rank (see Middleton nd). The point I wish to make here is that what dominates the Karembola postcolonial imagination *is* the micropolitics of interpersonal relationships, seemingly 'old-fashioned', if not exactly 'ahistorical', questions of responsibility and social control. Incest permeates relations within and between Karembola villages, but it seldom, if ever, colours their interactions with representatives of the state, urban elites, or newly emergent entrepreneurs. Indeed, for want of education and money, rural Karembola have comparatively few such links.

## Making the Self Live

On the surface, Karembola appear to entertain few doubts as to which kind of cultural practice is most likely to promote well-being and prosperity. 'Foreign ways kill', they insist, 'but ancestral custom makes the self live.'[18] Yet it is clear that the living also experience taboos embodying the past as a burden (see also Cole 1998; Feeley-Harnik 1991). The risks attached to incestuous practice give graphic expression to the dangers of ancestral regeneration for people who live in a 'foreign land'. Incest may make the past ever present, but it also registers a deep uncertainty as to whether past cultural practice remains socially productive today. Yet Maraze's mischievous laughter as she declared that 'we Karembola love to marry in tabooed relationships', perhaps partly in defiance of *vazaha* custom (see below), suggests that taboo breaking also celebrates the subversive vibrancy of a people who have survived in modern Madagascar with a remarkable degree of cultural and political autonomy and who do largely manage to make themselves live in a 'foreign land' by 'following ancestral custom, if imperfectly' (see Middleton 1997).

It is tempting to trace out this paradoxical, shifting take on contemporary predicaments in the way Karembola invoke incest to explain poverty, famine and drought. As I noted, the shortage of water, the very source of fertility and life, is frequently blamed on incest. Linking the material world to a moral economy of persons, Karembola explain that the rain does not fall, and ground springs have dried up, because of all the broken taboos. Yet it could be argued that for almost 70 years the aridity of the Karembola (= incestuous activity?) has been chief guarantor of its people's cultural and political autonomy. 'What brings you to this thirsty land?' Karembola ask of strangers who venture there.

Unable to resolve the tension between taboo breaking and taboo keeping in their own lives, Karembola can only puzzle at *vazaha* who 'have no taboos yet do not marry kin' (*tsy manam-paly, kanefa tsy manambaly longo*). They wonder whether this paradox is somehow linked to the special knowledge and magical powers *vazaha* possess, enabling them to generate extraordinary power and wealth. They weary of their efforts to penetrate the mystery of the difference between Karembola and *vazaha*, however. For if the (alleged) increased incidence of unregulated incest indicates that Karembola are forgetting ancestral custom, the fact that taboo breaking still causes moral blame shows that Karembola can never really hope to become *vazaha*, that is, 'people without taboos', or 'people with wealth'. Or perhaps even non-relational selves.

If Karembola incest discourses today address the kinds of arguments around similarity and difference between Europeans and Africans, and their innate capacity for transformation, that characterised many colonial discourses on labour, development and capitalism (see, for example, Comaroff and Comaroff 1992: 391), so too the *ambiguities* in Karembola incest discourses find an echo in *vazaha* discourses. Close kin endogamy, often confused with incest, was an important theme of colonial discourses on Madagascar (see Thomas 1996: 14–16, 161). In colonial ethnology, it was frequently interpreted as evidence of cultural insularity, of minds, societies and economies 'closed' to penetration by the modern state and national economy (see, for example, Frère 1958). Yet, in the case of the Deep South, these discourses also associated closure with wealth and fertility in the shape of many cattle and people whose potential in the market as labour and commodities remained unrealised. Simultaneously productive and unproductive, there is a profound ambiguity in how *vazaha* have imagined the Deep South. Even today, a conviction persists among other Malagasy peoples that this is a land not simply of buried water but also of buried gold, of people who survive its aridity on account of their magical skills and mystical powers, a people who mask an immense wealth in (apparently invisible) cattle by dressing in loincloths and sandals of cattle hide. Outsiders have never been able to decide whether the Deep South is resource-rich or resource-poor (Middleton 1999).

Contemporary narratives around development and modernity continue to forge connections with discourses on incest. As Feeley-Harnik notes with reference to Sakalava–Merina conflicts, marked regional differences in incest categories, as well as ambiguities of opinion, are highly controversial in contemporary Madagascar, being used to characterise or condemn whole people and regions as the outcome of legitimate or incestuous, fruitful or deadly unions (Feeley-Harnik 1991:84–8, 172–6; 1997:168). In the Karembola case, there is an interesting convergence between emic and etic discourses since the attribution of illegitimate couplings as a practice typical of southern Malagasy peoples features in *both* Karembola *and* non-Karembola narratives.

## Conclusion: Incest and Postcoloniality

I began this chapter by asking how the intense, often explosively emotional, concern with the nature of moral and personal relatedness that has dominated the late-twentieth-century Karembola imagination relates, if at all, to broader historical questions of moral and political economy. I suggested that incest is a 'master symbol' for Karembola subjectivity, not because it opposes local cultural values of solidarity and sharing in a clear-cut way to contrasting modes of reproduction, or, alternatively, because it indicates the breakdown of 'traditional' behavioural codes; rather, the power of Karembola incest discourses and practices as a way of imagining contemporary predicaments lies in the indeterminate value they assign to kinship. The value controversies they express are incapable of final resolution because Karembola can never decide how best to make themselves live. Experience shows that the outcome of any option is unpredictable. Ancestral custom can render the tabooed union fertile, but equally the 'unknown', 'unseen' taboo deriving from ancestral times can render the apparently fertile union sterile.

As I indicated, Karembola contemporary predicaments are highly uneven, neither unremittingly good nor uniformly bad. Karembola are neither as impotent as they claim to be nor as powerful as they would like. The indeterminate potentialities of incest discourses and practices metaphorically express such broader paradoxes. They speak to the experience of farmers and herders exposed to the contingent events of a dryland ecology, whose diet in a good year is superior to that of many inhabitants of Madagascar's cities but who in a bad year starve. They resonate with the uncertainties posed by migration: is it safer to 'stay put in an arid land', eating 'ancestral foods' and 'people of known provenance', or might a Karembola be more likely to 'see wealth' by venturing further afield? Registering the essential arbitrariness of all power, they also encapsulate the contradictions in Karembola historical experience: of colonising agents so extraordinarily powerful that they changed the landscape overnight, yet of states so weak that Karembola have effectively remained 'lords in their own domain'. Potentially fertile or infertile, polluting or purifying, its infinite, highly contingent possibilities lend themselves to a fluid, imaginative play on the range of options Karembola have of making themselves live.

Reflecting on ethnography at the end of an era, Gupta and Ferguson (1997:5) recommend an approach that, 'rather than opposing autonomous local cultures to a homogenizing movement of cultural globalization', seeks 'to trace the ways in which dominant cultural forms may be picked up and used – and significantly transformed – in the midst of the field of power relations that links localities to wider worlds'. The emphasis, they urge, should be 'on the complex and sometimes ironic political processes through which cultural forms are imposed, invented, reworked, and transformed'.

Irony of this kind is clearly evident in the *doany* cults. It also constitutes a major strand in Karembola mortuary ritual, most notably in the monumental tomb building where the hard physical labour men undertake for the recent dead parodies the types of work Karembola, 'who, like cattle, do not know paper', perform for *vazaha* in the national economy (Cole and Middleton 2001). Practices and discourses around incest also reflect upon power relations that link Karembola localities to wider worlds. Just as kin stand symbolically for strangers in Karembola rituals, so the struggle between the house and paths beyond obliquely encodes the contrasting generative possibilities offered by migration and engagement with national economy over stasis, by cultural plurality over homogeneity, by fixed identities over fluidity. Karembola themselves explicitly make the connection whenever they conjoin the issue of incest to broader narratives of modernity, political impotence and cultural decline.

However, while contemporary incest discourses and practices do incorporate ever-widening referents, it would be wrong to see these as their essence. As I have said, the endless stream of incest histories that flowed through my notebooks construed and clarified for Karembola their densely textured, inward looking subjectivities. I should not care to argue that the main reason for anthropologists to become interested in incest in the Karembola context is on account of its enigmatic capacities for fusing the local and global and modernity's dilemmas (see, for example, Geschiere 1999:216). Karembola incest discourses locate sickness, poverty and failure in localised landscapes of individuals caught in intricate webs of mutual influence, and only secondarily in the wider frame. The relationship between the local and the global is occasional and metaphorical rather than direct and metonymical.[19]

Throughout this chapter, I have taken it for granted that I have been describing 'postcolonial' subjectivity/subjectivities. Yet in many ways it could be said that Karembola do not inhabit that imaginative space we call the 'postcolony'. Certainly, Karembola communities have a very different 'feel' than that evoked by Mbembe in his seminal essay on the 'postcolony' (Mbembe 1992). Earlier I indicated some structural reasons why this is so. While I do not wish to make light of the poverty, drought and famines Karembola have experienced, or the local incidence of conflict and dissent, the fact is that 'postcolonial' Karembola have not lived through anything comparable to that experienced by many other Africans in recent decades (see, for example, Malkki 1995; Werbner 1991). As in a Jane Austen novel, civil war, ethnic violence, state political terror, genocide, obscene disparities of wealth and even, for the most part, politicians, are all noises off. Or, as Karembola say, with no trace of irony, 'there's no disturbance here' (*tsy misy tabataba ty eto*).

Yet it is a question of emphasis. Deceptively 'traditional' symbols of sexual taboos and marriage alliance are entangled with and take on significance in relation to wider forces. Highly personal subjectivites concerned with moral rights and duties, and with intimate bonds between individuals, do incorporate political consciousness. One thinks of Mbembe's observation: 'the post-colony is made up not of one single "public space" but of several, each having its own separate logic yet nonetheless liable to be entangled with other logics when operating in certain specific contexts' (Mbembe 1992:4). What the present case study underscores is the need to recognise that this 'entanglement of logics' works out in very different ways in specific contexts. As Werbner notes, postcolonial African discourses, experiences and strategies vary immensely. Highly specific and locally created forces preconfigure personal knowledge and understandings, and historically specific local languages, rich in cultural idioms images and metaphors, put their distinctive imprint upon postcoloniality (Werbner 1996:2–3). As Ortner reminds us, 'Every culture, every subculture, every historical moment constructs its own forms of agency, its own modes of reflecting on the self and the world and of acting simultaneously within and upon what one finds there' (Ortner 1995:186).

So what is the particular character of social subjectivities powerfully felt as incest? What are the specific implications of incest discourses and practices for how people problematise social value, identity and personhood? What local understandings of power, agency and social relationships do these discourses reveal? At first sight, the parallels between them and witch-finding divinations are multiple and suggestive.[20] Like witchcraft, Karembola incest discourses and practices register uncertainty around intimacy and generative processes. 'There is the same confusing mixture of intimacy and bewilderingly wide horizons' (Geschiere 1999:320). Witchcraft and incest also share the same fundamental unknown, indeterminate potentiality, being neither unambiguously good nor evil. Indeed, incest can become a kind of sorcery (*voreke*) since it too 'kills people' (*mamono ondate*), although, unlike some Malagasy peoples (Bloch 1971:67; Feeley-Harnik 1991:174), Karembola do not directly equate the two. This may be because for Karembola incest also has a less clear-cut *opposition* to kinship values than witchcraft. Whereas witches 'eat' others for selfish reasons, becoming the prototype of the nonrelational person who consumes human productive and reproductive potential (Shaw 1997:3; cf. Apter 1993:118; Auslander 1993:178; Bastian 1993:138–9), in Karembola constructs of the prototypical relational person, kin are urged to 'eat one another' in endogamous, potentially incestuous unions which please the ancestors.

If modern witchcraft discourses and practices in many parts of Africa relate strongly to unequal access to *new* emergent forms and sources of power and wealth (Geschiere 1999:212; cf. Apter 1993; Auslander 1993; Matory 1994), Karembola, by contrast, are preoccupied with incest – that is, with the indeterminate nature of procreative processes – because local inequalities of wealth and power rest primarily on the manipulation of seemingly 'traditional' networks of 'gift exchanges' based upon the bodily reproductive powers of people and cattle, rather than upon access to political office, to education, or to new kinds of entrepreneurship. The fertility and infertility of sexual unions dominate the Karembola imagination because Karembola 'cultural projects' are 'unmodern', and social value is conceived as wealth in people and cattle. Managing the difference between deadly and blessed unions drives an intense micropolitics of household, lineage and village because marriage and children are both 'stakes' and matters of deep uncertainty (cf. Whyte 1997). Yet incest discourses and practices clearly also enact the problematic of making oneself live by traditional modes of production and reproduction in 'a foreign land'.[21] If witchcraft proliferates in modern sectors where it addresses the articulation of new forms of wealth with old intimacies (Geschiere 1999:212), Karembola locate their poverty in the surfeit of (unregulated) age-old intimacies that constantly saps their wealth in people and livestock. The multiple, uncertain potentialities of incestuous practice express both the power and centredness that stem from being enmeshed in a deep web of connectedness, and the disadvantage and impotency that stem from peripherality to other social worlds.

I do not know whether incest figured equally prominently in colonial and precolonial Karembola subjectivities or whether substantially different incest discourses have emerged during the last forty years. It seems unlikely, given the political and environmental history of the Karembola region, that uncertainty – the condition Karembola gloss as 'never knowing' (*tsy hae teña*) – is peculiarly (post)modern, the product of or the response to (recent) global processes of social, material and cultural transformation.[22] Not only has the 'power of indeterminate meaning' (Geschiere 1999) long been central to local social and cultural practices (Middleton 2001); but most of the afflictions – aridity, famine, sickness, infertility and high infant mortality, poverty – for which incest today serves as an explanatory idiom are also *de longue durée*. Indeed, Karembola themselves show an interesting ambivalence as to whether these are modern or endemic predicaments. While it is tempting to see late-twentieth-century incest practices and discourses as registering late-twentieth-century moral and political dilemmas, the ancestors, Karembola tell us, also broke taboos as they grappled with comparable ambiguities around authority, reproduction and social control. In short, the 'real peculiarities' of *postcolonial* Karembola subjectivity will be grasped only when colonial and precolonial Karembola subjectivities have been better studied and understood (cf. Ranger 1996).

## Epilogue

For seventy-odd years, the 'play possum' strategy adopted by Karembola has been successful, largely because theirs is a 'thirsty land' where others have had little reason to go. It is a strategy that will require drastic rethinking, however, if Rio Tinto Zinc (RTZ) (in the shape of its subsidiary Canadian QIT, now at Fort Dauphin) casts its search for ilmenite deposits further west. Ecologists, too, are eyeing the 'megadiversity' (Mittermeier 1988) of the Deep South with growing proprietal interest, and ecotourists are passing through the region in ever greater numbers, 'eating lemurs', informants report, 'on the way'. The promotion of this industry by the World Bank and International Monetary Fund (IMF) will require Karembola to renegotiate their relationships to outsiders. AIDS is the third shadow upon the horizon, and one that can be predicted to interact with local incest discourses and practices in particularly powerful ways.[23] Finally, it is very likely that these new experiences of *vazaha* power and money will be mediated in no small part by the evangelical Pentecostalist churches which are growing rapidly all over Madagascar.

## Notes

1 At the time of my fieldwork, many Karembola traced the origins of 'independence' (*fahaleovañe teña*) as a political discourse to concepts and practices which the French had introduced at the time of conquering Madagascar. As they saw it, these 'foreign ways' (*atao vazaha*) had undermined 'ancestral customs' (*fomban-drazañe*) by censoring the very obvious truth that there are primordial differences between kinds of Malagasy people, the noble and the enslaved. This is one of many ways in which Karembola represent the colonial and the postcolonial periods as indistinct.

2 For the comparable Merina concept of *hasina*, see Delivré 1974; Bloch 1986.

3 Whenever I use the term 'incest' in this chapter, I mean those sexual relations that Karembola themselves define as taboo (*faly*).

4 Unlike other Malagasy peoples for whom all close kin unions are considered to be in various degrees incestuous (Bloch 1971:52–4, 57, 58; Huntington 1978; Feeley-Harnik 1991:186–229; Kottak 1980:201; Lavondès 1967:82; Thomas 1996:181), Karembola state very clearly that unions between first and second cousins (other than matrilateral parallel cousins) require no sacrifice because 'there is no taboo'.

5 Karembola use the term *faly* to denote both the taboo and the broken taboo.

6 *Manin'aze Ndriañanahare lehe mañota faly ondate; kanefa le fa misy lio, tsy hañahe; tsy misy handra, tsy misy hakeo fa vita an-añombe*. It should be noted that Karembola distinguish two kinds of sacrifice. The *efe-paly* (from *mañefetse*, 'to separate' or 'to divide', *faly*, 'taboo') simply removes the moral blame, and restores the taboo, when people have committed incest. If the couple commit incest again, another sacrifice is required. By contrast, the more expensive *soroñe fanambaliañe* ('marriage sacrifice') takes away the taboo for good. It enables the couple to marry, thus transforming an accursed union into a fecund, blessed one. Since expense alone differentiates these two kinds of sacrifice, however, Karembola can never be sure that they have performed the appropriate one.

7 The logic behind Karembola incest prohibitions is difficult to grasp, partly because

Karembola understandings of procreation, and particularly of the role of blood in creating human relatedness, are very vague. Incest prohibitions are not based on kinship in any simple sense since marriages between the children of brothers (*anak'mpirahalahy*) are held to be the ideal. Moreover, blood is a fluid that has the potential to couple people in both fertile and infertile ways. References to ancestors dominate the local rhetoric of incest and social reproduction, but they also link and divide people in highly ambiguous ways.

8  Although goats have been herded in the region since at least the seventeenth century, and have the advantage of multiplying rapidly, Karembola insist that they are non-ancestral and polluting, and can never substitute for cattle in the sacrifices to the ancestors and the gods that ensure social reproduction (*tsy avy an'hazomanga ty osy*, 'goats do not come to the prayer-post').

9  I was told that people are ashamed to admit openly to incest. They usually disclose the particulars in a roundabout way, saying 'so-and-so's blanket covered me'.

10  *Ho mate avao fa faly loza, añombe tsy mahavita aze*. At this moment, it became very clear that 'brother–sister' marriages should actually take place *between* houses (that is, between patrilateral parallel cousins) rather than *within* one house. Karembola generally mask this inner boundary on endogamy in a number of ways.

11  Although Karembola say that cases of incest have grown more numerous, and the consequences more difficult to control, they generally insist that the taboos themselves have not changed. In this respect, Karembola incest discourses are less wholeheartedly 'historical' than the Eastern Nuer incest discourses studied by Hutchinson (1985). It is difficult to know whether Karembola perceptions of the unchanging nature of their incest taboos are justified. We lack the rich documentation for earlier periods of Karembola history that Hutchinson is able to draw on for the Nuer in the shape of Evans-Pritchard's ethnography. There seems to be no *a priori* reason to suppose that incest categories, core practices, and the representational forms through which social bodies have been constituted, have altered in recent decades. Hutchinson found that, while Eastern Nuer had been redefining various categories of incest over the previous 50 years, among Western Nuer they had remained close to those described by Evans-Pritchard (Hutchinson 1985:27). The point is that the semantics of contemporary Karembola incest discourses and practices depends upon the putative ahistoricity of 'ancestral' custom imagined as a relatively simple set of timeless, immutable taboos, based on primordial connections, which people today break. This is crucial to the constitution of Karembola identity as a people 'still following ancestral custom but getting it wrong'.

12  It would be interesting to know whether the spirits of Sakalava monarchs divine incest quite so frequently as the cause of sickness and misfortune when 'at home' in north-west Madagascar. Certainly, incest is little mentioned in published accounts of spirit possession there (see, e.g., Sharp 1993; Lambek 1998).

13  At the time of my fieldwork, incest was among the most common explanations given for difficulties with pregnancy, miscarriage, still-birth or birth defects. It also figured often in conversations as a possible cause of death, although Karembola practise few if any burial divinations.

14  Significantly, while East Coast Betsimisaraka think that a single sacrifice can make good multiple transgressions (Jennifer Cole, personal communication), Karembola insist that each fault has to be named and dealt with separately. This reinforces the sense Karembola have of never being able to disentangle the massive skein of intimacies that constituted Karembola personhood 'long before the French arrived'. In contrast to certain African Pentecostalist discourses (see, e.g., Meyer 1999), Karembola incest discourses and practices constitute a subjectivity that denies the possibility of ever breaking with the past.

15  I should like to stress that Karembola obsessions with incestuous activity are very different in tenor to contemporary Western discourses/practices around the sexual abuse of children

by adults (Jean Comaroff 1997, La Fontaine 1998). This is because the alleged incidences of 'parent–child' incest I recorded generally involved young adults of different *genealogical* generations but of similar age. For instance, I began this chapter with a case of 'mother' and 'child' incest. Although they belonged to different generations, in other respects the pair were ideal marriage partners because they were close agnates (FFBD/FBSS) of similar age. Indeed, in many ways it could be argued that the widespread taboo breaking helps to adjust the discrepancies between generation (category) and relative (biological) age that inevitably arise with close kin endogamy. But clearly there is more to Karembola incest discourses and practices than practical reason, as this chapter shows.

16 See, e.g., Cole (1999:116) for similar use of the term *politique* in East Coast Madagascar, and Barthes (1957:140) for francophone Africa.

17 In this respect, Karembola diverge markedly from the Malagasy of the west coast, among whom history is said to be the privilege of royalty, and genealogical knowledge among commoners rarely extends beyond three generations (Astuti 1995:84; Baré 1977:51; Feeley-Harnik 1991:57, 69–88; Lavondès 1967:102).

18 *Mamono ondate fomban-bazaha. Mahaveloñe teña fomban-drazañe.*

19 Englund and Leach (2000) recently complain of 'the extent of ethnographic ignorance in the perspectives organised by modernity's meta-narratives' (p. 226), and are critical of the 'alleged need to "situate" the particular in "wider" contexts' (p. 226). Clearly, I share their caution about imposing metropolitan narratives on lived experience without careful empirical enquiry into how people themselves feel and think about their lives. However, I do not wholly share their affirmation of the 'subject's authority in determining the contexts of their beliefs and practices' because I have indicated very particular structural reasons that help explain why Karembola have been able to live in 'Anthropology-land' and construct the kind of subjectivities they have. Moreover, while I share Englund and Leach's wariness regarding unwarranted shifts in analytical scales (see Gable 1995), I do think that the highly localised and inward-looking nature of Karembola incest discourses and practices are usefully and indeed necessarily examined in the context of, and perhaps even partly read as *countering*, broader histories of the region, particularly the experience of labour migration.

20 It would be wrong of me to suggest that contemporary Karembola subjectivities focus on 'incest' to the exclusion of witchcraft. Witchcraft accusations and rebuttals are in fact very common. But, with the exception of *anciens combattants* (World War II veterans who are thought to be particularly likely targets because they enjoy a regular cash income in the way of a small pension and special entitlements to purchase land), most of the cases I recorded related to the so-called 'atemporal concerns' of traditional African ethnography (Shaw 1997:3), with rivalry between co-wives in polygynous unions especially prominent.

21 Karembola incest discourses focus more upon the problematic of their own social reproduction in a modern age than upon the problematic nature of Western technology and wealth, perhaps because rural Karembola do not live cheek by jowl with obscene wealth. Indeed, their idea of the luxury enjoyed by *vazaha* is that they eat only tiny morsels of bread and tinned meat, imagery that seems to bear the imprint of the colonial era rather than the late twentieth century. To indicate the level of technology and consumer goods available to rural Karembola at the time of my fieldwork, I should like to record that the sound of a radio turned full volume actually figured in several rituals as a symbol of conspicuous consumption. Karembola villages are without electricity, running water, and television.

22 See Whyte's careful study (1997:204–5) of Bunyole, Uganda for a similar observation.

23 Recent studies suggest that HIV prevalence is still very low in Madagascar, according to the *UNAIDS/WHO Epidemiological Fact Sheet on HIV/AIDS and Sexually Transmitted Infections* (Madagascar, 2000 update). This is puzzling, since 40 per cent of Malagasy women are currently estimated to have a sexually transmitted infection, a statistic far higher than, for example, in Uganda or Zambia.

# References

Althabe, Gérard (1972), 'Les manifestations paysannes d'avril 1971'. *Revue française d'études politiques africaines* 78(June):71–7.

Apter, Andrew (1993), 'Atinga Revisited: Yoruba Witchcraft and the Cocoa Economy, 1950–1951'. In Jean Comaroff and John Comaroff (eds.) *Modernity and its Malcontents: Ritual and Power in Postcolonial Africa*. Chicago: University of Chicago Press.

Astuti, Rita (1995), *People of the Sea. Identity and Descent among the Vezo of Madagascar*. Cambridge: Cambridge University Press.

Auslander, Mark (1993), '"Open the Wombs!": The Symbolic Politics of Modern Ngoni Witchfinding'. In Jean Comaroff and John Comaroff (eds.) *Modernity and its Malcontents: Ritual and Power in Postcolonial Africa*. Chicago: University of Chicago Press.

Baré, Jean-François (1977), *Pouvoir des vivants, langage des morts. Idéo-logiques Sakalava*. Paris: François Maspero.

Barthes, Roland (1957), 'Grammaire africaine'. In *Mythologie*. Paris: Editions du Seuil.

Bastian, Misty (1993), '"Bloodhounds Who Have No Friends": Witchcraft and Locality in the Nigerian Popular Press'. In Jean Comaroff and John Comaroff (eds.) *Modernity and its Malcontents: Ritual and Power in Postcolonial Africa*. Chicago: University of Chicago Press.

Bayart, Jean-François (1996), *L'illusion identitaire*. Paris: Fayard.

Beidelman, T. O. (1971), 'Some Kaguru Notions About Incest and Other Sexual Prohibitions'. In Rodney Needham (ed.) *Rethinking Kinship and Marriage*. London: Tavistock.

Bloch, Maurice (1971), *Placing the Dead. Tombs, Ancestral Villages, and Kinship Organization in Madagascar*. London: Seminar Press.

— (1986), *From Blessing to Violence. History and Ideology in the Circumcision Ritual of the Merina of Madagascar*. Cambridge: Cambridge University Press.

Chabal, Patrick (1996), 'The African Crisis: Context and Interpretation'. In Richard Werbner and Terence Ranger (eds.) *Postcolonial Identities in Africa*. London: Zed Books.

Cole, Jennifer (1998), 'The Work of Memory in Madagascar'. *American Ethnologist* 25(4): 610–33.

— (1999), 'The Uses of Defeat: Memory and Political Morality in East Madagascar'. In Richard Werbner (ed.) *Memory and the Postcolony*. London: Zed Books.

Cole, Jennifer and Karen Middleton (2001), 'Rethinking Ancestors and Colonial Power in Madagascar'. *Africa* 71(1):1–37.

Collier, Jane and Sylvia Yanagisako (eds.) (1987), *Gender and Kinship: Essays Towards a Unified Analysis*. Stanford, California: University of California Press.

Comaroff, Jean (1980), 'Healing and the Cultural Order: The Case of the Barolong boo Ratshidi of Southern Africa'. *American Ethnologist* 7: 637–657.

— (1985), *Body of Power, Spirit of Resistance: The Culture and History of A South African People*. Chicago: University of Chicago Press.

— (1997), 'Consuming Passions: Child Abuse, Fetishism, and "The New World Order"'. *Culture* 17: 7–19.

Comaroff, John and Jean Comaroff (1992), *Ethnography and the Historical Imagination*. Oxford and Boulder: Westview Press.

Comaroff, Jean and John Comaroff (1993), 'Introduction'. In Jean Comaroff and John Comaroff (eds.) *Modernity and its Malcontents: Ritual and Power in Postcolonial Africa*. Chicago: University of Chicago Press.

Covell, Maureen (1987), *Madagascar. Politics, Economics and Society*. London and New York: Frances Pinter.

Cruise O'Brien, Donal B. (1996), 'A Lost Generation? Youth Identity and State Decay'. In Richard Werbner and Terence Ranger (eds.) *Postcolonial Identities in Africa*. London: Zed Books.

Csordas, Thomas (1990), 'Embodiment as a Paradigm of Anthropology'. *Ethos* 18:5– 47.

De Boeck, Filip (1999), 'Identity, Expenditure and Sharing in Southwestern Zaire'. In Birgit Meyer and Peter Geschiere (eds.) *Globalization and Identity. Dialectics of Flow and Closure.* Oxford: Blackwell.

Delivré, Alain (1974), *L'histoire des rois d'Imerina: interprétation d'une tradition orale.* Paris: Klinsieck.

Edwards, Jeanette, Sarah Franklin, Eric Hirsch, F. Price and Marilyn Strathern (1993), *Technologies of Procreation: Kinship in the Age of Assisted Conception.* Manchester: Manchester University Press.

Englund, Harri and James Leach (2000), 'Ethnography and the Meta-Narratives of Modernity'. *Current Anthropology* 41(2):225–39.

Feeley-Harnik, Gillian (1991), *A Green Estate: Restoring Independence in Madagascar.* Washington and London: Smithsonian Institution Press.

— (1997), 'Dying Gods and Queen Mothers: The International Politics of Social Reproduction in Africa and Europe'. In Maria Grosz-Ngaté and Omari Kokole (eds.) *Gendered Encounters. Challenging Cultural Boundaries and Social Hierarchies in Africa.* New York and London: Routledge.

Feniès, J. (1957), 'Migrations Tandroy'. *Bulletin de Madagascar* 7(138):923–40.

Ferguson, James (1985), 'The Bovine Mystique: Power, Property, and Livestock in Rural Lesotho'. *Man* (new series) 20: 647–74.

Franklin, S. and H. Ragoné (eds.) (1998), *Reproducing Reproduction: Kinship, Power, and Technological Innovation.* Philadelphia: University of Pennsylvania Press.

Frère, Suzanne (1958), *Madagascar. Panarama de l'Androy.* Paris: Aframpe.

Gable, Eric (1995), 'The Decolonization of Consciousness: Local Skeptics and the "Will To Be Modern" in a West African Village'. *American Ethnologist* 22(2):242–57.

Geschiere, Peter (1997), *The Modernity of Witchcraft: Politics and the Occult in Postcolonial Africa.* Charlottesville and London: University of Virginia Press.

— (1999), 'Globalization and the Power of Indeterminate Meaning: Witchcraft and Spirit Cults in Africa and East Asia'. In Birgit Meyer and Peter Geschiere (eds.) *Globalization and Identity. Dialectics of Flow and Closure.* Oxford: Blackwell.

Gudeman, Stephen and A. Rivera (1990), *Conversations in Colombia.* Cambridge: Cambridge University Press.

Gupta, Akhil and James Ferguson (1997), 'Culture, Power, Place: Ethnography at the End of an Era'. In Akhil Gupta and James Ferguson (eds.) *Culture, Power, Place: Explorations in Critical Anthropology.* Durham and London: Duke University Press.

Huntington, Richard (1978), 'Bara Endogamy and Incest Prohibition'. *Bijdragen tot de Taal-, Land-, en Volkenkunde* 134:30–62.

Hutchinson, Sharon (1985), 'Changing Concepts of Incest among the Nuer'. *American Ethnologist* 12:625–41.

Hyden, Goran (1980), *Beyond Ujamaa in Tanzania: Underdevelopment and an Uncaptured Peasantry.* Berkeley: University of California Press.

— (1983), *No Shortcuts to Progress. African Development Management in Perspective.* London: Heinemann.

Jackson, Michael (1982), *Allegories of the Wilderness.* Bloomington: Indiana University Press.

Jackson, Michael and Ivan Karp (eds.) (1990), *Personhood and Agency: The Experience of Self and Other in African Cultures.* Washington, DC: Smithsonian Institution Press.

Kottak, Conrad P. (1980), *The Past in the Present. History, Ecology, and Cultural Variation in Highland Madagascar.* Ann Arbor: University of Michigan Press.

La Fontaine, J. (1998), *Speak of the Devil: Tales of Satanic Abuse in Contemporary England.* Cambridge: Cambridge University Press.

Lambek, Michael (1993), *Knowledge and Practice in Mayotte. Local Discourses of Islam, Sorcery, and*

*Spirit Possession*. Toronto and London: University of Toronto.
— (1998), 'The Sakalava Poiesis of History: Realizing the Past through Spirit Possession in Madagascar'. *American Ethnologist* 25(2):106–27.
Lavondès, Henri (1967), *Bekoropoka. Quelques aspects de la vie familiale et sociale d'un village malgache*. Paris: Mouton.
Lévi-Strauss, Claude (1969, 1949), *The Elementary Structures of Kinship*. London: Social Science Paperbacks/Eyre and Spottiswoode. Translated from the French by J. Bell, J. von Sturmer and R. Needham.
Malkki, Lisa (1995), *Purity and Exile: Violence, Memory and National Cosmology among Hutu Refugees in Tanzania*. Chicago: University of Chicago Press.
Matory, Lorand (1994), *Sex and the Empire That Is No More: Gender and the Politics of Metaphor in Oyo Yoruba Religion*. Minneapolis: University of Minnesota Press.
Mbembe, Achille (1992), 'Provisional Notes on the Postcolony'. *Africa* 62(1):3–37.
Meyer, Birgit (1999), *Translating the Devil: Religion and Modernity Among the Ewe in Ghana*. Edinburgh University Press/IAI.
Middleton, Karen (1997), 'Circumcision, Death, and Strangers'. *Journal of Religion in Africa* 27 (4):341–73.
— (1999), 'Who Killed "Malagasy Cactus"? Environment, Science, and Colonialism in Southern Madagascar, 1924–1930'. *Journal of Southern African Studies* 25(2):215–48.
— (2000), 'How Karembola Men Become Mothers'. In Janet Carsten (ed.) *Cultures of Relatedness: New Approaches to the Study of Kinship*. Cambridge: Cambridge University Press.
— (2001), 'Power and Meaning on the Periphery of a Malagasy Kingdom'. *Ethnohistory* 48(1–2):171–204.
— (nd), 'Memory, Alliance and Landscapes of Power in the Karembola (Madagascar)'.
— (ed.), (1999), *Ancestors, Power, and History in Madagascar*. Leiden: Brill.
Mittermeier, R. A. (1988), 'Primate Diversity and the Tropical Forest: Case Studies from Brazil and Madagascar and the Importance of Megadiversity Countries'. In E. Wilson and F. Peters (eds.) *Biodiversity*. Washington, DC: National Academy Press.
Ortner, Sherry (1995), 'Resistance and the Problem of Ethnographic Refusal'. *Comparative Studies in Society and History* 37:173–93.
Parkin, David (1986), 'Violence and Will'. In David Riches (ed.) *The Anthropology of Violence*. Oxford: Basil Blackwell.
Piot, Charles (1999), *Remotely Global: Village Modernity in West Africa*. Chicago: University of Chicago Press.
Raison-Jourde, Françoise (ed.) (1983), *Les Souverains de Madagascar: L'Histoire Royale et Ses Résurgences Contemporaines*. Paris: Karthala.
Ranger, Terence (1996), 'Postscript. Colonial and Postcolonial Identities'. In Richard Werbner and Terence Ranger (eds.) *Postcolonial Identities in Africa*. London: Zed Books.
Riesman, Paul (1986), 'The Person and the Life Cycle in African Social Life and Thought'. *African Studies Review* 29(2):71–138.
Rowlands, Michael and Jean-Pierre Warnier (1988), 'Sorcery, Power and the Modern State in Cameroon'. *Man* 23:118–32.
Sharp, Lesley (1993), *The Possessed and the Dispossessed. Spirits, Identity, and Power in a Madagascar Migrant Town*. Berkeley: University of California Press.
— (1995), 'Playboy Princely Spirits of Madagascar: Possession as Youthful Commentary and Social Critique'. *American Anthropological Quarterly* 68(2):75–88.
Shaw , Rosalind (1997), 'The Production of Witchcraft/Witchcraft as Production: Memory, Modernity, and the Slave Trade in Sierra Leone'. *American Ethnologist* 24(4):856–76.
Stoller, Paul (1995), *Embodying Colonial Memories*. New York and London: Routledge.
Strathern, Marilyn (1988), *The Gender of the Gift: Problems with Women and Problems with Society in Melanesia*. Berkeley and Los Angeles: University of California Press.

Taussig, Michael (1980), *The Devil and Commodity Fetishism in South America*. Chapel Hill: University of North Carolina Press.

Thomas, Philip (1996), 'Place, Person, and Ancestry among the Temanambondro of Southeast Madagascar'. Unpublished Ph.D thesis, London School of Economics.

Tronchon, Jacques (1986), *L'Insurrection Malgache de 1947*. Paris: Karthala.

van Binsbergen, Wim (1999), 'Globalization and Virtuality: Analytical Problems Posed by the Contemporary Transformation of African Societies'. In Birgit Meyer and Peter Geschiere (eds.) *Globalization and Identity. Dialectics of Flow and Closure*. Oxford: Blackwell.

Werbner, Richard (1991), *Tears of the Dead*. London: Edinburgh University Press.

— (1996), 'Introduction. Multiple Identities, Plural Arenas'. In Richard Werbner and Terence Ranger (eds.) *Postcolonial Identities in Africa*. London and New Jersey: Zed Books.

Whyte, Reynolds Susan (1997), *Questioning Misfortune: The Pragmatics of Uncertainty in Eastern Uganda*. Cambridge: Cambridge University Press.

# ◎ Afterword

## The Personal, the Political and the Moral
### *Provoking Postcolonial Subjectivities in Africa*

## Paul Stoller

Memorable moments have become rare commodities in the academy. Even so, a scholar may occasionally paint an indelible image that charts a new intellectual course. Sometimes an academic may even use humour to inspire an audience of students or colleagues. I remember one such occasion at an academic conference during which the late Peter Rigby, a man of enormous wit and erudition, discussed a panel on pastoralism and social change in Africa. The most striking aspect of the papers, according to Rigby, was the indisputable fact that no matter the degree of social upheaval or ecological ruin, pastoral peoples seemed able to adapt to changing circumstances. Wanting to underscore this poignant point, Rigby – with characteristic panache – compared pastoralists to cockroaches. 'You can relentlessly spray them or trample them,' Rigby said, 'and just when you think they're dead, they dust themselves off and walk away. The pastoralist,' he stated, 'is a kind of social cockroach.'

One can say the same sort of thing, I think, about the resilience of the autonomous subject, a notion which suggests that individuals, using reason, continuously and freely construct and reconstruct the world. For several generations, modernists have bludgeoned the autonomous subject with batteries of sophisticated anti-humanist analysis. Indeed, challenges to the autonomous subject have come from some of the most revered scholars of the twentieth century. Claude Lévi-Strauss, for one, has used the structuralist analysis of kinship and myth to open a conceptual gulf between the infinitely variable behaviour of subjects and the more immutable dimensions of putatively universal binary oppositions. In Lévi-Strauss's world the texture of the subject's action is less important than the conceptual relationships that action implicates. Subjects, then, lose their subjectivity and become, to paraphrase Clifford Geertz (1973), cerebrally savage. For Roland Barthes

225

(1972) the forces of the social world constrain writing, which is never context-free, such that authors are dispossessed of their writerly being – their subjectivity. This fact compels them to write in the intransitive voice. Conceptually speaking, the sentence 'I eat' is transformed to the intransitive 'This eats itself.' Taking the process a step further, Michel Foucault famously proclaimed the veritable 'death' of the author, who, like Barth's scribe, is condemned to write in the intransitive voice. Caught in the tangle of the episteme, 'dead' authors lack the autonomy to create, for their expression is forever constrained by an always already discourse.

In many African contexts this anti-humanist world view is somewhat appropriate, for the African subject's autonomy can be highly constrained by forces beyond individual control. More often than not African land is not 'owned' by an autonomous subject, but by a group of which the individual is only a small part. This collectivist notion of 'ownership,' in fact, restricts social relations. Lack of the subject's autonomy is evident in at least two other (West) African domains: oral poetry and sorcery. Among the Songhay people of Niger and Mali it is said that wordsmiths or griots are not the 'owners' of words, but are 'owned' by the words that they commit to memory ( Hale 1999; Stoller 1997). No one person, it is said, can possess something that belongs to everyone, something that has the power to link past and present. Songhay sorcerers, the illustrious *sohanci*, are said to eat power, but that power also eats them. By eating power they are 'owned' by it (Stoller 1989, 1997). In this sense many systems of African social relations, oral poetry and sorcery are, to borrow from Derrida, always already there, which, in turn, constrains social autonomy.

Despite the felicity of these West African examples, the anti-humanist design of the poststructuralist project is one that is perhaps too narrowly drawn. In collectively oriented societies, there is space, after all, for the fascinating tension between individual desire and group will. In the same vein, West African griots respectfully recite their always already 'old words', but with individual variation and flair. Sorcerers follow the recipes of their ancestors, but are variously effective. Why is it that clients prefer particular griots or sorcerers?

How, then, can we account for the subject's incomparable resilience? One could say, at the risk of creating a phrase a tad too purple, that the subject's subjectivity is subjected to the subjunctive. As Susan Reynolds Whyte suggests in her admirable contribution to this volume, subjectivity begets subjunctivity, an indeterminate space in which social relations are continuously entangled, in which irrational emotions are expressed. Within the subjunctive frame, as Gregory Bateson (1972) might have put it, poetry displaces the bloodless discourse of academic plain style. No matter how hard scholars try to eliminate human imperfections, we seem unwilling and perhaps unable to dismiss our subjectivities.

Which brings us to the varied and stimulating chapters in this volume, *Postcolonial Subjectivities in Africa*. Space precludes a thorough analysis of each and every essay in the volume. Here I attempt to tease out some general themes underscored by the essays and then suggest how these themes – by subjecting the subject to the subjunctive – take us back to the philosophical future.

A key issue that almost all the chapters consider is that of identity, a notion that has become as slippery and polysymous as the concepts of culture or society. So much as been written about the construction and politics of identity that one wonders what yet another essay on the subject might contribute. What distinguishes the treatment of identity in this volume is that authors' comments on it are based upon long-standing field study, which means the question of identity becomes, like most postcolonial worlds, multi-perspectival. The authors consider identity within small and large institutional contexts (Middleton, Wilson), as an embodied phenomenon (Whyte, Nyamnjoh, Wilson and Behrend), as a ramification of war, state and tribal politics (Hutchinson, Okazaki and Durham), as part of intersubjective dynamics (Nyamnjoh, Lambek, Whyte) as well as a central component in the cultural construction of the state (Durham, Wilson). In each case, though, the struggle for identity creates subjunctive frames within which identity takes on a surfeit of meanings, each of which has a particular social, cultural and political ramification. In this way, the essays underscore the prodigious difficulty of coming to terms with the perplexities of the postcolonial human condition.

Like identity, the issue of power has a voluminous literature. What more might be said of such a thoroughly considered social phenomenon? Here again the essays in the volume demonstrate forcefully that there are no unidimensional theoretical solutions to complex postcolonial problems. Two of the authors describe power in terms of the state production of cultural discourse (Wilson, Apter). Here the state uses its considerable symbolic repertoire to promote certain images that reinforce legitimacy. Images that subvert hegemony are erased. Put another way, the postcolonial state produces images that subject cultural themes to inclusion, exclusion, memory and erasure. By the same token, state power in postcolonial Africa also subjects people – to tyranny and tragedy (Hutchinson, Durham, and Okazaki). And yet power, the chapters demonstrate, is not the exclusive province of the state, for individuals also exercise a will to power, using it to rein in a world gone wild with change (Lambek, Whyte, Okazaki).

In postcolonial Africa, of course, the proliferation of mimetic technologies has made cultural production an increasingly important cultural resource. Accordingly, the issue of power has become more and more linked to the ability of individuals, groups and the state to reproduce culture. As the chapters in the volume demonstrate, there are a variety of highly creative moves that individuals and groups make to manipulate the mimetic faculty to meet various socio-cultural goals. In postcolonial Africa this manipulation provokes some remarkable symbolic inversions. In Kenya young men prize photographs depicting them dressed like African American gangsta rappers – a copy of a transcultural reality that transfers to them the putative prestige and force of African American rap culture (Behrend). In the same vein Congolese youth living along geographic, ethnic and cultural borderlands adopt powerful and forceful filmic images (cowboys, gangsters, ninjas) to make sense of the indeterminate powerless spaces in which they live (de Boeck 1999). The aggressive subjectivity produced in these spaces is defined by the subjunctive, for people make copies of reality in order to grasp a modicum of control over its indeterminate ever-changing nature (see Taussig 1993, Stoller 1997).

As individuals attempt to copy reality to control it (if only for a sliver of time), postcolonial institutions produce an airbrushed reality in order to subject their subjects to an all-encompassing institutional discourse. In Nigeria the state used FESTAC to construct 'a public' for 'public con- sumption'. In this case the Nigerian state choreographed a nation to present to the world, a nation which bore little, if any, connection to local-level Nigerian social life (Apter 1999). In South Africa, the state, through its Truth and Reconciliation Commission, constructed a bureaucratic truth to create a 'fictive' ideology of reconciliation – a kind of symbolic penance for the atrocities committed during apartheid (Wilson 1999). In both cases, postcolonial African states manipulated modern media to shape a national imaginary devoid of cultural depth and political specificity. Despite the prudence that these states used to shape their 'objective' and 'highly visible' tableaus of reality, alternative versions of social life – the subjunctive subjectivities of individuals and groups – rose to the surface to stain carefully designed portraits.

The spectre of postcolonialism in Africa not only challenges our tried and true notions about identity, power and expressive culture, but also compels us to reconsider epistemological frameworks. Given the almost unlimited exchange of photographic, filmic and electronic images across the globe, it is no longer sufficient to study one group of people in one place using one analytical orientation (de Boeck 1999, Behrend, and Wilson 1999). The essays in the volume – not to forget the papers read at the conference that are not here included – demonstrate the need for epistemological flexibility. In the face of a conceptual chaos brought on by the uncertainties of the postmodern condition, there is also an epistemological need for scholars to attend more to lived experience (Whyte, Lambek) and practical wisdom (Whyte, Lambek). Such a move embodies a phenomenological shift toward narrative discourse in which intersubjective dynamics are densely detailed.

Although the chapters paint a rather murky picture of the workings of African postcolonial worlds, it is clear that our received categories – discourse, identity, subject – are not up to the task of making sense of contemporary postcolonial incoherence. It is also clear that despite the diligence of postcolonial states and poststructuralist scholars to erase subjectivity from the conceptual landscape, people in Africa defy their efforts by continuing the struggle to construct subjectivities.

Why all this construction and struggle? One could focus on modernism. The modernist project, which triggered the formation of totalitarian states, has, after all, profoundly dehumanised society (Lyotard 1984). In these dehumanised social contexts, which have been broadened and deepened by the postmodern condition, many human beings have lost their way. Wandering in the fog of obfuscation, they have lost sight of what is important. Here and there, the wise ones find their way to a clearing – spaces where they fashion stories, laced with subjectivities, which restore some of that lost dignity. This ongoing process of restoration is central, I think, to the contemporary human condition.

Between the lines of this fascinating and stimulating group of essays we are, in the end, reminded of the felicity of looking back to the philosophical future. Scholars of the postcolonial and postmodern condition are all to often caught in webs of discourse that obstruct the path of our classical mission – the quest for wisdom, the knowledge that enables human beings to live well. African sages have long understood the scholar's burden. In a variety of ways the chapters in this volume brilliantly provoke us to again take up that classical burden. Are we up to the challenge?

## References

Apter, Andrew (1999), 'Producing the People: National Culture and the Public Sphere in Nigeria'. Paper read at 'Manchester '99: Visions and Voices'. Manchester, 27–31 October.

Barthes, Roland (1972), 'To Write: An Intransitive Verb'. In Richard T. de George and Fernande M. de George (eds.) *The Structuralists: From Marx to Lévi-Strauss*. Garden City, NY: Doubleday.

Bateson, Gregory (2000, 1972), *Steps to an Ecology of Mind*. Chicago: The University of Chicago Press.

De Boeck, Filip (1999). 'Postcolonial Subjectivities in Kinshasa: Reflections on Pentecostal

Churches'. Paper read at 'Manchester '99: Visions and Voices', Manchester, 27–31 October.

Geertz, Clifford (1973), *The Interpretation of Cultures*. New York: Basic Books.

Hale, Thomas (1999), *Griots and Griottes*. Bloomington: Indiana University Press.

Lyotard, Jean-Francois (1984), *The Postmodern Condition*. Minneapolis: University of Minnesota Press.

Stoller, Paul (1989), *The Taste of Ethnographic Things*. Philadelphia: University of Pennsylvania Press.

— (1997), *Sensuous Scholarship*. Philadelphia: University of Pennsylvania Press.

Taussig, Michael (1993), *Mimesis and Alterity*. New York: Routledge.

Wilson, Richard (1999), 'The TRC's Truth Making Machine'. Paper read at 'Manchester '99: Visions and Voices'. Manchester, 27–31 October.

# ◎ Index

Abu-Lughod, Lila 144
Abumbi II John Ambe 126
accountability 86, 154
Adok 89
**Africa**, artistic traditions of 46; capitalism
and 122-4; civility in 139-40, 150,
163; creative intersubjectivity in 135;
cultures of 227-8; East 31, 45; francophone 65, 149, *see also* France; gender
and generational roles in 211; globalisation and 112; health in 171; liberation movements and 68; literature of
68; memory crisis 19, 39; microcosm
of 112; oral literature of 226; photographic images of 44-5, 72; relational
self in 201; religions of 66; state in
150; subjectivity in 171-2, 226; technology and 227-8; witchcraft in 122-
4, 193, 204, 207, 226
African Advisory Council (Botswana)
(AAC) 157
African-American culture 5-6, 49-55,
58-60, 60-1n, 228
African Rights organisation 77
**agency**, ambiguity of 4-5, 163;
autonomy of 20, 143, 149; children
and 116-17; and civility 139-40, 142,
164-5, 187-8; collective/communal
111-19, 126, 130, 135, 143, 152,
162-3, 164, 165; colonial 214;
competing understandings of 111,
114, 117, 120, 127, 129; conceptual
difficulty of 37-8; and contingency
176; and conviviality 11-12, 111-13,
115, 117-18, 126-7; cultural 135,

216; and dependency 111, 124;
divination and 176; domesticated 12,
114-16, 119-26, 134; and dreaming
64; and empowerment 111-12, 122,
125; and ethnicity 140; family and
126-7; globalisation and 135; and
history 36, 135, 140, 216; hybrid 14,
165; and identity 66; and independence 124; individual 3-5, 65-6, 111-
12, 117-20, 130, 135, 143, 149, 155,
161, 162-3, 164, 165; and inequality
120; intersubjectivity and 111-15,
117-18, 120-7, 134-5, 184; local
effects on 216; of mediums 4-5; and
misfortune 176-9, 181, 204; moral 2,
13, 20, 25, 64, 117, 140, 148, 152; in
multicultural societies 11-12; and
narrative 174; negotiated 134-5, 143;
political 64; postcolonial reconstructions of 19; and power 13, 78-9, 188;
reductionist views of 135; and
resistance 70, 78-9; and social
memory 19; and social structures 134;
solidarity and 121; and spirit possession 37-9, 176-8; state and 140, 158;
and subjection 37-9, 181, 186, 188;
and subjectivity 78-9, 113-15, 117,
119-20, 186, 216; and subjunctivity
175-7, 185-6; and trouble 174; and
uncertainty 142-3, 158, 165, 174-6,
188, 204-5; undomesticated 122-4;
vulnerability of 11; Western 135
**agriculture**, agro-pastoralism 85; mechanised 63, 67, 70; plantation 122, 197;
subsistence 195, 198